THE
P
L

Decca A
for the
the Pap
is her fir

NORTH
MOBILE

East Ayrshire
COUNCIL

DECCA AITKENHEAD THE PROMISED LAND

Travels in search of the perfect E

FOURTH ESTATE • *London*

First published in Great Britain in 2002 by
Fourth Estate
A Division of HarperCollins*Publishers*
77–85 Fulham Palace Road,
London W6 8JB
www.4thestate.co.uk

Copyright © Decca Aitkenhead 2002

10 9 8 7 6 5 4 3 2 1

A catalogue record for this book is available from the British Library.

ISBN 1-84115-337-0

Typeset by Rowland Phototypesetting Ltd, Bury St Edmunds, Suffolk
Printed in Great Britain by Clays Ltd, St Ives plc

To the dancing bear

Contents

CONTENTS

Acknowledgements

Thanks are due to many. To Charlotte Raven and Terry King, for all the obvious and more. To my agent, Clare Alexander, and my editor, Clive Priddle, without whom this would undoubtedly not have happened. To Matt and Neill Aitkenhead, to everyone at Fourth Estate, and to all those we encountered on the journey, many of whom contributed unknowingly, and most of whose names have therefore been changed. To Nigel McGowan, for the programme. And, lastly, to Glenn and Brendan, for Strangeways.

Foreword

I came across the original outline for this book recently. *The Promised Land* would apparently be a bold and original study of happiness. Ecstasy, the proposal explained, was all about happiness; it was joy in a pill. I had divined that travel was also about the quest for happiness. To combine the two in a journey looking for the perfect E would, I suggested, reveal infinite truths about the essential nature of both. There was also some spin along the lines of 'subverting the genre' of travel writing – which for all I knew could even be true, as my grasp of the genre was flimsy to say the least. The form needed to move on, I announced – to the underbelly of abroad, where traditional travel writing feared to tread. This would be hardcore cool.

I don't know why I wasn't more surprised that anyone took the document seriously. I do remember being slightly thrown by ethical/legal questions about ecstasy as drug abuse, though. As if I was a drug user or something. That is what clubbers are, of course, but it is not what we consider ourselves to be. Few think of ecstasy as an actual drug, and most differ from their drug-taking predecessors by taking it without reference to a political or sociological subtext. It is unadulterated hedonism we're after, and the fact that it involves an illegal substance is an inconvenience rather than a position.

I would say that most of us frequently forget it is even illegal. Ecstasy is technically a Class A drug, like heroin, but taking it does not imply deprivation or deviance, and its use has never been confined to a particular category of person. If anything, ecstasy tends to work the other way, not as the product of a social category but the creator of one. It isn't expensive or addictive, nor likely to make you experiment with the possibility that your arms are in fact wings. Furthermore, people who sell pills to clubbers seldom subscribe to the unpleasant stereotype of the drug dealer, usually because they are one of our friends. Most clubbers have sold a few Es to each other at one point or another. The dealer is just someone who sells more.

Certainly, I have known clubbers who ought never to have gone near it. There was one boy from Leeds you could set your watch by; he'd dance on a podium all night long, happy as a butterfly, but come quarter to eleven on Sunday morning would start to sob, and not stop crying until Tuesday. And I remember a boy that nobody knew at a party in London, years ago. After everyone else had left he was still dancing on top of the fridge, refusing to come down; we tried knocking him out with Valium, but even after seven or eight of them he was still up there on the fridge and in the end had to be carried out, still kicking and dancing as he went. We found the Valium hidden in the teapot a few days later, but never saw the boy again.

Nevertheless, some of the happiest times of my life have come through clubbing. This book would not have happened otherwise, but it did present the question of whether there was something inherently wrong with chemical happiness. Quick hits, cheap highs – what did I think? I don't know. Sometimes I think it's an interesting question to which I do not know the answer, and sometimes I don't even know if it is an interesting question. I said I would look into it.

And then, suddenly, the terrible realisation dawns. I am *writing a book about drugs*. How could this have happened? There is no excuse for bringing another drugs book into the world. It cannot be a book about drugs. Perhaps it is really a travel book. Come to think of it, though, I never read travel books either. What did I think I was doing?

The defence I can offer is that this is not a book about taking drugs, but rather about trying to find them. Anyone who has sat through their friends' drug anecdotes will know that the entertainment to be had from such stories lies in the part where they are trying to get hold of the stuff. It is downhill all the way once they've taken it, and I have tried to spare any material of that nature. There will be no detailed exploration anywhere of what this or that E was like. This may strike some as an illogical omission, given the nature of the book's central quest, but I am sure it is preferable to the alternative of leaving it in.

Was this, in the end, an investigation of happiness? Rather to my surprise, it seems that it was. The relationship between different cultures and ecstasy revealed diverse ideas of happiness more effectively than I could have imagined, and the search led us to places we would never have found on any other journey. How much happiness it bought for ourselves is another matter. It was less predictable than that, and as a consequence a great deal more interesting. We were almost arrested in Thailand, and nearly shot in South Africa. We kept company with sex tourists and murderers, made friends with gangsters and racists, found some of the finest clubs in the world, and witnessed some of the worst dancing in evidence anywhere on the planet. The journey established beyond any doubt that the happiness of clubbing is not purely chemical, though there were times when I wished it was. We would have had a much easier time had it been that simple, but as it turned out the truth was more involving.

The conventional thinking on any drug-fuelled good time is that while you are enjoying it, you fancy that all this fun has nothing to do with the drugs. That it's only when you look back with hindsight, having fallen out with everyone involved, that you realise it was just that – a drug binge – and everything else a chemical illusion.

I seem to have reached the opposite conclusion about ecstasy. If anything, I think I had overestimated its contribution. Clubbing isn't about a drug so much as people and place and time – and so, perhaps, is this.

FALSE PROMISE

CHAPTER 1

Strangeways

It is traditional for ecstasy books to begin with an anecdote about the author's first experience, but I would like to start with Paul's.

It happened in 1998, some years after my own, and some months after we started going out together. Paul had accomplished the rare feat of reaching thirty without contact with drugs of any sort beyond the usual alcohol and cigarettes. This was quite an achievement, but one which, with regard to trying ecstasy, I felt presented a problem. People who try ecstasy like it enormously. Quite overnight, they turn into clubbers who buy twelve-inch vinyl and know the names of DJs and define their very existence by the pleasures of the weekend. There are a few exceptions, but those tend to be fragile souls – a description no one would apply to Paul. He has a hearty appetite for excess, backed up by a robust constitution, and there was every reason to assume that, once initiated, he would swiftly advance to the ranks of clubland's most committed enthusiasts. I foresaw ecstasy mayhem, M25 benders, arms in the air. He would, as they say, be mad for it.

All of which would have been ideal had we been idle undergraduates. As it was, we were soon to be married. Paul was a press photographer with a mortgage, and I was a journalist with more years of clubbing behind me than I liked to count. I doubted whether either of us could accommodate a headlong dive into the world of neophyte clubbing, and it seemed rash to risk it. I'd had my share; Paul had enjoyed himself without it. There was no compelling case for introducing him to ecstasy.

We consulted friends, but opinions varied. Charlotte felt we should let sleeping dogs lie. Terry couldn't see the problem. Nigel said if I didn't take Paul clubbing then he bloody well would. What was I talking about?

Until this point, Paul hadn't minded a great deal either way. It was news to him that such a thing as clubbing existed, as distinct from proceeding to a nightclub after the pub closed, and though he vaguely recalled something about ecstasy in the late eighties, he had paid little attention and assumed it had not taken off. Having been at first puzzled by our passion for clubbing, he'd become amused by the grandiose accounts of its epiphanic possibilities. Now, fired up by Terry and Nigel, he began to wonder what he'd been missing.

I bought some Es. There was a party that weekend in Covent Garden, and as we set off Paul took half a pill. Es these days are seldom strong enough to bother taking in halves but, this being Paul's first time, I imagined it would be enough. By the time we'd arrived at the party he hadn't felt a thing, so I handed over the other half. An hour later, still nothing. Bored now, Paul took charge of the bag. Two hours and two more pills later, still nothing. I couldn't think what had gone wrong.

Context! That was it. We needed a bass line, and flashing lights. Abandoning the party, we caught a cab to the Power House, and on the way he took another pill. Now they were all gone, and after an hour or so in the club he was still reporting nothing. I found a dealer and bought more. Paul took a fifth. I was dumbfounded. Towards the end of the night, he was willing to concede that he did, possibly, feel a mild tingling in his left foot.

Perhaps we should have left the matter there. Paul was satisfied with the discovery that he had been missing nothing after all, and I, although put out, was pleased to have acquired hard evidence that pills these days really were rubbish. It is common to hear clubbers complain that they don't make ecstasy like they used to, but the lament is always offset by the worry that the fault lies within us – that we have done something bad to our neurons, or messed up our internal chemistry, thereby rendering us immune to the charms of MDMA. To compensate for the loss of impact, we of course take more pills, then worry that we are only making matters worse. So when friends heard that Paul had taken five Es on his first outing, they were amazed but also privately reassured. In many respects it was a happy ending. Paul looked immensely hard and could now let the matter rest.

But the incident had left him wondering what we had all been talking about, for the discrepancy between his experience and my version of the life-altering years I'd spent clubbing was too great to be accounted for with allowances for exaggeration. Either something had gone wrong that night or his girlfriend was a mad fantasist. For my part, after the initial relief that Paul had not turned into a teenage raver passed, I felt terribly disappointed. Now, more than ever, I wished he could know what clubbing in Manchester had been like.

The early nineties blessed Manchester with first-class ecstasy and a dance scene famous across the world. Most celebrated of all was the majestic Hacienda, less a nightclub than a ship of state; but the best clubs are usually their followers' secret, and Manchester was full of hidden enclaves. One such was the gay village around Canal Street, then blossoming from a fleabitten red-light haunt into a sparkly Eden of bars and clubs. In the summer of '93, two new dance clubs opened and the village exploded. Paradise Factory was a proper club, with famous DJs and industrial-chic décor, and the first half of every Saturday night would be spent there, saying hello to everybody – 'Hi, faaaaab outfit!' But the second half was always spent asking the critical question: 'Going to Strangeways after?' I don't know why we bothered, because the answer was always yes.

Strangeways was not a proper club. Run by an older, gay couple from Lancashire, it operated from 3 a.m. to 9 a.m. on a Sunday morning in a camply shabby venue called Central Park. Central Park was an ageing wine bar wedged beneath a multi-storey car park next door to the bus station, and for six nights of the week we wouldn't go near it. On Sunday morning, though, with dawn breaking outside over the city, 400 of us would be careering about on the threadbare carpets, whooping and twirling as the DJ crashed on another record. DJ Shane couldn't mix exactly, but he had the best record collection in Manchester, and nobody cared about technicalities when he would play classic after shameless classic – My Friend Sam, Brothers In Rhythm, Donna Giles. Strangeways anthems were always belting thunderstorms of piano and bass, and between tunes Shane would dash out of the DJ box to dance, a joyful choreography of abandon spinning on the stage.

Clubbers do not dance 'with' each other in the traditional sense. They shape their own space and move from the hip, dancing more with their midriff than their feet; the energy is fevered, but the movements themselves have composed symmetry. Some clubbers keep their elbows bent and tucked to their sides, rocking their upper bodies with their shoulders, swaying with a bounce of the knees. Others will have one arm outstretched above them, and others both, their head moving one way with the beat and their shoulders the other. Often a clubber will stay fixed to one spot for several hours, dancing but never moving their feet; or they may take small, sliding steps backwards, or kick forwards, their alternate soles at right angles to the floor. House music has generated a globally recognisable genre of dancing, instantly distinguishable from disco or pop, but within it the variations are limitless. When a club works best, it is a mass moving as one.

Strangeways' dancing was fanatical but fluid, and always generous, with none of the fidgety camp of an old-school gay club or the repetitive techno mania of today. More than that, it was endlessly imaginative. Whole personalities could be dissolved into the angle of an elbow or the turn of a head, and clubbers would dance absolutely everywhere – on the bar, the pool tables, the toilet cisterns. The toilets were the nerve centre of Strangeways – as they are in all good clubs – and it was easy to spend the whole night in them, only to emerge, puzzled and blinking, when the music went off and the lights came up.

Strangeways was never advertised, and we were ferociously proprietorial about our secret. Nearly all of the faces were the same every week, known to one another by a complex and evolving system of nicknames. These were essential, as for some reason half the club was called either Mark or Paul. So there was Sandwich Heaven Mark, and Gold Waistcoat Paul, but even these at times became confusing; for example, Long-Haired Marcus Who's Got Short Hair Now was distinguished from Short-Haired Marcus. I am afraid to say that any straight newcomer to the club was discreetly but closely monitored. If we didn't like the look of him, a girl called Pippa would usually take the matter in hand. Pippa was astonishingly beautiful, and her trick was to sashay up to the offending party and dance very seductively, very close. Then she would begin to dance out of time. This is harder than it sounds, and amazingly effective, sending the poor man sloping off in embarrassment. On the other hand, if we liked the look of a stranger – and this is possibly even worse, now I think about it – one of us would sidle up and gently *spell out the rules*.

I can't imagine now what most of the rules were, but I think the main one was to do with sex. Gay sex, within reason, was fine, but otherwise we were very anti-sex. Strangeways covered two floors, with upstairs reserved for the techno loons – a male crowd with very short hair, tight tops and fierce faces, and their music frightened the life out of us. Unmentionable things went on up there, but downstairs was devoted to dancing and gossiping and admiring one another's spangly new outfits. Although very much a gay club, Strangeways had a sizeable contingent of honorary straight members, and we took our privilege extremely seriously – hence the vigorous prosecution of the No Bothering Girls rule.

The summer Strangeways opened, I found myself in sole charge of a gigantic flat in south Manchester. The other housemates were away until October, and so every week when Strangeways closed the club would relocate to the flat, spilling out over the fire escapes and down into the garden, a sparkle of sequins among the shrubbery. Decks were set up in the living room, and DJs would play all day and into the night, until the last ones standing had collapsed into a heap on the floor among the ashtrays and coffee mugs. We could lie there for hours, stroking each other's hair, marvelling aloud at how much we loved each other. It was our favourite topic of conversation by a mile.

There was absolutely no doubt about it in our minds: we were the luckiest people alive. We had the best club, the best DJs, the best friends, the best city, the best Es, the best everything. These weren't friends – this was *a family*. It was always disconcerting to go clubbing anywhere else and discover pockets of clubbers who were under a similar impression about their own scene. In nightclub toilets in Leeds and Liverpool – even Portsmouth – we heard people telling each other that *they were a family* too! We were amazed. Surely not! *We* were the lucky ones and it was our time.

I had started to worry about our time in my late teens. The eighties had been problematic for me, pop-culture-wise for having been just too late for the punk/mod option, and ill suited to Duran Duran, I seemed in danger of sailing through my youth without catching a single contemporary wave. Bob Dylan records had a certain retro kudos in the sixth form, but I didn't wish to be stuck with my parents' record collection for the rest of my life. This looked increasingly likely to be my fate, though, and by the time Strangeways appeared over the horizon I'd more or less resigned myself to it. But then, suddenly – at last – it was our time! This beautiful club full of captivating people, on a drug our parents never had, dancing to music we had *only just invented*. I thought I would die of pride. Strictly speaking, the club belonged to its promoters, Glenn and Brendan, but we all presumed a de facto sense of ownership and guarded Strangeways like a precious jewel.

The happiness was very precise, had a particular quality. Ecstasy

creates a curious sense of timelessness, suspending you in a moment
of perfection without past or future. It is distilled happiness, freed
from the gravity of time, a weightless euphoria. Paradoxically, the
effect of this is one of profound nostalgia, for you find yourself griev-
ing for the moment even as you are experiencing it. The perfection
of ecstasy is irreproducible, analogous to nothing.

This premature nostalgia possibly explains dance culture's weakness for the notion of the classic. A club that is mourning itself
even as it dances is highly susceptible to its own memorial – and so
records not even six weeks old were declared 'classics' and revival
nights were hugely popular. 'Back to '93' on a flyer was guaranteed
to attract queues around the block, even when we were only halfway
through '94.

Strangeways had its share of unlikely followers. A pair of poodle
groomers from Plymouth used to turn up most weekends, sometimes
with a prize poodle in tow. When it got out that the pooches were
worth thousands of pounds, some of the club's shadier characters could
usually be found in the toilets plotting elaborate kidnap schemes. A
piano tuner from Birmingham also put in regular appearances, and
would loiter by the DJ booth all night, beseeching Shane to play
some 'lovely piano tunes'.

And then there was a vet from Liverpool, who would come every
weekend. He was straight, and rather conventional (although he and
his fiancée used to turn up in extraordinary rubber contraptions).
But he stays in my mind because of something he said once in
Strangeways' very early days. It was a simple remark, but it caught
me because I hadn't thought about it before. Dancing near the stage,
he looked across and said, suddenly, that in the very heat of his
happiness he felt desperate sadness. 'And I know it's because I never
want this to end.'

Well, it did end, of course, and with a bang. Glenn and Brendan
were the surprise victims of a hostile takeover, sprung on them out
of the blue one Sunday morning. As the club began to empty, the
bouncers began to hand out flyers announcing that, as of the following
Saturday, Strangeways would be known as Safeways and its members
would have to re-register. Lord, what a drama! It was quite literally
handbags at dawn, with everyone shrieking at everyone else and an
almighty scrap in the car park. What eventually emerged was that a
rival promoter had put in a bid for the Sunday-morning slot. The
owner of the venue had accepted. Glenn and Brendan were out.

We were stunned. No one could believe it at first, but by lunchtime a campaign committee had assembled and was plotting revenge in a bar on Canal Street. We were hopping mad, and on Monday morning, phones were ringing in Safeway supermarket's legal department, informing them of the misappropriation of their brand name by a most disreputable little outfit. All week, disputations were dispatched to beg, bully and finally threaten the new promoter. And when the doors opened the following weekend there we were on the pavement, holding up placards, picketing the club.

Looking back, what amazes me is that we did not for one second consider it irregular to be picketing a nightclub in the middle of a cold February night. Far from it, we sent undercover spies in to catch any of the Strangeways faithful having a traitorous dance, and scabs were instantly blacklisted. The new promoter – although this too now seems bizarre – must have anticipated some kind of boycott, for he bussed in several coachloads from Liverpool to fill the club and continued to do so week after week. It was a desperate spell. In the usual way of these things, the picket slowly flagged and the protest eventually splintered. People started to drift back in. A few stood firm, but relationships split up and friendships were poisoned.

Glenn and Brendan tried to revive Strangeways in various different venues, but the spell had been broken. Our one enduring victory concerned the new club's name. Safeways the supermarket was having none of it, and the name was changed Danceteria, but by then it no longer mattered, for our beautiful club was lost.

By the second half of the nineties I had moved to London, where dance culture was becoming a business machine, no longer something you could lose your heart to. For a time, I would go back to Manchester every weekend and go clubbing with my friend Terry. Terry was one of Strangeways' defining personalities – a personal triumph of self-invention, larger than life, with something of The Great Gatsby about him. When I met him, he was building Manchester's first gay bookshop, but he soon grew bored of it and it burnt down not long afterwards. Terry's enthusiasm for adventure is without equal, and when Strangeways closed his solution was to open a new club in the village, staffed with the old Strangeways faithful. DJ Shane was back behind the decks, Linda the dealer was in charge of accounts, and for a brief, intoxicating spell it was Strangeways all over again.

But though much admired by the patrons for his tendency to snort drugs off his own bar, Terry was recklessly impatient with licensing laws, and it wasn't long before the whole thing ended in tears. By then, clubs all over Manchester were closing down. The Es were getting worse, bars and beer were back in fashion, and the city was in the grip of a gang war. Gangland shootings claimed the clubs one by one, and when the Hacienda closed down, just days after its fifteenth birthday, Manchester's reign was over.

I didn't expect to fall in love with clubbing for a second time. But it was around this period, in basements dotted around north London, that something loosely known as underground garage began to stir. Introduced to it by a friend, Nigel, I was completely bowled over. In its principal features the scene was nothing like the village in Manchester, for this was *Lahn*-dan, all puffa jacketed up, snorting charlie off car keys. Black teenage boys, stringy white girls at their sides, skulked about with their hands up their Moschino jumpers, pretending to hide shooters. But, for all that, there were amazing echoes of Strangeways.

Underground garage revolved chiefly around the after-party circuit, a post-club collection of events in unspeakably ramshackle venues. Our favourite was Philip Lane, which kept the same sort of hours as Strangeways in a disused bakery tunnelled underneath a road in Tottenham. We would arrive on a Sunday morning, and find a chaotic assortment of clubbers clustered in this dank hole in the ground, dancing to hauntingly wistful garage. Underground garage is now known as speed garage, and with its transfer to mainstream popularity seems to have lost much of its delicate subtlety. At its birth, though, it had the urgently authentic claim of an organic sound, improvising intimate passion out of the most unpromising raw materials. Somebody from Philip Lane would drive to France to buy drink to sell through a hatch in the wall, and after working all night in the West End DJs would arrive and play for free, occasionally coming to blows behind the decks over whose turn it was next.

Philip Lane had the familiar narrative of joy and squabbles associated with a Sunday club and a sense of shared ownership; Nigel's indignation knew no bounds, for example, if he wasn't allowed to MC all day. Like Strangeways, it had also succeeded in uniting a thoroughly disparate crowd in a common passion. This is a rare feat, as most clubs achieve the opposite, assembling an identikit crowd who fail to find anything in common at all. And, again like Strangeways, underground garage was a secret. But slowly the scene spread, colonising West End clubs and ultimately lording it on Radio One, where Spoony and Timmi Magic were suddenly DJ superstars. At some point Philip Lane was closed down – by the police, I imagine, to nobody's great surprise – but its spirit survived in pockets, and when Paul decided to give clubbing another chance, it was the garage scene he fell for.

His first sample of ecstasy had been particularly poor, but the quality of Es comes in cycles, and London shortly enjoyed a good run. Paul was persuaded to try again, and before long could be found in record shops in Hackney on a Saturday afternoon, buying Amira and Todd Edwards. We would go to Costa Nostra and Sun City, winding up at another after-party in Hornsey on a Sunday afternoon, and we had a fine time. But underground garage nights were always hit and miss, and I knew clubbing could be better than this. God only knew, the Es could.

Somewhere in the world, there had to be something more like Strangeways to show Paul. It was a hopeless dream to be stuck with, though, for while I could play Paul 'Peace and Harmony' for ever, the spirit of Strangeways – its fierce commitment to its own euphoria, and the effortless pursuit of happiness, was untranslatable. The pursuit of happiness as a reason for living is a relatively recent orthodoxy, and though we are all of us engaged in the quest, most of the time it is surprisingly difficult to achieve. Strangeways was the moment when it came easy.

When we met, I was a columnist for the *Guardian*, Paul a photographer for Reuters. At the turn of 1999 we bought a flat in north London and rapidly accumulated a startling collection of things – sofas, cutlery, a colander. In the spring we were married, and soon the century would be turning, and there were conversations about having children. And still, in spite of myself, a small part of me was waiting for the last dance.

I think it was originally my friend Charlotte's idea. I met Charlotte Raven at Manchester University, and on graduation we moved to London together, became journalists, and shared a flat for some years. The limpness of media social circles took us both by surprise, and we were prone to wistful recollections of Manchester nights, and theatrical, slightly camp despair about what was to be done. She can't remember if it was her idea or not, but we had a joke that one of us should take the matter in hand and go round the world in search of the perfect E. After a bad day or a disappointing night out, one or other of us would come home and announce that that was bloody well it – we were off to find the perfect E. It was nothing more than that, a throwaway line that would be shouted from the bathroom, and I'd forgotten all about it by the time I married Paul.

By then I'd also managed to acquire a literary agent, on the doubtful understanding that at some point I would come up with an idea for a book. We would meet for lunch from time to time, but of course I never did have any ideas. It was during one of these lunches that Charlotte's name came up. Something my agent said reminded me of our old joke about the perfect E, and I threw it out casually, a token gesture intended to imply that I had been giving some thought to the problem of what to write about. Within the week, I appeared to have written a long proposal persuading publishers that it would be an excellent plan to send Paul and me round the world buying drugs.

On the day the plan was agreed, we invited Terry and Charlotte round to break the good news. Charlotte arrived first. She is extremely delicate, but can be surprisingly noisy when roused, and wanted to know if we had thought the matter through.

'How is it going to *work*?'

When Terry arrived, he was absolutely scandalised.

'An *ecstasy shopping spree*, disguised as a book?'

As far as Terry was concerned, this was nothing but an unbelievable scam. Charlotte had come round to the idea by then, though, and tried to defend it – 'No, Terry, I think it's meant to be a cultural prism' – but still he was having none of it. Terry was far from suggesting that this was cause to reconsider, however; that the idea was a scam was the primary inspiration for his enthusiasm. If there was hoodwinking to be done, he wanted in on it, and immediately booked himself on a flight to join us in San Francisco.

I at least had the good sense not to show them the proposal I had written, for I think they would have both died laughing. After they left that evening, though, there was a slightly uneasy hour while Paul and I considered their reactions. To be honest, we were a little taken aback, and decided not to tell anyone else what the journey was about. In private, though, we were still beside ourselves with excitement.

We even packed a bag of favourite records, so that when we found the perfect E we would be able to whip out the perfect tune. Half were Strangeways classics, the other half speed garage. DJ Shane lent us Brothers In Rhythm, Juliet Roberts, The FPI Project and Joe Smooth's 'The Promised Land'. Tina Moore, Y-Tribe, Todd Terry and Doolally went in the garage half. We couldn't decide which was the perfect tune, but there was much hilarity anticipating the scene when its moment arrived – the pair of us in some exotic club, trying to persuade the DJ to play our record. *What* a lark.

I clean overlooked what a bore it would be to drag a record bag around with us. It is hardly surprising, then, that I also missed the less obvious but more ominous metaphor of being burdened with the baggage of old times. Clubbers often talk about their early days with ecstasy as a honeymoon – a golden time, the halcyon period between discovery and disenchantment. Looking back now, perhaps I should have questioned the wisdom of attempting a second honeymoon, still less with someone who wasn't there on the first. Paul was extraordinarily patient throughout the trip. At times, though, he must have felt as if he was being dragged around the world looking not for the perfect E but for a previous spouse.

CHAPTER 2

Piano. Cheesecake

Any clubber who has been buying drugs for a while imagines they're getting better at it with experience. It certainly gets easier, and as time passes you find yourself telling amusing anecdotes about the occasion you mistook a head bouncer for a dealer, or about the wretched night you wasted looking for a man in a student dance, armed only with the information that he was on a murder charge and had false teeth. But the crucial point about these mishaps is that they took place a long time ago, and as you chuckle away – what a *fool*! – what you are really saying is that you are now something of an expert. Expert drug buyers do exist, and I don't doubt the celebrity smack addicts on chat shows who boast of being able to arrive in any small English town and find heroin within the hour. But most of us would be hard pressed to find the police station in that time, for despite our fond self-regard, it gets easier to buy drugs only because we've made friends with more people who sell them.

I liked to think of myself as an old hand. Paul assumed the reason he was hopeless at buying drugs was inexperience. Only as we stood in the middle of Detroit, a city that appeared to have no one living in it – and certainly no one I knew who sold Es – did the folly of our thinking begin to dawn. It is probably a good thing neither of us knew then what the miscalculation would mean. But with Paul waiting expectantly to hear our next move, it was already too late. 'Easy,' I smiled brightly, 'we'll find a bar, and ask someone to point us towards a good club.'

We had arrived in Michigan early that morning. 'Welcome to *Deeee-troit*,' sang the pilot's hopeful drum roll. 'Mo-toooor *City*!' Some

14

cities need no introduction, and Detroit is evidently not one of them, for nobody can say the name without adding 'Motor City'. It would be an odd enough tic even if it were true, but on the long drive in we saw not one other car. For a long time we didn't even see a city, either, just a flat grey plain of hinterland. Then we turned a corner, and suddenly, like a child's pop-up book, there it was.

At first glance, Detroit looked a little like Gotham City. Art deco skyscrapers loomed out of the unnatural flatness of the earth, their outlines sharp in the sunshine, but something was not quite right about the buildings, and what was missing, we soon realised, was light. Boarded up with plywood, the towers cast only shadows, and as the thicket deepened a cold gloom fell over the car. It was like stumbling into a stage set of a ghost town, colourless and deadly still; even the parking lots were boarded up, and the streets ran silent and empty. Reaching the river, we drew up outside what looked like a concrete multi-storey car park. The taxi driver got out, swung open the rear door, grunted something through his nose, and to our great surprise what he had apparently said was: 'This is your hotel.' The multi-storey car park was the Renaissance Center, Detroit's proudest civic jewel.

That had been some hours ago. We'd checked in now and were outside again, exploring what our map described as the city centre. There had clearly been a mistake. Walking up one derelict street then gingerly down another, we re-consulted the map. Becoming increasingly wary, Paul led the way past more rows of boarded-up shops, picking around the jagged gaps where sections of streets were missing completely – and soon it became quite plain that the only two people on the streets of downtown Detroit on a sunny Saturday were a lone British couple, clutching a map and beginning to look quite nervous.

After about an hour, we found a sort of concrete shed with thrash metal pounding out of an open door. It looked like a bar, but it was hard to tell, on account of being pitch-black inside. Tiptoeing in, we waited in the dark, and in due course a heavy young man with a spike through his chin lurched through the gloom. When he'd recovered from the surprise of seeing customers, he explained that downtown got 'kind of quiet' on a weekend, and chuckled softly to himself as he poured drinks. Foreigners in his bar were apparently some form of private joke.

'Would you know of any good dance clubs we could go to?' He stopped pouring and looked up.

'You're kidding, right?' I shook my head and smiled encouragingly. He handed over a copy of the city's listings magazine, the *Metro Times*, we bought a box of matches, and under a tiny pool of light read through the column of club entries. It was an unexpectedly short list.

Most of the descriptions sounded more like a threat than a promise ('Six hours, one DJ, one room'), and almost all the clubs were billed as 'old skool'. Different categories of dance can be identified by their deliberate misspellings; variants of hip-hop tend to contain a 'ph' where there should be an 'f' – hence phat beats, phunk, etc – and anything to do with techno is peppered with the letter 'k'. There seemed to be an awful lot of 'k's in these listings. Really hardcore techno, the type that makes your ears bleed, is spelt hardkore – and this word appeared on every other line. As we turned to leave, the barman called after us.

'Don't get shot, now.'

Outside on the deserted street, blinking in the sunlight, a kind of nervous hysteria set in. Paul wanted to know just how fierce a techno night in Detroit would have to be to qualify for the distinction of 'old-skool hardkore'.

When a lone taxi idled past on Monroe Street, there was some confusion as we tried to explain that we wanted a tour of the city. Geriatric, one-armed, the driver squinted through the cracked glass partition. '*Huh?*' With a doubtful shrug of his stump, he took us on a loop through more urban desolation, and still we saw no one. We did find a dance-record shop after about an hour, but it was empty save for the owner, a kindly man who looked thoroughly alarmed to hear we planned on going clubbing.

'You guys sure you know what you're doin'?'

Paul chipped in that he was from Glasgow, so there was no need to worry. When the man had turned his back, I got a long, questioning stare.

The only person he would be willing to approach for drugs, Paul announced once back in our room, was an obvious undercover cop, in the hope that we might then be arrested and taken somewhere safe. Face-down on the bed in a fit of morbid speculation, he conjured visions of derelict nightclubs full of gangsters. It seemed entirely likely. Even the hotel was spooky, like a graveyard for seventies executive tat, the reception staffed by women in beige nylon who looked as if they'd been crying, and the lifts by spotty bellboys done up in Victorian fancy dress. A ghost of better, more American times still lingered in places – so our room was the size of a badminton court, with two bathrooms, two TVs, and floor-to-ceiling windows gazing down upon the river. But everything was the colour of boiled brown rice, and the sunken bath looked more like a coffin. When Americans swear, as they are inclined to, 'You get what you pay for', they are clearly not thinking of the Renaissance Center Marriot, Detroit.

A cosmetics company was staging a teambuilding get-together that weekend, and painted saleswomen with enormous hair streamed out of the lifts, shooting wolfish looks at Paul. One of the women said 'fucking', and they all laughed, nervous, high-pitched little peals. On a sofa in the foyer a glum bride sat by herself smoking a cigarette. Dinner was served in a revolving restaurant with panoramic views, but the only sign of human life below was a litter of tail-lights glowing in the dark, queuing up at drive-thrus.

I had read somewhere that Motor Lounge, in the east of the city, was the 'sixth best club in America' and this was our nervy choice. We took our time getting ready to go out, fussing about and propping ourselves up with bogus enthusiasm, but had more or less run out of steam by the time we pulled up outside a plain redbrick building on a dank street corner. In the inky midnight, coils of steam were slinking out of manholes, playing in the shadows. Huddled on the back seat of a cab, Paul asked our driver to wait a few minutes, just in case, and when a bouncer fixed plastic tags to our wrists, Paul suggested this was to assist the hospital with identification later. Shooting a last, thin grimace, he went inside first. Following him down a narrow passage, I found him standing very still, staring at the scene before our eyes. It was a few minutes before either of us could say a thing.

Around 250 white teenagers filled a small hall decorated in the style of a student beer-cellar. The boys were dressed for a boy-band audition and the girls for babysitting. Even the few trying to affect vacant nonchalance were careful not to trip anyone up and everyone smiled sweetly. A number had made it on to the dancefloor, where they observed each other's space politely while dancing a kind of epileptic hoedown – furious jerking of arms and legs, like speeded-up breakdancing. One girl was dancing like a string puppet; another boy took a great sprint on to the dancefloor and kept running, doing laps around it, waving his arms about. As each dancer launched into a new flailing of limbs, the others would gather round in an admiring circle; when the record ended, the dancer would give a rueful smile and it was someone else's turn. It was clear that no one had taken any drugs – not just tonight, but ever – and doubtful whether anyone had even had a drink. Motor Lounge resembled nothing so much as a Christian youth-club disco.

In due course, the house music descended into demonic Detroit techno, but there was nothing to suggest that anyone noticed the switch, and if the DJ had broken into Abba I suspect the crowd would have carried on politely bobbing along. Hours passed. We kept waiting for Paul's gangsters to arrive, but they never came, and when the thought occurred to us that the two meanest-looking people in the club were probably ourselves, we left.

The case for going to Detroit had always been slightly opaque. To most Americans the city is famous as the murder capital of the USA – and, although strictly speaking this is no longer statistically true, it's not far off. It is the American Dream's nightmare, a city where capitalism has gone famously wrong and from which half of its population has fled. To a certain type of clubber, however, Detroit is hallowed ground, for it is the birth place of Kevin Saunderson, Derrick May, and techno. The step-sister of house music, techno is an amphetamine-fuelled fury of metallic beeps and to some clubbers it sounds divine. Personally, I think it sounds like the devil drilling holes in dustbins, and I would never have gone near Detroit had it not been for an old friend who insisted I'd got the wrong end of the stick *altogether*. When they say *techno* in Detroit, he assured me, what they *mean* is any kind of electronic music. It could be house, garage, even disco. We'd love the place. It had this fantastic 'kicking urban vibe'.

We spent a long time looking for the kicking urban vibe, and having hunted high and low, I would now defy anyone to find it. The DJs who invented techno are said to have taken their inspiration from the movie *Bladerunner*, and this sounds plausible, as the *Bladerunner* set is what the city looks like. Stretched so thinly over such a huge map, whole sections have worn threadbare until they scarcely exist – and so one of Detroit's more ironic tragedies is that while its citizens can no longer make a living from cars, they can't live in Detroit without owning one. 'Jeez,' people say, 'I couldn't survive without my car. You gotta have a car.' And they are essentially right. But the longer you spend there, the more this starts to sound like the relationship between a junkie and smack.

Ambitious boulevards fan out from the city centre, and whichever one you choose leads straight into derelict dystopia, where the shops look less as if they closed down than simply gave up, and bad debt lingers like a smell on every corner. The only businesses that have managed to remain open in any number are transmission-repair shops and strip joints. One, Venus, was advertising a 'Golden Oldies' night, giving us something to puzzle over. Similarly puzzling are the new shops dotted amid the debris selling beauty products for nails, which have the smack of *Titanic* deckchair rearrangement. The only stately buildings left standing are churches, but these are heavily outnumbered by the low-rent, mission variety – Repent Ye Now shacks, the last refuge of the desperate. Tattered roadside billboards advertising the services of pawnbrokers and loan sharks have survived, like cockroaches after nuclear attack.

Detroit looks as if it has been the victim of some freak natural disaster that left it standing but turned it inside out. The further you go from the middle, the more it looks like a city, and after about ten miles you reach a place where there are cars and people and parking meters on the streets, and bars along the pavement, and restaurants with live music and air conditioning, full of jaunty waiters serving oversized meals to white-toothed young men and women who laugh loudly but tidily. The houses here are smaller and closer together than the creaky hulks marooned in the wastelands downtown, and the people who live in them are in the majority white. These are the suburbs, where everyone with enough money fled after the race riots of 1967, and from where they have stubbornly refused to return. It is quite possible to meet people in the suburbs who have visited Europe more recently than they have downtown Detroit, and those whose jobs don't allow them that luxury treat the city centre like a contaminated site. They park underneath office blocks connected by glass skywalks, and drive home in cars fitted with security devices that engage central locking when the engine starts up.

The mystery of Motor Lounge's Christian disco took no time at all to clear up. Dance music in Detroit meant black music, and with race relations as they were most of the downtown clubs had closed by the time of our visit. Those still open were taking no chances, and only nice white kids from the suburbs were welcome. We were wasting our time. I was mortified with embarrassment by the false start, but Paul was simply relieved. We gave up and drove to Chicago.

Ecstasy is the street name for a chemical called MDMA, or methylenedioxymethamphetamine. Invented in 1912 by a German pharmaceutical company and intended only for use as an ingredient in other drugs, it was effectively forgotten for several decades. After

19

World War Two it reappeared briefly in a handful of medical journals and was later tested by the American military as a Cold War truth drug. Then, once again, it was forgotten.

A Californian chemist re-synthesised MDMA in 1956. Alexander Shulgin was an unusual individual – a licensed pharmacist with a major drug company, but also a hippie – and for the next thirty years he operated a drugs laboratory from his home. By the late seventies, the Californian therapeutic community was prescribing MDMA to patients in psychotherapy, but still hoping to keep it a secret, fearful that widespread use would lead to abuse and attract the attention of the authorities.

'Let's face it,' wrote Timothy Leary. 'No one wants a sixties situation to develop, where sleazy characters hang around college dorms peddling pills they falsely call ecstasy to lazy thrill-seekers.'

But of course there were plenty of people who couldn't wait for such a development, and the elitist hippies' secret was soon out. Businessmen in Texas began marketing ecstasy as a club drug, and on the East Coast it became a feature of the gay black dance scene. The media got wind, then the authorities, and in 1985 the Drugs Enforcement Agency issued an emergency ban making MDMA an illegal substance.

Had they moved sooner, it is possible that none of us would have heard of ecstasy today, but they were too late. Followers of Bhagwan Shree Rajneesh were using the drug, and with branches of the cult scattered across the world ecstasy had already spread to Europe. The cult communities still thought of it as a therapeutic tool, though, rather than as a recreational drug. The credit for the missing piece of the ecstasy equation – music – goes to Chicago.

In the mid-eighties, DJs at a club called The Warehouse were inventing what soon became known as house – computerised dance music, like techno, but more soulful and textured – and with its happy marriage to ecstasy, modern clubbing was born. Since then, over the years house music has splintered into so many subgenres – hard house, deep house, trance, handbag – that 'house' is no longer a definition so much as an umbrella term. Unfortunately, the same, could be said of 'ecstasy'.

Ecstasy comes in a pill. Every tablet bears an imprint – a logo, if you like – and has its own name. In 1990 you might have had a White Dove, bearing a tiny engraving of a bird, and these days you might get a Mitsubishi, bearing the triple-diamond indentation of the automobile logo. Occasionally, you still come across ecstasy in capsule form. Capsules were popular in the early nineties, for there was a feeling that you got more for your money and you will still hear clubbers speak wistfully of Dennis the Menaces (black and red), or Rhubarb and Custards (pink and yellow).

Manufacturers of ecstasy have demonstrated a nice instinct for topicality. As Oliver Stone's *Malcolm X* was released we had Malcom Xs, imprinted with a large X, and Pterodactyls were issued to coincide with the release of *Jurassic Park*. In the run up to the 2001 general election, pills bearing the Euro symbol were popular, and if Britain ever has a referendum on its currency, no doubt Es will appear with a pound sign on them. Manufacturers are nothing if not inventive, clearly, but sadly it's not only the names they change. Though there is far greater choice on the market nowadays, the impression of consumer empowerment is illusory – for as soon as a wider variety became available, the quality began to vary drastically.

When manufacturers began tampering with Es, they would substitute the cheaper ingredient of amphetamine for MDMA. Then came a spell when pills were laced with a hint of barbiturate, followed by a short but nasty batch of Es containing ketamine, a devastating veterinary anaesthetic. A particularly sneaky substitute is something called MDA, a derivative of MDMA. Popular with drug dealers, it mimics the effects of its chemical cousin for the first fifteen minutes until, very suddenly, it's over – giving the unlucky clubber just enough of a glimpse to tempt them back to buy another. A typical dud pill nowadays contains little more than glucose and caffeine, but MDMA is still out there and the quality of Es widely varies, each new brand quickly acquiring a reputation on the club scene. When Leah Betts died after taking an Apple, dealers assumed their stocks would be worthless, but on the contrary, everyone wanted one. Apples, it was agreed, must be really something.

In other words, buying ecstasy has become a lottery. It's an endlessly frustrating game, and one that goes most of the way towards explaining why a world tour felt necessary simply to find a decent pill. I was absolutely certain we'd find some in the States. America had invented the drug as we know it, after all, as well as a philosophy for giving customers what they want. It seemed a safe bet. We were a little concerned, admittedly, to buy some club guides in Chicago, which took the editorial line that the clubs would be good if it weren't for the people in them. There were no details of the nature of the shortcomings, though, and all the signs for Chicago's scene looked promising. When Friday night came, we set out styled more like hikers than clubbers, bulging with flyers and maps. Any old E would do now to get us up and running, and the sooner the better.

We went clubbing all weekend long. I don't know how many clubs we went to, but we trawled through an enormous number, all crawling with armies of gargantuan security men, who patrolled the premises like sniffer dogs. Wherever we were, King Kong would walk past every two minutes and this strategy apparently worked, for there wasn't so much as an aspirin in sight. We seemed alone in finding this offputting, though, and became increasingly confused by the people we found in each club. We were starting to see what the magazines had meant, for you have to question a club's commitment to its own enterprise when it fills itself up with people better suited to be in a game-show audience. In one club, Crobar, a British-sounding man who was presumably the promoter got hold of the microphone in the DJ booth. 'This is fucking Crobar!' he roared. 'Make some fucking noise!' The crowd obliged with a polite murmur, but appeared baffled and mildly alarmed.

'Anyone under the influence of drugs,' warned signs in several clubs, 'will be arrested.' It was a threat I'd never seen before, and in any case seemed quite unnecessary here. Clubbers all over the world are nothing if not resourceful, and if they wanted to take ecstasy in Chicago they would. But there was nothing to suggest that any of them did. Instead, they liked to bring along toys – light sticks, sparkly skipping ropes, dummies – filling up the clubs with their props, and happy to leave it at that. The point of ecstasy is to create a formless space and see what can be made of the emptiness, but to a nation raised on orchestrated fun, this was beginning to look less appealing than I'd imagined.

American schoolchildren aren't allowed to spend their school holidays hanging about, but are sent away to summer camp for a marathon of wholesome group activities – and that's only the start of it. Most British undergraduates will agree to act like fools for Freshers' Week, but the nine-legged pub crawls are usually over once term begins. Americans, on the other hand, are encouraged to join fraternity and sorority groups, whose job it is to organise keg parties and other high jinx so that their fun is efficiently choreographed right up until the day they receive their degree.

When British students go home for a lie down at Easter, Americans are on Spring Break – an allegedly riotous week on a beach in Florida or Jamaica that consists of strictly scheduled misbehaviour. Monday

is Wet T-Shirt Contest day, Tuesday is Sunset Booze Cruise, and
so forth. On no account must a Spring Breaker be left in the lurch
with an idle hour, and MCs are posted along the beach with micro-
phones to commentate on what fun everyone's having. While we
were in Chicago it dawned on me that all the people I knew from
the UK who fell in love with America and moved there share one
common trait: they are basically dull souls who would very much like
to be thought otherwise but find this hard to pull off at home, where
they are left to their own devices. In America, however, they have
only to subscribe to a vigorous programme of social capers and they
can pass themselves off as whacky guys.

We ate an awful lot in Chicago. We couldn't help it, there was just
so much food everywhere we went, and much of it had the giddy
confection of a menu dreamt up by children. Ice cream came covered
in chopped up Mars bars, and we passed a bar whose sign read: 'Eli's
– Lunch. Dinner. Piano. Cheesecake', the sort of sense of priorities
you dream about as an eight-year-old. We couldn't find ecstasy for
the life of us, but we could have Black Forest Gateau with Smarties
on top at four in the morning if we liked, and these two things began
to seem related. The families I've known who are mystified as to why
anyone would want to get drunk ('Doesn't it just make you *silly*?')
conceive of a party as an occasion for excessive overeating, so that
the more they eat, the more successful a party it is, and there were
echoes of this here. Eating too much was an approved social over-
indulgence, and no matter how much you ate, nothing could go
wrong.

It is probably no coincidence that although Americans invented
ecstasy and house music, few of them thought to put the two together.
It was only when both were imported to Britain that clubbing as we
know it was born. Americans still haven't worked out what to do with
their twin inventions, and though we continue to read that US club
culture is at last about to 'take off', I wouldn't count on it. As Paul
has since pointed out, it's only a shame I didn't think of that earlier.

On our last weekend we made one final attempt, at a club called
Karma. Like all the other venues, Karma had mastered the appearance of a serious nightclub. And, also like all the others, it had let in
a bizarre medley of types, all engaged in extraordinary kinds of dancing. A young woman seemed to be impersonating a toy soldier;
another looked as if she thought her clothes had caught fire and was
trying to put them out. A fat man moved across the dancefloor as if

he was swimming underwater, and the one next to him appeared to be putting on an imaginary space-suit. Everyone gave the impression of suffering from a severe spinal defect, so that their bodies gave way at critical but unexpected moments – rather as if they'd all taken three steps out of their wheelchair before remembering they couldn't walk.

One of the loveliest characteristics of a dance club is the way it merges into fluid unity; it is an unmistakable quality, hard to describe, but beautiful and always affecting. I couldn't actually remember the last time I'd seen a dancefloor like these ones in America. People were dancing in pairs or individually, but never with . . . and as I searched for the word, Paul finished my sentence. 'The music'. And that was it; they were all fractionally out of time. We weren't looking at dancing at all, but at a laborious expression of good manners.

Bizarrely, though, people were pretending to have taken ecstasy. Everywhere we turned, they were chewing like mad, rubbing each other's heads, and waving neon light-sticks in friends' faces. There was much stomping and blowing and again and again we'd be convinced someone was on drugs, but realise up close that all they'd done was learn to look as if they were. They acted out the pretence with tireless attention to detail – although there wasn't much they could do about the abysmal dancing.

But it was even more bizarre than that. They weren't all pretending – some of them *really had taken an E.* Not many, but a few, and they were dancing every bit as fabulously badly as the rest, simply managing to chuck themselves out of their invisible wheelchairs slightly quicker. I have a friend who claims that every boyfriend she's had has been so lacking in rhythm that even with MDMA coursing through him he was unable to locate a beat. I'd never witnessed the condition until Karma, and we couldn't believe our eyes.

The idea when buying Es in a club is to approach someone who has clearly taken one, apologise for the indelicate nature of the enquiry, and ask if they know anyone selling anything. But Karma was so far beyond chemical redemption that the risk of actually finding Es, then being stuck there until they wore off, was terrifying. Neither of us liked to admit this to the other at first, so we shuffled around for a while. I said I thought I had a headache, Paul was struck by a sudden craving for Black Forest Gateau, perhaps with Smarties on top. And thus it was that we made our excuses to each other and left.

★   ★   ★

There was no point in trying to pretend otherwise. Chicago was a disaster. Detroit had been a farce, and the entire trip was beginning to look like it might be a terrible mistake. Putting aside the uneasy thought that at this rate we'd soon be home, we abandoned Illinois and flew on to San Francisco. The West Coast's contribution to the musical side of club culture was modest, it was true, but San Francisco had been the home of ecstasy's early pioneers. Furthermore – and this now seemed much more important – the city was famous for its prodigious consumption of drugs.

CHAPTER 3

Just a Bitch Slap

Visitors to America often have the sensation of having stumbled into a film set. Sometimes I think Americans experience the same problem, for their teenagers have only to open their mouths and out comes MTV, but with the Mayor of San Francisco, the sensation is overwhelming. Willie Brown is the prototype movie star's black liberal, a sleek package of good looks that glitter with cheeky authority. Just to add to the confusion, he is great friends with Sharon Stone in real life. His very name sounds like a screenwriter's fancy, and just before our arrival even his own city appeared to have mistaken him for an actor, for it had re-scripted his election campaign as a cliffhanger.

Mayor Brown had been anticipating a smooth return to office. The darling of gay, liberal and black San Francisco, he was enjoying a comfortable campaign until one week before polling day, when a militant gay contender called Tom Ammiano announced that he would run. Almost 50,000 voters wrote Ammiano's name on the ballot paper, forcing the mayor into a tense run-off battle. Even a lame election campaign can send a fever through a city, and a run-off is like an operatic duel. We arrived to find San Francisco upside-down with the thrill of it all.

'I've got *The LA Times* on the phone every day, *The New York Times* . . . Honestly, it's just gone *mad*,' panted Joey as he welcomed us in. Joey ran a guesthouse with his boyfriend, Simon, in the Mission district, and had been appointed a mayoral commissioner during Brown's first term. A fine example of a young civic queen, he ran off a breathless checklist of his public duties while showing us to our room, then snatched a quick fag before dashing off to the gym. Joey was outraged about California's ban on smoking in public, and dying to be booked for the offence so that he could 'take it all the way'. He flew about the guesthouse, leaving a gossipy trail in his wake ('Tom should have waited; it's his turn next time. It's just not *fair* to make the gay community choose. It's a bit *much*'), with Simon drawing up the rear. The less pretty half of the duo, Simon spoke to us only once and that was a week or so later, when Terry had just flown in. Stunned from a cigarette-free flight, Terry was smoking a brace of Camels as we welcomed him. 'We've found you the only hotel in town where you're allowed to smoke,' I was boasting, when Simon leapt out over the counter, swooped on the Camels and bore them off at arms length as though carrying a pair of hand grenades. 'You'll get us arrested!' he hissed.

But this was some time off, and on our first day in San Francisco Paul was convinced that Joey – effervescent, gay, libertarian Joey – would know where to get hold of the very best ecstasy. Historically, gay politics in San Francisco are closely related to the politics of hedonism, and this knowledge informed the new optimism blooming within Paul. Only reluctantly was he persuaded to leave the matter until we went out to dinner with Joey. Simon wouldn't be coming, Joey explained, as he had some housework to do.

The night began in Beauty Bar, in the heart of the Mission. It was exactly the kind of bar you would hope to find in San Francisco, a kitsch recreation of a fifties beauty salon, fitted with period hairdryers and dotted with manicure trays. The toilets were wallpapered with old newspaper adverts for beauty products, and across a collage of cuttings exhorting tight waists and porcelain skin someone had scrawled, 'I cannot be all of this'. A headline asked, 'When Is Casual Too Casual?' 'NEVER' had been added.

Joey drank cocktails. He was a handsome man in his early thirties with Latino-cropped black curls and skin the colour of tea, groomed into an all-American package of Hilfigger and Gap. When he talked of his business plans, his black eyes fizzed with ambition. Presently a friend of his passed by, a hairdresser called Robbie, peroxide blonde but possibly wiser than his tan suggested, and soon we were swept into laughter on his wave of camp exclamations.

'I went on three dates with unemployed men since August,' he volunteered, as if unemployment were a personal fetish.

Why were they unemployed?

'Ex-*actly*!'

27

Like many gay entrepreneurs, the pair were a likable confection of orthodoxy and excess. 'Here's a tip,' advised Robbie. 'Only buy cocaine from someone who has a job. Never buy it from an unemployed person.'

After Robbie left, the three of us moved on to Foreign Cinema. Foreign Cinema is another Mission showpiece, a restaurant designed like an old mill, built around an open courtyard where subtitled films are screened via an old-fashioned projector. The evening was mild, and we took a table outside. Joey introduced us to a string of owners and maitre d's, and gave excitable waves to groups of diners dressed in matt black. As more cocktails arrived, he became fluttery, and began to confide his suspicions about one of the managers, a young man with a sweet smile who, Joey explained, had recently got married.

'See?' whispered Joey, over his glass. 'See the way he keeps glancing at me, when he thinks I'm not looking?' The manager in question had been busy with tables inside for at least an hour, and I had to say that I hadn't noticed, but Joey was convinced. 'I know it's going to happen, I just know it. Sure, his wife's a sweetie and all that, but you know – newlyweds, huh? It's always the way.' He gave a conspiratorial snort, and ordered another round. I liked Joey a great deal, but saw now with terrible certainty the direction the night with him would take. I was reaching my cocktail limit, but Paul was steaming along, blissfully unaware. With a broad wink in my direction, he leant over and got down to business.

'The thing is, Joey, we haven't got all that much time in San Francisco. You know Decca's doing this travel book. Well, it's got a slightly, ah, unusual angle. You see, we've been sent to find the best ecstasy in the world.' Pausing for effect, he gave him a light pat on the arm, and ploughed on. 'Now, you're clearly a man who knows what goes on in this town. Do you think you could steer us in the right direction?' Joey looked taken aback. He glanced at me, and looked back at Paul.

'We-ell,' he began cautiously, 'that's really not my scene. I just smoke pot. I don't think' – and then his face lit up. 'But, hey, you know what? I know a few people around town. What do you say we have another cocktail and see what I can come up with?' Paul grinned, waved for a waiter, and leant back in his chair, just out of reach of the kick I aimed under the table. I smiled – 'That would be wonderful, thank you so much' – and resigned myself to the inevitable.

It was late when we stumbled out of the restaurant. Joey had done all he could to keep us there, but Paul was under the impression that

Joey and he had an understanding, and was eager to get off. Well after midnight, when Paul had interrupted yet again – 'Now, Joey, about those Es' – our host could defer no longer, and we poured into a cab and set off to a club he knew called Liquid. First, though, we had to drop back at the guesthouse, so that he could roll a joint and change outfits again. Simon was sitting very still in the corner of their living room as we clattered in, and remained stony quiet as Joey danced around the apartment showing off his walk-in wardrobe, his collection of sunglasses, his stash of pot. Paul trotted after him, keeping up a stream of baffled compliments. After three joints, Joey found an outfit he was happy with, an improbable sort of homeboy concoction topped off with a floppy hat. 'Da-daah!' he cried, gave a bow to the mirror, blew Simon a kiss, and led us off in another cab.

Pulling up a few blocks away on 16th Street and South Van Ness, we found a crowd milling on the pavement. This is a common sight outside San Francisco nightclubs, as everyone has to go outside to smoke, and Joey breezed through and marched us to the bouncer. I took this for a promising sign, but he wasn't proposing a little freelance business – merely congratulating the man on the birth of his new baby. We admired the infant photos until we had run out of things to say, and still Joey seemed keen to linger at the door and smoke another joint. Paul took him by the arm and led him firmly inside.

Liquid wasn't a large club, just a bare, rectangular room with a bar along one side, a low stage at the rear and a pool table near the door, but it was nothing less than an epiphany. The closest we'd come so far to Americans moving in unison had been a line of treadmills in a Chicago gym, but here fluid harmonies of dancers packed the floor. More gay than straight, they wore vintage denims and trainers, and bursts of laughter bubbled through the club.

'Do you like?' Joey beamed.

'It's stunning –' I began, but Paul was already shouting above the music.

'Now, my friend, about those –'

'Let's dance!' With a pina colada balanced on each shoulder, Joey bore him off into the throng.

The night took its predictable course. I was gently sobering up, Paul was crashing around, roaring about Es, and Joey was getting increasingly giddy.

'More cocktails! Let us lie on the pool table!'

At one point he sent Paul off to ask the newly paternal bouncer if he knew where we could get anything. When Paul returned looking somewhat shaken and sheepish, he was swept away back on to the dancefloor. Through a crowd of heads, I could see Paul staggering in circles, now wearing Joey's hat so low on his brow he was unable to see. The next time Joey nipped outside for a joint, I grabbed Paul's hand.

'Home time, I think.'

'Really?' He blinked. 'But Joey says there's this guy he knows, has the best stuff, gonna be here any minute now. Joey says he really doesn't want to let us down.'

We found him whispering giggles to the bouncer outside.

'Thanks for a lovely night. It's been great. It's just that I'm a bit tired now, so we're going to go home.'

'Oh! No, hold on, wait a minute. I've remembered this other club I know. It's an after-hours place; I'm sure we can get some there. If not, we can definitely get speed. It's just around the corner. And if that doesn't work, I know another place we could try.'

'No, really, thanks, but it's no problem. And we don't want any speed.'

'But I'm sure we'll find Es. And I think you should buy something now, anyway. After all the trouble I've been to for you.' He turned to Paul. 'I've been to a lot of trouble, you know.' He turned to hail a cab, and I pulled Paul into a doorway.

'Sweetheart, of course he claims he can get you whatever you want now. He'll say anything to keep you out with him. He doesn't have a clue where to get pills – he never did – he's been stringing you along all night. He just wants to get you pissed. He thinks you fancy him, and that all that shouting in his ear about drugs is a closet come-on. Now he's trying to make out you owe him something.'

'Oh, fuck. Hook, line and sinker.'

'So let's go home.'

'Right. Definitely.'

'To this after-hour club, then?' shouted Joey. Paul turned, confused and off-balance, spotted him, and gave a wobbly wave. 'Great! But look, there aren't any cabs. Let's just walk home, eh?'

We set off on foot along Mission. By 17th the buzz of Liquid had faded into the darkness, and the pavement was deserted except for a man asleep in a wheelchair. I pulled my coat tighter; Joey and Paul fell silent. When a night-bus drew up at the next corner I could feel Joey's wave of relief as he bundled us on board – but as I fumbled for change, without warning he stepped smartly back, taking Paul with him as the doors snapped shut. They re-opened – 'You getting on, or what?' the driver barked – and began to close again. Just in time, Paul pulled me off, but already I had seen what was happening. Behind Joey stood a tall black man in a large coat.

The bus pulled away. The three of us stared at the man. It was 3 a.m. on a scruffy crossroads in the wrong part of the Mission, and the only other people I could see were beggars and prostitutes looming in the half-light of doorways. For a second, Joey visibly lost his nerve. Just inches away from his intended tête-a-tête, here he was instead, saddled with the pair of us and his rash promise to buy drugs from this giant. He looked panicky. Then he squared his slender shoulders, sidled up, and asked the man if he was selling anything.

The dealer was all smiles and efficiency. Oh yes, he said, but only cocaine. Addled by this unexpected turn of events, and swaying slightly, Paul turned to me. I gave a weak shrug. Men claiming to sell cocaine on street corners at 3 a.m. are never selling anything of the sort, and right then $40 seemed like a price worth paying to get us off this street and back to the guesthouse, where the discovery that we had in fact bought baking powder should bring the ludicrous night to a close. I nodded. The man began to rummage in his pocket, and Paul leant over and asked if it was rock. Oh yes, said the man, it's rock all right. Delighted, Paul began to hand over the money, but by then I had realised the mistake. By 'rock', Paul meant a lump of high-grade, uncut cocaine – a wildly optimistic request under the best of circumstances. What the man meant by rock was crack cocaine.

Joey apologised, explained the misunderstanding, and we were turning to walk away when he asked the man if he could suggest anywhere else we might find powder.

'Sure. Try right over there.' Beckoning over his shoulder like a policeman giving directions, he pointed at a patch of mosaic beneath his feet. 'Same kind of stone he'll be standing on, but just round the corner.' Joey thanked him, and he smiled pleasantly.

'No problem, goodbye now. You take care. Stay safe.'

And so around the corner we went, a caravan of misunderstanding and calamity, tottering along in Joey's floppy hat through the flotsum of bums and hookers and Big Mac boxes. Sure enough, on another mosaic paving-stone stood an extremely tall black man wearing large glasses and an anorak. There was nothing of the street in his clothes or his demeanour, and he had the bearing of a rather serious-minded preacher. Beside him stood a faintly deranged-looking skinny black woman with long hair scraped into a high pony-tail and a face all squashed out of shape, her eyes sunk into the seventies, her lower lip jutting into next week. She was spinning in circles, spewing up chatter like a tipsy teenage girl, and her face lit up as she saw us approach.

'Where you *from*, let me hear that *acc*-ent, where's that *from*? London! London, Paris . . .' She broke off and turned to Paul, who was mumbling something to the preacher man.

'He a good man! He ain't gonna rob you or nothin'.' In the same breath she was back to me.

'You know, my ambition is to go to London. I only have three ambitions in life. To go to London, Paris, and own a Jag-war. Yep! A Jag-war. I already had a Rolls-Royce, I had a rich godfather, you see, but I ain't never had a Jag-war. That's my ambition.' I tried to edge away from her to hear what Paul was saying to the man, but she launched into an agitated tangle of a tale about a friend of hers.

'People say to me, what you doin' wit' a white guy? And I say, that ain't no white guy, that's my friend –' Joey's head snapped up.

'White's a colour!'

'White ain't a colour!'

'Oh yes it is.'

'No it aint!'

'Yes it is.'

Slipping away, I went in search of Paul and the preacher, who had disappeared. I found them around the corner, deep in conversation in a doorway but as I approached, though, hard on my heels came Joey, and hard on his the woman. The preacher's face fell as he saw the rabble descending. It was impossible to find out what had been said, as the woman was holding forth once more on her Jag-war ambitions.

'Come on,' I whispered to Paul. 'Let's call it a day.'

'No, no, it's fine.' He swayed gently. 'We were just having a nice chat about things. Oh, and he says he's got some great pills.'

But Joey was having none of it. Having lost his place in the proceedings, he pouted and glared angrily at everyone. 'If the deal was *going* to happen, it would have *happened* by now. Come on.' He tugged Paul's arm. 'This stinks.' The preacher watched and listened calmly, but when Joey tried to bustle Paul away he took a quick long stride, blocking their path. All at once the dealer looked ominously vexed.

'Excuse me, sir,' he said to Joey. His voice was very low and very quiet.

'I'm not *sir*,' Joey flounced back. 'Who are you calling sir?'

'I'm calling you sir' – the baritone was icily soft – 'because I am trying to be polite, and speak diplomatically, and go about my business properly with good manners.' He leant down until his mouth was inches from Joey's ear. The woman fell silent, and took a half-step back. 'Now you, sir, are being rude and arrogant. I am trying to talk to you as a human being, and you are not doing me the same courtesy. Now please, leave me alone to get on with my business.' There was a frozen pause.

'*I* don't deal with humans,' Joey huffed, tugging on his hat. '*I* deal with feelings.'

The next pause was broken by the woman, sounding altogether less sure of herself.

'This a good man,' she bleated. 'He ain't gonna beat you or rob you.' Paul looked at her with bleary incomprehension, started to sway again, and I turned to the man. 'Excuse me, you can talk to me. I'm his wife.' But then the woman was erupting back in my face – 'Oh, your accent!' – and in the confusion I heard Joey tell Paul we were leaving. If Paul could feel anything by this point, it looked like relief, but as we turned to walk away he made a fatal mistake. 'Sorry,' he told his new friend bashfully. 'Looks like we're done here. I've been told.'

'Who told you?' the preacher asked very quietly. Oblivious to all that had passed, Paul lifted a finger and pointed it to Joey. 'Him.'

The preacher took a smart step up, swung his arm back, and gave Joey a great big swat around the face.

He fell to the floor. The woman let out a shriek, and everyone scattered. A second later Joey was back on his feet, fumbling in his pocket and dancing, wild-eyed and flushed like a boxer. Christ, I thought, I don't believe this, he's got a gun – but worse, what he pulled out was a phone. He stabbed out a number, and within moments was gabbling hysterically to the police, still dancing and too distracted to see that half a dozen men had appeared from alleyways and were heading towards the commotion.

I flew off down the street, followed by Joey when he saw what was coming, but Paul was still wandering in an amiable daze on the corner. I screamed at him to follow, and he ambled out into the traffic; I turned my gaze, only to see Joey not fleeing but chasing the preacher. The preacher had his head down, taking long, loping strides, with Joey galloping after him, still talking into the phone. I looked back and saw a gang of men heading down the street behind me. The gap closing, I was running out of breath, and couldn't even see Paul any

33

more – when from nowhere, a cab pulled up and the door swung open. I yelled for Joey and Paul, and seconds later we were all safely inside.

'Well, thank Christ for that.' As the doors swung shut I sank back in the seat and began to give the address of the guesthouse, counting the minutes until we'd be home, but Joey shouted a stream of directions over the top. To my horror, I saw he was still on the phone. Waving directions to the driver, he relayed co-ordinates to the police, and soon we were weaving back to the original scene, combing the alleyways with Joey's head out the window.

'Is that him?' he squealed.

'Is that who?' mumbled Paul, sinking asleep with his head on my shoulder.

'Look, guys,' the driver started, 'I don't want no trouble, I just put you out here, OK?' But Joey was glued to the phone and took no notice, so up and down the alleys we went, my head now in my hands. The taxi driver tried again. 'Look, I really don't have time for this. I drop you here, OK?' But as he pulled over, one, two and then three police cars appeared, a cavalry of lights and sirens blocking each end of the alley, so that the only people successfully entrapped by the whole exercise were ourselves. The driver too had his head in his hands now, and was cursing softly in Spanish under his breath. He switched off the engine.

'Well,' I spat at Joey. 'I wonder what we'll say when the cops ask us why we were talking to the guy in the first place.' Paul woke up, rubbing his eyes.

'Oh yeah.'

'Oh, don't worry about *that*. I already told them: he asked us for money, we said no, and he socked me in the jaw. Just like it happened.' Three heads were now in hands. Joey got out the car, exchanged words with an officer, and the police cars pulled off. With great reluctance, Joey got back in and told the driver to take us home. We pulled away.

'Phwew!' Joey giggled, rubbing his knees. 'What a drama!'

'God, mate, I'm sorry you got hit,' offered Paul. 'That's awful.'

'Hit? Hit? That didn't hurt! If it hadda hurt I'd have hit him back, only I thought he had a gun. No, that didn't hurt. Look, it's not even red. That was just a bitch slap.' Then, seconds later, 'I can't believe he hit me! He hit me!' And so home we rode, with Joey, torn between the shabby indignity of it all and high on the glamorous drama, unable to decide which way to fall but inclining towards the latter. We said goodnight at the foot of the stairs, and halfway up he turned and visibly swelled. '*Wait* till Simon hears about this!'

'Do you know,' Paul slurred as he collapsed into bed, 'in the taxi Joey had his hand on my leg. Can you believe it? What was that about?'

CHAPTER 4

Aspirins and Vitamins

The first days in San Francisco slipped by fresh and mild. We cycled over the Golden Gate Bridge, followed the election campaign, and idled about, eating burritos in our fingers and watching Mexicans trade fake greencards in doorways. Awed by the mansions on Nob Hill, seduced by the glamorous seediness of SoMa, we rode the cable cars, ate out in laundrettes, sailed up and down in trams, and got lost in the pink and pale-blue streets at least once every day. It is an astonishingly pretty city, like a psychedelic Brighton, its gracious villas giving way as you climb the hills to a higgle-piggle of pastel terracing.

Joey and Simon's guesthouse stood in the heart of the Mission neighbourhood, just southwest of the city centre. Traditionally working class, low rent and heavily Latino, the area is a scruffy cauldron of vice, with none of the romantic pedigree of the Castro or the Haight, and until recently would have been an unlikely home for an ambitious gay couple. By late 1999 fashionable gentrification was under way, however, and Joey considered himself its bohemian ambassador. His place covered three floors of darkly Spanish design, and would have evoked an old Barcelona townhouse, heavy and sombre, had it not been for the dishes of jelly babies and candy twists sprinkled liberally in every corner.

Joey's recovery from our adventures had been impressively brisk. Already up when we came downstairs the following morning, he was busy with election paperwork, citric aftershave mingling with the smell of coffee, and fresh lilies on the mahogany dining table. I was curious to see how he would process the previous night, but he batted it away with a light laugh and a shake of the head, and at breakfast addressed the larger share of his attentions to me. Over croissants, he talked about the mayoral campaign and the political pressure on both candidates to show resistance to the corporate march of super-stores and Starbucks in neighbourhoods like the Mission. Neither Brown nor Ammiano could afford the impression that commerce was the cause closest to his heart, he explained. The other campaign issues Joey listed – Was Brown anti-fat people? Should transvestite nuns be allowed to march on Good Friday? – would have sounded about right in Manchester's Student Union bar.

The mayoral election made explicit San Francisco's character, but it is palpable everywhere. In the Tenderloin district, the poor and drug-addicted queue up for food handouts, but even in their desti-tution they carry themselves with a dignity that suggests they know they do not have nothing. In the Financial District stands the Trans-america Pyramid, a statuesque commercial building, the highest in the city. Property values in San Francisco arc dictated by the quality of view offered, thus offices conventionally command more rent the higher up they are. It would stand to reason that developers would wish to maximise the space available at the summit, and yet this shimmering building has been built in the shape of a spire.

The other great thing about San Francisco, Paul and I both thought, was that there obviously really were a lot of drugs around. It would be difficult to say exactly how we formed this impression. People weren't dancing through the streets off their heads, but there was something in the general mood that implied we would have no trouble in our search, and none of the prudish chill of most American cities with regard to depravity. Ecstasy was not going to be a problem. So confident of this were we that we decided to forget about the hunt for a while. It could wait until Terry arrived – flying in from Man-chester for a weekend with characteristic gusto for the promise, as he put it, of 'a right old carry on'.

It would have been a wise plan, but sadly was not one we quite managed to see through. The day before Terry was due to arrive we hired bicycles, and by mid-afternoon had ended up lost again – this time in a grassy uptown square framed by Italian cafes and antiquarian-bookshops. A young man stopped to ask if we needed directions, and we fell into conversation. He had floppy blonde hair like a surfer, and a manner like a *Lonely Planet Guide* dispensing information. As he rattled on I could feel Paul gearing himself up.

'Sounds as if you know this town well. Do you know where we can get any ecstasy?'

'Yeah, sure. Go to the corner of Haight and Masonic.'

'Really?'

'Sure. Know where it is?' We nodded, hugely impressed.

'You'll have no problem.' We thanked him – 'Any time' – and he sauntered off.

Needless to say, the sensible thing at this point would have been to go home. The weekend would soon be upon us, Terry would arrive, and we could set about finally buying some Es in a more plausible fashion. Had anyone told me they'd tried to buy drugs off the street in the old hippie quarter on the advice of a surfer, I would have blushed. Yet there we were, half an hour later, alighting from a bus at the corner of Haight and Masonic, making hopeful eyes at strangers in the dusk.

If Disney ever builds a sixties hippie themepark, it will look like this corner of Haight Ashbury. The intersection is the bullseye of the neighbourhood, made famous more than thirty years ago for its free love and pot but which has since been turned into a lifesize souvenir of itself. Tie-dye and incense shops line the roads, next to vegan coffee shops and other gestures towards the quarter's former life. Red-eyed teenagers squat on the pavement, smoking wistfully and talking rubbish. Dogged lesbians buy African poetry in the book-stores, and German tourists buy novelty lighters. I could not believe we were going to try and buy drugs here.

I am always amazed by the number of people who equate social status with drug proficiency. From an ability to build wittily sculp-tured spliffs, or to infiltrate trifle with hash, are limitless personal attributes inferred by such people. According to their social code, if a clubber takes more than ten minutes to buy drugs it is a personal catastrophe – and the code is popular among clubbers, because it represents a new ladder of social opportunity most of us stand a chance of scaling. A hearty appetite for drugs and a modicum of dexterity with a packet of Rizla is all it requires. I'd rather smoke my own foot than subscribe to this view, however – and so it is not easy to explain why I was wandering up to two stoned teenagers squatting on the floor outside a vegetarian-candle shop. The truth was that I didn't relish having to tell Terry that we'd failed to buy a single E.

One teenager was halfway through a ramble: 'That's the point of Rainbow, man. You just are what you are –' when he looked up, broke off, and thrust a flyer in my face.

'It's a party, man, you're gonna love it.' I studied the flyer.

'How do you know?'

'Er, because you will.' His Jimi Hendrix T-shirt covered his knees.
'But you don't know us.'

He thought about this for a moment. 'I know you love to party.'

'OK, then,' said Paul, 'can you tell me where we can buy some drugs?'

'We-e-ell.' He studied us. 'Are you a cop?'

'No,' sighed Paul, 'I am a British tourist now very bored of trying to buy drugs.'

'Oh, OK, what do you want?' We told him, and he cheerfully bounded off up Masonic to find some, pausing only to give instructions to the young boy with him who couldn't have been more than thirteen years old. 'Watch them, yeah?' he ordered, 'and don't forget the only rule: no offering anything to kids.'

Minutes later he was back, panting with excitement. 'They're $25, man; they've got a butterfly printed on them; they're excellent.' He clearly had no idea about ecstasy, and the pills were clearly going to be useless, but there comes a point where these transactions assume a logic of their own. Another whey-faced, catatonically stoned teenager approached, and this was of course our man's friend. We took a stroll around the corner together. With money and pills ready to exchange, he spoke his only words.

'You sure you're not a cop?'

'No,' replied Paul, 'I am not a cop.'

'Oh, OK,' and he handed over the pills. Back at the guesthouse, we found that they had a sugar coating and looked a lot like headache pills; and that their butterfly logo bore an uncanny resemblance to that of a pharmaceutical brand. We took them, had some supper and went to bed, reflecting the following morning that it was an achievement of sorts to set out in search of the best E in the world and manage so soon to come across the worst.

Terry's visit got off to a strained start. He flies with tremendous enthusiasm, so tends to arrive dazed more by his own exuberance than any effects of long-haul confinement. He took the view that anyone game enough to come all this way for a weekend should be entitled to smoke a cigarette in bed, and when Simon confiscated his Camels in reception it rather took the wind out of his sails. He was still smarting when Joey cantered up to our rooms to say hello. There was a wary tension as the two shook hands and sized each other up; the pair shared Spanish good looks and not dissimilar ambition, but Terry was none too sure he liked the look of Joey's extravagant charm, and after a few taut minutes Joey retreated, still flashing smiles but looking slightly taken aback. As the door swung shut Terry cocked one eyebrow. 'I see.'

He declared he had no patience with jet lag, so the three of us set off on foot through Delores Park for the Castro, the famous gay district. It was a crisp Saturday morning, and soon Terry was exclaiming at the gayness of it all. 'Look at that!' he whooped, face pressed up to the glass of a gym on Market Street, 'And look at him!' We bounded up Castro and down Noe, Terry seizing my hand, now skipping, then stopping dead to stare at some new vision of delight. In truth, the Castro's heyday was over years ago, seen off chiefly by Aids, but also by an uneasy feeling that it was time the gay community grew up; the infamous bath-house quarter of the seventies has been tamed into little more than tasteful restaurants and furnishing stores, and looks like a West Coast Hampstead. But, for all that, it is still the Castro, and Terry was in no mood for disappointment.

Soon Terry was ready to hear grand tales of ecstasy triumph. 'So,' he asked between mouthfuls of pancake in a diner, 'let's have it. What's been the best so far?' I studied the tablecloth and considered a quick fiction, but abandoned the idea and mumbled the bare bones of the truth.

'What?' Terry reached over for more syrup. Not looking up from my plate, I repeated my tale. He stopped eating, put down his cutlery and gaped.

'Not a thing? Three weeks, and not a thing? No! You are joking, aren't you?' He tossed back his head and hooted. 'Well, sod that. Give me half an hour in this town and I'll sort us out. Honestly!' He gazed at us, shaking his head.

I tried to explain – 'You don't understand, Terry, you ask people about drugs in this country and they look at you like you're some kind of lunatic' – but he was having none of it, and called for the bill in a flounce of amused impatience, like a wife who's come home and found her husband making a hash of the ironing.

'Was everything all right?' asked the waiter. Terry glanced at the bill and looked up.

'Will you get us arrested if we ask you a question?' The boy, a freckly baby-faced blonde, made a nervous bash at coquette eyes.

'Er, no, fire away.'

'Do you know where we can buy ecstasy?' The waiter thought hard, and offered a sheepish grin. 'That's the only one I don't think I can help you with,' he whispered.

'What about cocaine?'

He gazed helplessly. 'Oh. That's the other one. Sorry.'

The rest of the day passed with more whooping and shopping in the Castro. Terry had it in his head that the Cult Boys, a troop of gay models along the lines of the Chippendales, were signing calendars in a gift shop, but when we got there it turned out to be the calendar's photographers doing the signing instead. Terry's attention turned to a display of bottles of pheromone scent, apparently guaranteed to make him irresistible to other men.

'Does it really work?' Paul asked.

'My husband certainly thinks so,' preened the man behind the counter.

'But that doesn't prove anything, does it? Presumably he finds you attractive anyway.'

'Well, he finds me more so when I'm wearing it.'

'But surely,' Paul persisted, 'the real test is to wear it with someone who doesn't like you?' The man stiffened, and glared. 'There has been some *actual* scientific research.' Terry snorted, but bought a bottle anyway.

Passing another shop, we spotted a pair of Dior sunglasses in the window, their oversized rims encrusted with diamante. I was transfixed, and the shopkeepers, a pair of gentle antique queens, were thrilled. 'You can have $25 off, because you love them so much!' Next door was a vaguely New Age vitamin shop, boasting pills that sounded like amphetamines.

'Will I feel them working?' Paul demanded.

'Oh yes,' the assistant smirked. Two each, and two hours later, we couldn't feel a thing. In a store on Market an elderly, bird-like woman sold us another brand. 'Half of one of these and I'm flying!' she giggled.

'Any idea where we can buy some drugs?' Terry asked as we paid. 'Frankly, we've been reduced to buying bloody vitamin pills, and we were rather hoping for something stronger.'

She shook her head kindly. 'Ooh, sorry, dear, I'm afraid I'm the last person to ask.'

Joey sealed his fate early that evening. Terry was ready before us, so headed down to Beauty Bar for a drink with Joey. He was back within ten minutes, quivering. Joey had ordered him a cocktail – then made him pay for it! Terry looked like he had just accidentally drunk some-one else's urine, and Joey was henceforth relegated to an irredeemable object of contempt.

Unfortunately, I'd been banking on Joey to point us in the right direction for the evening, and soon we found ourselves trawling the Castro aimlessly. It was a damp, fuzzy night, and behind every window we could see only more people eating more food; we passed noodle bars, bistros, pizza parlours and even a sausage emporium, but not a single bar or club. Even in the Castro, Americans' overwhelming urge was apparently only to eat. Just as I was about to suggest a quick dash back to see Joey, Terry made a lunge down Market Street and grabbed a passer-by. Where should we go to get a drink and some music, he demanded.

'Well,' said the young man, smiling slowly at him. 'If you came back to my place I sure could show you a –'

'No, no. We just want to go to a bar.'

The man shrugged. 'There aren't really any good bars in the Castro. I guess you could try Midnight Sun. That's really Ralph Lauren . . .'

'Marvellous.'

We found Midnight Sun a few blocks away, on 18th.

'Right then.' Terry leant over the bar and bellowed. 'Just where do we have to go to find a good time?'

'That all depends what you mean, honey,' the barman batted back. He wore a full beard, but spoke like a drag queen.

'I want to go somewhere with beautiful boys and have fun. Obviously.'

'We-ell. That still depends what you mean. My idea of beautiful is a big hairy lumberjack type, and fun is being tied up in a dungeon with a bottle of poppers duct-taped to my nose. Define your terms.'

Terry giggled. 'That sounds fantastic.'

'Ah-ha, no.' Stepping in briskly, I shook my head. 'What he means is, to go to a nice club with beautiful men where you can jiggle about and dance and smile at people and take drugs.'

The man glanced at me, abruptly disengaged. 'Well, I can help you with everything except the last one.' He pulled a face. 'That's so *eighties*. But if you must, go to Club Universe.'

It was pouring with rain when we arrived at Universe. Outside was the usual semi-circle of clubbers, shivering in tight white T-shirts and smoking sodden cigarettes. Inside, the club was huge, designed, like the Hacienda, along industrial-chic lines, and fully appointed with pumping Euro house, a podium dancer in chaps and a cowboy hat, and all the usual trappings of a gay dance club. Terry was in raptures – 'Give me five minutes' – and was gone, his shimmery disco shirt swallowed up into the dancing. Paul and I shuffled about on the edge of the dancefloor.

Half an hour later he was back, fuming.

'Now this *is* a joke. I went straight to the back of the stage, and there was a man in one of these stupid cowboy hats, *obviously* selling drugs. So I say, "Will you sell me some drugs?" And he says, "No. I don't know you. You could be anyone. I've never seen you before in my life." So I told him, I said, "Bloody hell, this is ridiculous. I've come all the way from England to this bloody place for the weekend and all I want is an E, and you lot are so uptight about it, it's an insult."'

Paul struggled not to laugh while Terry continued. 'So he says OK, and tells me to stand there and wait, because his mate's got them but he won't hand them over just now. So I stand and wait, and, bugger me, a whole queue starts to build up behind me. And it's obvious what's happening, and those gorilla bouncers are standing around, and then the dealer cocks his bloody hat and dances off!'

Terry disappeared again, and was back ten minutes later in a new bewilderment of dismay. He had found a dealer who'd told him that yes, he had Es in his pocket, but didn't dare take them out and hand one over, for fear of being seen. The rest of the conversation, as reported by Terry, went: 'This is ridiculous. You're a drug dealer and you're too scared to hand over drugs?'

Drug dealer: 'Yes.'

Terry: 'Well, if you don't watch out I'm going to steal them out of your pocket.'

Drug dealer: 'Go away.'

Now Paul was equally indignant, for it was two minutes after two and the bar had stopped selling alcohol. Bouncers in black bomber jackets were already shining torches into people's glasses and ordering them to drink up; commando-style squadrons patrolled the room, fingering their flashlights restlessly. When it reached the point where four of them were circling us, we stalked out in disgust. There was a horribly damp silence in the back of the cab.

The whole weekend was collapsing into ruins. I might have been right about San Francisco's overall indulgence of vice, but had overlooked a recent shift in police attitudes towards recreational drug-use. Paul had spotted various stories in the press about a police reappraisal of policy, but I'd dismissed them as standard election-time empty posturing. This was proving to be a horribly careless miscalculation. The city was in the grip of an almighty crack-down on drugs, a concerted and meaningful operation quite unlike the token gestures the British police occasionally make. One club had already been closed following drug-related arrests, and the threat hung over several more, so dealers were minimising their risk by magnifying suspicion. We had a serious problem on our hands.

Terry started on the driver.

'Frankly, I have to say that your clubs are absolutely bogshite awful. You can't smoke, you can't drink, you can't take drugs. It isn't a nightclub if you can't do any of that.' The driver glanced up at him in the rearview mirror.

What followed is unclear. I'm a woeful drinker, prone to collapse, and had kept pace with Paul and Terry only on the assumption that we would shortly be buying something that would bring me round. I folded on to the floor of the cab, but I have an image of Terry leaning forward in a whispering huddle with the driver, then sitting back in a brighter mood, announcing that he had new plans for the night. We could go home, but he was off to another club – and at some point we must have dropped him off, because when we got back to the guesthouse he was gone. I was fast asleep; Paul carried me out of the taxi, then off the pavement, up the stairs and into our room.

The next thing I remember is waking up in bed and hearing Terry and Paul run through the intervening hours. Terry's indignation had scaled new heights. The taxi driver had taken him to a sex club, where he'd arrived in high spirits, only to be issued with a laminated list of dos and don'ts – 'And half these things I've never done in my life, don't even know what the buggers are' – then counselled by a man in a lab coat before being allowed to take his clothes off. 'It was like going to the clap clinic. I just danced around in a towel for a bit and left.'

Drifting off again for a minute, I re-awoke to hear Paul saying: 'So I got her into bed, but then I woke up and found her naked, trying to climb out of the window in her sleep.' I listened on with surprise as he described pulling me down and steering me into the bathroom along the corridor. 'I must have fallen asleep,' he continued, 'because the next thing I know someone's banging on my door, and I thought it must be you or her, but when I open it there's the little queen from the next-door room standing there in his boxers. And he's looking a bit scared, and he says to me, "I'm sorry to disturb you, but would you mind coming and getting your wife out of my bed? I woke up and found her getting in, and I keep asking her to get out, but she won't wake up."'

*   *   *

The Mission was at its most exotic on Sunday mornings. San Franciscans referred to it as a transition district – meaning a poor part of town teetering on the cusp of gentrification – but while some considered the imminent overhaul a promise, and others a threat, either way it was still in its infancy. If you turned your eyes upwards, it looked like Havana, red paint peeling off wooden balconies and salsa floating down from cracked windows, but the scruffiness below was less sultry. Concrete thrift-stores sold plastic stereos, burritos, nylon bridesmaids' dresses and jumbles of Catholic bric-à-brac behind windows promising 'NU 2U2'.

Saturday night would bring white faces on to the streets, pretty young bohemians in upturned jeans, but by Sunday morning they were gone again, and the air grew thick with the smell of Mexican cooking. Young men in cowboy boots clipped along with moody girlfriends on their arm, and entire families would fill cafes for a Hispanic variation of brunch, a pungent marathon lasting late into the afternoon, until sleeping toddlers in shiny dresses had to be carried home crumpled and stained. Outside on the pavement, tramps laid out weekend wares on blankets, but who would buy their kitchen-roll dispensers, ballgowns and telephone wires was never clear.

That Sunday we woke late and grumpy. I was reluctant to go down to breakfast for fear of running into our next-door neighbour, and Terry was grumbling about how I'd been the only person to end up in bed with a gay man so far, and if the bugger wasn't so ugly he'd have tried climbing in himself. 'So much for those fucking phero-mones.' Paul was moderately cheerful until we broke the news that he had to get up because we were going to another club. He lay in bed, duvet over his head, moaning softly into the pillow.

The T-Dance at Endup had been running from 8 a.m. every Sunday for nearly a decade. A clubbing institution is usually one of two things – a corporate museum, like the Ministry of Sound, for instance, or one of the best clubs in the world. Paul was in no doubt at all about which of these the T-Dance would be; nor could he be dissuaded from the view that there was something unhealthy about going to a nightclub before lunch. Stumbling bleary-eyed through the Mission, Terry kept up a babble of optimism – 'It's *bound* to be just like Strangeways.' Paul would only stuff his hands deeper into his pockets and stare at the ground.

CHAPTER 5

Faaab Sunglasses

There is a common misconception among ecstasy's critics that the drug has supernatural powers and can transform the dreariest night into nirvana. This, oddly enough, is what they have against it. If only it were true. The chemical reality is more mundane, and after a few halcyon weekends late in 1992 I had already started to see that such powers had been drastically overstated. Less than six months after taking up clubbing, I was ready to call it a day.

Manchester University was undergoing a demographic upheaval at the time. When I applied, in the late eighties, it was a soundly respectable Northern institution favoured by politicos with a taste for redbrick and working-class football. Then I spent a year abroad. I was away when *Newsweek* ran its 1989 cover story about Madchester, city of ravers and flares and pills, and I missed the sudden craze for T-shirts that read 'And on the seventh Day, God Created MAN-chester'. So it came as quite a surprise when I came home to find that I'd enrolled in the first choice of every public-school kid who had failed to get into Oxbridge and wished to spend their trust fund and the next three years in pursuit of a fashionable reputation.

The Student Union's rowdiest event was traditionally the Freshers' Week meeting of the Labour Club, but the year I arrived it had to be abandoned in deference to the riot going on along the corridor. A new society called Freedom to Party was signing up members, and the entire floor rapidly assumed the flavour of an impromptu rave, as enthusiasts with ghetto blasters and whistles danced on filing cabinets to demonstrate commitment to the cause. This was probably the closest any of them had ever come to affiliation with a cause as such; but, despite the vaguely political suggestion of the name, Freedom to Party in truth confined its activities to organising student raves. It claimed overnight distinction as the university's largest society on record.

Under Freedom to Party, the student dance scene in Manchester enjoyed a racy cachet among a certain public school type all over Britain. It was dominated by thin, languid boys called Crispin or Rupert or Toby who liked to pretend that their names were actually rather ironic. They didn't care to see themselves as posh, and appeared to be under the impression that if they took enough drugs they wouldn't be. They displayed little enthusiasm for less worldly undergraduates though, but always liked to have one appropriately seamy Mancunian friend to bring along to parties. Most of them were of the opinion that failure to wash one's hair for a week amounted to kicking the system and shared a daring taste for clubs in the poorest parts of town, where they would have been more thrilled than troubled by the thought, had it ever occurred, that their new trainers cost more than an average month's pay.

To be fair, a number of them were highly creative, and their raves were lavish bacchanals. But they always wound up feeling guilty back in somebody's flat afterwards, telling each other how disgusted their dad would be if he knew what they were up to. This sentiment never tempted them to decline his next cheque, however, nor interfered with their belief that they were quite the most radical, dashing young adventurers of their day. Manchester functioned for them as a kind of finishing school, where they could grow their hair, take drugs and acquire a collection of amusing ethnic outfits before taking up residence in the right part of Notting Hill.

Over time, a handful became good friends, but *en masse* they served as an effective deterrent. Given that anyone who took ecstasy endorsed their idea of sophistication, I was well into my second year before I tried it, and the months that followed were somewhat dislocated. At the weekend, I would enter a bogus chemical complicity with these student ravers, then spend the following week going about in disguise. It was a confused spell. Ecstasy is a delight, but it cannot eclipse all sensibility, and there is something very wrong about socialising with people you wear hats and hide in doorways in order to avoid the next day. By Easter 1993, I was embarrassed and bored. I went out for one final night of clubbing, confident that it would be my last – and the evening sprang into a chaos of clubs and car journeys and confusions, ending in the gay village, outside the only club still open at 4 a.m. It was a shabby little place none of us had heard of called Ethos.

Ethos was Strangeways' predecessor, an after-hours gay club run by the same couple, Glenn and Brendan, in a literally underground venue. We'd only intended to go in for a quick drink and a dance, and I was quite unready for what lay at the bottom of the stairs. The sticky warren of rooms stank of amyl nitrate, and wherever you turned, on every available surface, people were dancing. They were dancing on the bar, on the beer crates, on the pot plants, and as I watched I was shocked with a jolt of inexplicable recognition. I'd never been anywhere like this, yet it felt like coming home, and that was the night that the possibilities of clubbing first suggested themselves. My companions thought Ethos seedy, and probably do not remember it. I fell in love with it, and had little cause to think of those students ever again – until Paul and I found ourselves at a rave on a beach in Thailand, after almost a decade had intervened.

Back then, my discovery of Ethos had seemed like a haphazard accident of timing, but I found it repeated time and again in different ways over the coming years. Wherever you go in the world, you will find clusters of clubbers at the end of their tether, unable to remember the last time they had a decent pill, and about to quit. It is then, just as their patience is snapping, that a wondrous new E appears on the market, and all talk of retiring is lost in the stampede of excitement. So the cycle goes on. Ecstasy is not an addictive drug, and this must be a source of disappointment to its manufacturers so there is the suspicion among some clubbers that the cycle is not so much a coincidence as a calculated form of marketing. The idea sounds far-fetched, and yet I would be tempted to agree – were it not that the conspiracy of timing stretches beyond chemicals to the quality of clubs themselves. So far beyond, in fact, that it followed us round the world, putting in an appearance on a bad-tempered Sunday morning in San Francisco. For a fleeting moment that afternoon, I thought we had cracked America.

We found the Endup on the corner of 6th and Harrison in SoMa. From the outside, the club appeared to be just a concrete building on a bald, noisy intersection, but once inside we found ourselves in an eccentrically meandering venue filled with deep Chicago house. At one end of the dancefloor were leather sofas arranged round an open fire, and at the other a garden and courtyard; blissed-out clubbers were sprawled everywhere in between. Seldom can the sight of people who have taken too many drugs ever have been so welcome. Topless gay couples shared a Vicks on a sofa, a girl in cowboy boots with plaits to her waist was dancing in a tree, and everywhere we looked we saw glimpses of Strangeways.

Delighted, we installed ourselves in the garden, where Terry and Paul swiftly reached the decision that it was my turn to look for drugs. But before I'd had a chance to think about the task, our eyes were drawn to a man on the other side of the courtyard. Probably in his fifties, his thick, bleached-blonde hair fell to his waist, and fish-scale tattoos covered both his arms. He wore nothing on his top half, but his legs were covered in billowing green-and-gold silk culottes, and his toenails were painted fuschia pink. And he appeared for some reason to be waving at me across the crowd, waving his whole body like a drowning mermaid in drag. Then I saw that he was wearing sparkly sunglasses, and realised it was my new Dior pair he had spotted. He was flailing away, and I was smiling back weakly, trying to look the other way, but he kept on waving and waving. *Please God, no*, I prayed, cursing my sunglasses, *not the mad hippie*. Then a crop-haired young woman next to him was waving too, and the pair began chanting: 'Come over here!'

Terry couldn't believe our luck. 'Get over there and buy some drugs!'

Paul gave me a hefty shove from behind and over I trotted, singing, 'Hello! Faaab sunglasses!'

'Well!' the man beamed as I reached their table. 'We just said, "Look! Doesn't she look fabulous?" And then Mia here,' and he pointed to the young woman, 'she said, "I bet she's only got a bra on under that jacket?"'

'Of course!' I lied.

'Ha!' he said. Then he took a pair of black frilly knickers out of his pouch bag, sniffed them and put them on his head. Everyone around laughed uproariously.

'My name,' he said, stretching out his hand, 'is Lord Blueberry. How do you do?'

I shook hands with Mia, and with an older, blonde woman called Topaz, and various others who seemed to be with them, while Lord Blueberry smiled on, the underwear still on his head. I glanced over my shoulder at Paul and Terry. Huddled against the garden wall, the pair were making little cupped gestures with the palms of their hands to say hurry up when they thought no one was looking.

'Mia,' I started, 'I'm so sorry to ask you a boring question, but do you know anywhere I can buy some drugs?'

She smiled warmly. 'Yes, yes, of course. I'm sure my friend Dean will be able to help you. Here,' and she beckoned a tanned, blonde young man over to the table. 'This is Dean. Dean, this is Decca.'

Dean wore a sort of sailor's outfit made of lycra. Bending down he planted a lingering wet kiss on my cheek, began to stroke my hair, and purred, 'Of course I can help you.'

Club etiquette requires that when you first meet a dealer you should proceed on the pretence that he is going to fetch drugs from an acquaintance until he says otherwise, so I suggested he might know where I could find three Es. He winked admiringly. 'Three, eh?' Not wishing to appear a complete glutton, and assuming he might like the look of Terry, I gestured over my shoulder and explained that I was also buying for my dear, handsome friend over there, and for my husband. He removed his hand from my hair.

'You know what?' he snapped. 'I'm not really in the mood for walking around looking for drugs.' And with that he got up and left.

Mia had by now wandered off, and Lord Blueberry and Topaz were engrossed in some complicated private joke, so I trotted back to Paul and Terry.

'Well?' Terry prompted. I explained what had happened.

'You bloody fool! I could have told you he wasn't gay. Honestly, Decca, why couldn't you string him along until you had the pills? Now, get back out there and try again.' He sighed impatiently. 'And I'll just have to see what I can do.'

I wandered back off around the garden, hearing the same story from everyone I approached. Security in the club had gotten out of hand, they said. It was virtually impossible to buy anything. If you found a dealer, you had to leave the club with him and do the deal outside.

'But this is San *Francisco*! And we've come all this way.' Everyone nodded sympathetically and agreed it was very un-San Francisco, but the police had threatened to close down the club if they caught anyone dealing.

Paul's spirits had deflated again. I found him sitting on the floor in the shade of a tree, too hungover to speak, being eyed closely by two bouncers prowling nearby. Terry and I talked in whispers.

'*Well.*' He pointed to a well-built Latino man wearing a heavy overcoat, standing alone in a raised corner of the garden. 'There's a drug dealer up there. I'm absolutely certain he's a dealer. He's standing there by himself, and I've seen him follow four people out, and come back in again through the exit.'

'Then go and ask him.'

'No bloody way. Next time he goes out, I'll follow him.' When the man headed for the door, Terry shot off after him, leaving me dancing next to Paul under the tree, rather as if he were my handbag. Soon Terry was back again, hand over mouth, shaking.

'Well?'

'Well, I asked him.'

'And?'

'He said, "Congratulations. You've asked the only plain-clothes police offer in here. Why don't you try security next, and they'll take you down an alley and beat the crap out of you?"' Terry had to sit down next to Paul to recover.

Soon Mia appeared at my arm to check that Dean had sorted everything out. She seemed surprised to hear he hadn't, and for a moment looked thoughtful. A mark of a good club is the willingness of strangers to assume responsibility for each other, and for the first time since in America I felt a sense of this. Mia was cheerful and briskly purposeful, and looked like a Parisian art student, but claimed to be an underwater-photographer from Poland. She was terribly plausible, and I began to hope she would take charge of us.

'We're leaving real soon,' she said presently. 'Would you like to come back with us? I've got two pills at home, and I don't like to boast' – Paul and I looked at each other – 'but they really are the best Es in the world.'

As is often the way with these matters, real soon turned out to be some time, and tempers degenerated badly in the course of the next hour or so. During the period between a promise and its delivery in a club, it is hard to avoid your body language giving the impression that you are waiting for a train. I kept waving and smiling at Mia and her friends, keen to look as though we could have a good time without ecstasy but also hoping to remind her that we were still waiting. Terry became more and more worked up about the police-man. A bouncer with a bolt through his nose glowered our way, Dean started casting sour, distrustful looks, and Paul's hangover turned ugly. He lay curled up on the grass, hugging the tree trunk.

Eventually Lord Blueberry began waving again, so I made my way over and he gave me an enormous hug.

'We're getting ready to go now, Decca.'

'Oh! I think we're coming along with you. And going back to Mia's.'

'Marvellous! That's great. Mia, you know, she's like this to me,' and he clutched his hands – still holding the underwear – to his bare chest. 'These are hers. She took them off earlier, you see.'

But just as they seemed to be gathering themselves together, they began to dance again – great circling leaps, like Red Indians. Terry was getting extremely jittery – 'What the bloody hell are they up to now?' – and when they broke into a sort of voodoo rain-dance I thought he might explode. Then suddenly we were off, the three of us out of the door and standing on the pavement with Mia. Equally suddenly, something else was forgotten and Mia was gone again. Leaving a hysterical Terry with Paul, I followed her back inside.

I found her on the terrace in a clinch with Dean, who clearly had the twin intentions of stopping her from leaving, so that he could get off with her, and of warning her against us. He had spotted Terry following the undercover cop, and from what I could gather was under the misapprehension that we were in cahoots with the FBI. Stationing myself a couple of feet from the pair, I jiggled innocently, inching closer with every scowl he shot my way. If this went on for much longer, I would soon be standing on their toes, but Mia stood her ground, kissed Dean, and said a firm goodbye.

Lord Blueberry, Mia and a friend of theirs who looked like a truck driver were now all outside. We seemed finally to be on our way – when from nowhere Mia produced an old black bicycle.

'You get a ride with Topaz,' she called, jumping on, 'I'll see you back at mine.' And with a broad wave she wobbled off up the pavement. Moments later the truck driver let out a giggle.

'Oops. Look, Mia's fallen off.' Fifty yards up the street our saviour lay tangled in a heap, but as we looked she picked herself up, remounted, and sailed off around the block. And that, I was quite sure, was the last we would see of Mia and her lovely pills.

Dusk had started to fall. Other people were now leaving the club, and several glanced over at the curious group huddled under the amber glow of a streetlight near the door. Terry was still flapping about policemen and bouncers, and Paul was leaning against the wall, gazing around in despair. The truck-driver man, Don, was whispering to Lord Blueberry. They made an unusual pair, Don in his blue jeans and denim shirt, gold chain and cowboy boots, muttering to a psychedelic old hippie who was whispering back loudly, 'It is *not my fault*.' It seemed that Don, too, had an interest in Mia's two remaining pills. The atmosphere was getting very shaky, and it was now so dark that I couldn't see out of my sunglasses, but as they seemed to be the only thread left holding us to this group I didn't dare take them off.

'Would we be better off walking, Lord?' I tried. 'We could go on ahead if you like. Do you know Mia's address?'

'Yes. I know the address. But you do not want to miss *El Tarro*. *El Tarro* is an experience.' He folded fishy arms over his bare chest, and stared.

'*El Tarro?*' mouthed Paul.

'Ooh,' I blundered on. 'I'm sorry, it's just that I'm cold.'

'Well, you should learn to be patient. I have taught myself to be patient.'

'Tee-hee-hee.' I could hear myself gabbling. 'Ooh, I'm so cold. You must be freezing, Lord. Brrr!'

'No. I have a nuclear reactor inside me. Or maybe,' and he swept his hand in an open gesture, 'maybe I am cold and I just don't know it.' Paul rolled his eyes at the wall.

'Huh-huh-huh!' gurgled Don. 'Huh-huh! Don't you love the way he says these things? "Maybe I'm cold and I just don't know it?" That's so cool. Huh-huh! I love that.'

Just as I was certain we would never see our pills, out of the club stepped Topaz like a blonde blast of purposefulness.

'Honestly, I went back for them, and they had fresh drinks!' she giggled, pointing to a man and woman behind her. I stuck to Topaz like glue, and as we set off we chatted about how long the T-Dance had been running, and how many of us would fit into *El Tarro*, and I had begun to bask in this unexpected injection of sanity when suddenly she stopped dead and looked puzzled.

'Oh, that's funny. Have I missed my street?' My heart sank. Topaz had lost *El Tarro*.

I looked back over my shoulder at the crocodile tailing down the road after the mislaid *El Tarro*. There was Terry, wild-eyed in his shiny see-through gold shirt, still flapping about the policeman, and Paul, hunched up in a black leather jacket, looking ominously Glaswegian. Then came Lord Blueberry in his flowing silk culottes, followed by Don the chuckling truck driver, and then the last two – a Jerry Springer witch with hooded eyes and a heavy fringe, and clinging on to her hips a scrawny ginger man with shocking rotten teeth. At the front of this stood Topaz, middle-aged, with bright-pink cheeks and buck-teeth, looking like a community-college drama teacher. Beside her, stumbling along in the dark in diamante sunglasses, was me.

And then, almost by magic, there before us was *El Tarro*. *El Tarro* was an enormous and ancient Cadillac. Inside, the upholstery and dash-board had been carpeted with fake leopardskin; on the outside, the bodywork had been spray-painted from end to end. The background colours were ultramarine and lilac-pink, suggesting a cloudy summer's sky, and up the middle of the bonnet had been painted a gigantic, violently pink erect penis. Across the boot was painted a swollen vulva, also in vivid pink, and down one side of the car ran the words 'Harder, Faster', and across the back bumper 'Love and Nudity'.

'Just *look* at *El Tarro*!' sighed Topaz.

She and Lord Blueberry stood and gazed in fresh delight at the car. Their manner was difficult to place; they cooed at the car, but weren't being saucy, just delighted to be showing *El Tarro* to a new audience. Topaz pointed out each detail and Lord Blueberry smiled proudly, like a couple admiring their prize flowerbed. There was no suggestion that the thing was even mildly bizarre – just rather wonderful.

A quick head-count established that we made eight, one over *El Tarro*'s usual limit. Topaz took the driver's seat, Lord Blueberry and Don squeezed in beside her, and I found myself lying face-down, stretched along the laps on the back seat. With a whoop from Topaz – '*El Tarro, ride!*' – the car made a great lurch forward and leapt out on to the street. Don led a chant of 'Go Topaz! Go Topaz!', as the car bunny-hopped and swerved its way through several lanes of traffic, jerking to a halt at some red lights and sailing on through others. Topaz laughed away, lighting cigarettes and chatting to every-one on the back seat, looking straight ahead perhaps once a block, apparently having forgotten she was in charge. As we cruised through another red light a police car drew alongside. 'Hah!' Topaz whooped, '*Way* too much paperwork!' The police car fell back at once, and we lurched on in a chorus of cheers. 'I haven't been stopped since I got *El Tarro* painted,' she giggled. 'I guess they always think, "Too much paperwork".'

Still face-down, through the din I could dimly make out Lord Blueberry telling Topaz that this was our turn coming up. 'Our alley now, Topaz,' he repeated, louder and louder, 'O U R alley!' And when we were halfway past it she heard and slammed her right hand down, and *El Tarro* careered sideways, snaking around four cars, and shot off up a narrow alley. Half the car had mounted the pavement, and my head was between Terry's feet as we squealed to a halt, scattering crack addicts like rabbits. They regrouped at a safe distance to watch us fall one by one out of the car. Topaz dusted herself down briskly, and had resumed her commentary on *El Tarro* – 'Now, look at the lines, it really is a masterpiece. Not a single brushstroke!' – when I heard a noise, and turned round to see Paul doubled over, being sick.

It was hard to see how anyone could be living here, but Mia's face appeared from behind a steel door, and we followed her up a back stairway, past her bicycle and a jumble of janitor's junk, into a warehouse loft-apartment the size of a tennis court. Everything was painted purple or turquoise. There was very little furniture, but she had a jungle of pot plants and a stereo system the size of a small car. The three of us paused at the door, taking all this in, but Topaz, Mia, Don and Lord Blueberry swept past and made straight for the centre of the room, where they resumed dancing in circles, waving their arms like windmills. Trance music filled the apartment. As we watched, two barking dogs – more like wolves, really – jumped out of a cupboard and joined the dancing circle.

We were summoned to a sofa in the corner by the Jerry Springer hag and the scrawny man. Thinking that perhaps they had the Es, we sat down opposite, but the pair set about mauling one another, giggling and whispering between mouthfuls. Paul looked about to be sick again when the woman broke off, looked up, and seemed surprised to find us sitting there.

'Get up!' she growled, waving her arm at us. 'Get up and bap.'

'What?'

'Bap. *Bap!* Get up and bap!' The three of us looked at each other in confusion.

'What, dance, you mean?' Terry tried. 'Is that what you're saying? It's all right, we're fine for now. We'll dance in a minute, thank you.' It was the woman's turn to look confused.

'What d'ya say in England for dance? Bap, right?'

'Er, no.' Then she was really angry – 'You lie! You're lying!' The man next to her piped up.

'I'm Irish, and dammit, it's bap.'

'No, really, I don't think it is.' Terry and I searched for acceptable alternatives.

'Paul says groove,' I tried, 'but he's Scottish, you see. We don't really say that.'

'You're lying,' the woman hissed, then slumped back into the sofa and began nudging Paul's toe and winking at him.

After an uncomfortable few minutes we were rescued by Mia, who had tired of dancing and remembered the pills. 'Come this way,' she called, and led the three of us into the bathroom.

'Er,' Terry coughed. 'Those two on the sofa. Have they had any of these?' She stopped rummaging in the purple medicine cabinet and looked amazed.

'Are you crazy? Look at them. Do they look like they've had a nice E?' She burst out laughing. 'They're from *Indiana*.'

'Well, thank Christ for that. If you sell me anything that makes me turn like that I'll have you arrested.'

'Sell?' Mia repeated. 'I'm not selling you anything. These are a gift.' She split the two clear capsules open, divided the powder inside into three piles on a mirror and handed them over.

'Surely you understand. The Lord is with you.'

In the event, the only one the Lord was with turned out to be Terry. Half an hour later he was dancing on the sofa, rolling his eyes to the heavens and declaring himself in MDMA nirvana. 'You weren't kidding,' he sang to Mia as he set off around the room with one of the wolves. 'These really are the best Es in the world!'

I looked at Paul, who was staring at Terry in bleak disbelief. 'You neither?'

He shook his head. 'Not a bloody thing.' He nodded at Terry. 'Tell me. Tell me he's making it up. It isn't possible, is it?'

Another half-hour passed without development, and murderous looks began to flash across Paul's face as he studied everyone else's chemical adventure. I would have minded missing out much more had the afternoon been less diverting, but the scene was so bizarre it felt like being on drugs anyway. I was even warming to the mad witch on the sofa when Lord Blueberry, Mia and Topaz came to join us. Calmer now, they asked what we were doing in San Francisco, and I told them.

'We win!' The three bounced up and down. 'We win!' After several minutes of high-fives all round, they quietened down enough to explain.

'Doc Vadis is the ultimate dose-meister,' Lord Blueberry began, and at the mention of this name a hush fell in the room. Doc Vadis was a mysterious Californian chemist, Lord Blueberry explained, a kind of renegade potentate famous on the West Coast for cooking up the very best drugs. If we were looking for the best ecstasy in the world, we need look no further.

Lord Blueberry had known the legend only by name until a year ago, when he went to a party out in the desert. There a man had approached him with the words, 'I have been checking you out. And you know what? We are the only two people at this party wearing sunglasses. Weird, eh?' The two had got talking, and fell to discussing how many times each of them should have died.

'It was just then,' continued Lord Blueberry, 'when I was saying, "I'm immortal", and he was saying, "So am I", that Mia walked past and said, "Hi, Lord." And the man says, "No! Are you Lord Blueberry?" And I say, "Yes, who are you?" He says, "Why, I'm Doc Vadis!" And I say, "No!" It was incredible – a real spiritual connection.' The sofa went into new raptures at the retelling of this cherished tale.

Paul coughed. 'So, Mia, those pills you gave us. They were made by Doc Vadis?'

'You know what? I thought they were. But when I got back I realised that one of them was, but one of them was Dean's. Can you feel anything?' We all looked at Terry. He was dancing in the middle of the room, eyes shining, arms aloft, beaming rays of joyous wonder back at us.

'Oh,' I said softly, 'sweetheart, I'm so sorry. It looks like Terry got it all.'

The three of us returned to the T-Dance, where Terry proceeded to have a whale of a time. While he cantered around the dancefloor Paul and I made ourselves comfortable on a speaker in a corner, and gradually Paul began to feel a faint tickle of pure MDMA – enough, he agreed, for his first ever hint of what the fuss was about. The club itself came closest to Strangeways by far, and when we left at midnight we were counting the days until we'd be back with supplies from Doc Vadis.

Terry flew home on Monday a happy man, and on Tuesday we returned to Lord Blueberry and Topaz. They lived in the lower reaches of the Haight, on Castro, in a wooden villa crammed with lurid, surrealist pornographic paintings and wooden models of penises. While Lord organised drinks, Topaz flowed from room to room, discussing star signs, mental energy and her strange friends from Indiana – all in the same tone she'd used for *El Tarro*.

'This is what we call the Opium Den.' She showed us a room upholstered with silk cushions and psychedelia. 'Lord used to spend so much money travelling,' she continued, leading us down a passage, 'and then he thought, why not build a fantasy room instead? So here it is, kind of African. Hand-painted, one hundred per cent quake-proof.'

We sat on the floor of the replica Bedouin tent and talked about

San Francisco. 'After Aids,' Lord said, 'the city got hit real hard. When the sissies stop partying, everyone stops partying. But it's getting better again.' He thought the city's art was very disappointing, though. 'There's not enough repression. People get lazy and paint whales.' Paul wondered if Topaz felt cocaine was bourgeois.

'Not really. The only time I did was when I saw someone taking it with absinthe. I said to myself, "That's a bit much".'

In my experience, most modern hippies are frauds, but Topaz and Lord Blueberry were the real thing, and utterly charming. We spent days at their house, taking sunset rides in *El Tarro* and drinking vodka late into the night. As the week wore on there was much hushed talk of Doc Vadis, and arrangements were made to buy a supply of his finest on Saturday night. Topaz even thought there was a small chance we might meet the man himself. She didn't like to promise anything – Doc Vadis was a law unto himself – but would see what she could do.

It was now four weeks since we'd left London. Our progress had been a mixture of miscalculation and bad luck, mostly calamitous and occasionally farcical. We'd both had serious doubts about the entire enterprise. So it would be hard to exaggerate the level of suspense our excitement had reached when Saturday arrived and we rang on their doorbell.

The house was shrouded in darkness. It was minutes before Lord Blueberry came to the door, and he stood before us in silence. Swaddled in a long black cloak, ashen-faced, he looked stricken.

'What is it? What's wrong?' He hung his head and let out a low, mournful moan. 'Is it Topaz?'

He shook his head. 'Mia has just telephoned,' he said. 'Doc Vadis –' and his voice trembled. 'Doc Vadis . . . He is not the man I thought he was. Doc Vadis has gone home to his family – for, for *Thanksgiving*.'

Lord Blueberry was devastated. The great Doc Vadis – exposed, as a *square*! He was inconsolable – although possibly less so than Paul or I. With our outward flights booked for Monday, we would never taste the famous if flawed potentate's magic.

ON A PROMISE

CHAPTER 6

Lovely Girls

The Oriental Hotel in Bangkok is proud of its aristocratic past. It describes itself as colonial, even though Thailand has never been a colony, and is staffed by bellboys in magnificent pantaloons who actually wring their hands when they bow. We arrived there on our first day in Thailand, and were at once presented with personalised gold-embossed stationery in order that we could write letters home to prove that we'd stayed at the Bangkok Oriental.

From the air, the city looks like a First World forest of skyscrapers, but at street level the hauteur quickly gives way to an anarchy of dust and clamour and slums. It is exotic chaos – each street a bewilderment of noisy enterprise, sweatshops crammed in next to computer stores, a jewellery emporium, then a store selling safes. Tuk-tuks judder and screech, spitting oil into a mayhem of gridlock, while monks in orange robes and office girls in platform shoes barge each other out the way on the pavement. The smell is unbelievably foul. Sweet and nauseous, like meat putrefying in toilet cleaner, it creeps out of the river to hang in every breath. Oddly, the Oriental is the only place it fails to penetrate, and so, for all its pantaloons, Bangkok's famous landmark hasn't a trace of the city's defining sensation. Once inside its thick cool walls you could be more or less anywhere in the world – except, of course, Bangkok.

A few miles north along the Chao Phraya river lies another city landmark. The Kao San Road is a scruffy strip of budget hotels and shops that service the traveller economy, and is effectively what backpackers mean when they say Bangkok. Like a human Spaghetti Junction, it is their entry and exit point for Southeast Asia; in *The*

Beach, Alex Garland described it as a decompression chamber, and we were curious to see it. When night fell, more bellboys in eveningwear pantaloons swung open gilt-edged doors, and waved us into the greasy darkness.

We got as far as the pavement, and a line of parked tuk-tuks painted like fairground rides.

'Taxi?' A dozen drivers leapt out as if on fire, and began waving. 'Taxi? Taxi? Taxi?' The Kao San Road, Paul said.

'Why you go there?' called one. Draping an arm around Paul, he dropped his voice, suddenly confidential, and drew us aside. 'You stay here?' he pointed to the Oriental. 'Why you go Kao San?' His voice dropped again. 'You wan' marijuana?' It is sometimes hard to understand when Thais speak English, as it can sound as if they've had a minor stroke.

'No thanks,' said Paul. 'Do you have any ecstasy?'

'Wha'?' The man squinted. 'Wha' you say?' Paul mimed putting something in his mouth, then smiling and dancing.

'Come on,' I laughed. 'Let's leave it.' The man began to hop from foot to foot.

'Yes! Yes, yes!' He summoned another driver for a conference, then turned back to us, triumphant.

'Yes! Yes, we can get it.' A complicated debate then followed about whether or not we were all talking about the same thing, which seemed highly unlikely.

'You take pill, you no sleep all night, yes? No sleep, all joy. Tiny, red. Good to smoke?'

'What? No, you're meant to eat it.'

'Oh! Yes, good to eat too! Eat too! Top quality. One hundred per cent. You wan' heroin?' On and on it went, gradually drawing an audience of drivers, until I began to feel nervous. I've often thought it would be interesting to be arrested for drugs possession, but the curiosity didn't extend to Thai police cells, and Thai dealers have a reputation for selling tourists drugs, then reporting them to claim a tip-off fee. We handed over some money cautiously, agreed to meet again in half an hour, and retreated to the Oriental to reconsider.

The bar in the Oriental was hushed and burgundy. That evening a jazz band was playing. A breathless young Thai woman sheathed in sequins sang Western love songs, and at every table middle-aged white couples watched in silence. The women sipped cocktails through straws, holding the glass with both hands, never taking their eyes off the band. The men leant backwards, arms locked straight, palms flat, and from time to time their heads would swivel, as though every one of them was stranded on a blind date that had not worked out. We took a table, and Paul ordered a Mai Tai. Its arrival was clocked by a man on one of his scans, and his big red face lit up.

'Eh, that looks good. What's that one then? A what?' He studied his cocktail menu, then held it up for us, pointing. 'We had this one last. This one's next on my list.' Paul took a sip of his Mai Tai, and the man practically leapt out of the sofa.

'Eh, when I saw that I thought, oh, he's spoiling the wife. But it's for him! And she's got a lemonade, and you've got that!' He laughed and laughed, shaking his head. When he had subsided he leant closer. 'Beer man normally, are you?'

Satisfied, he went on. 'When did you get in? We got in this morning. Came from Yorkshire. Saw the King's palace. It's definitely not to be missed. Full of lots of different cultures. Different influences. Thai influences . . .' There was a long pause. 'Um, Cambodian. Very spectacular. Then we went to Papong.'

His frosted blonde wife perched stiffly at right-angles to the conversation. 'Patpong,' she corrected softly, without turning her head.

'Yeah, Patpong. Anyway, market were 'eaving, absolutely 'eaving. But it weren't as bad as what I'd thought it would be.' Patpong is Bangkok's famous red-light district, home of the ping-pong show. If he thought the vice would be very bad, I wondered why he'd wanted to go. 'But the shopping were amazing. We saw this bag' – his wife wordlessly produced a fake Prada handbag '– and we got the price right down to four hundred baht. Didn't we, love?' He talked us through the haggle like a fisherman reliving how he landed a shark.

'You've got to be hard,' murmured his wife through pinched lips. 'You've just got to be hard.'

'And it's flame-resistant!' cried the man, and she held it up like a magician's assistant, and lit a match to it for us to see.

'Normally we go to the Caribbean,' he went on. 'This is our first time East. The wife likes cocktails, you see, so we thought, well, let's go to Fooket. Eh, where are you going?' Paul told him we were aiming for Ko Samui and Ko Pha-Ngan, and he looked momentarily thrown.

'So you're on a *three*-centre holiday, then? Bangkok, Ko Samui, and – and the other one. Phew.'

As he was taking this in, I glanced up and spotted the tuk-tuk driver behind him at the window, face pressed to the glass, waving. Giving Paul a nudge, I tried to excuse ourselves, but the man was having none of it. 'Oh no, no you don't. Another Mai Chai, eh? For the wife! Ha-ha-ha.' Over his shoulder I could see the driver getting agitated, flinging himself from side to side and rapping on the window.

'So sorry!' I yanked Paul up. 'I don't feel well –' and we fled to the door, with the man's views on 'that Delhi Belly' echoing after us.

Outside by the pool, the tuk-tuk driver was bursting with pride.

'Top quality, top quality!' He handed over a tiny packet of silver foil, and we pocketed it doubtfully. 'Now, you wan' go see sexy show?'

Back in our room we unwrapped the silver package to find two minuscule, reddish-brown pills that smelt of chocolate and looked as though they came from a local pharmacy. We agreed that this would be the last time we ever bought anything on a street corner, stuffed them into a sock and went to bed.

Friends had been telling me about Thailand for a decade. Ko Samui was described as a tropical hedonist wonderland, and its neighbour, Ko Pha-Ngan, as a place of dreamy charm. Ko Pha-Ngan was famous for its monthly Full Moon rave, said by some to be a quasi-spiritual experience. By the late nineties it had assumed the status of Mecca for the ecstasy generation, and one claim was made of it so often that it came to be a form of mission statement. In effect, the claim was this: no matter how jaded or disenchanted you felt, however numb to ecstasy, a Full Moon rave would restore your clubbing innocence. The rave's wildest enthusiasts billed it as an ecstasy baptism. At the very least, it would be an epiphany of pleasure.

Paul had spent a week on Ko Samui ten years earlier. That was before either the gap year or *The Beach* had been invented, and he had stayed in a town called Chaweng, which he remembered as rustic and charming. After one night in Bangkok, we flew south to the island, and by dusk were driving down country lanes, black palm trees framed against a fading evening sky. We hugged on the back seat, faint with relief to be going somewhere unequivocally lovely at last, and wondering if it would still be light enough to swim when we arrived. But when the taxi pulled up to let us out, it was in a resort that looked unaccountably like Magaluf, Majorca.

Chaweng had a main strip – two miles of potholed road running parallel to the beach – lined with concrete restaurants and shops, and pubs called Fawlty Towers. Neon signs advertised PUB GRUB, cold beer in a PINT GLASS, and WESTERN TOILETS FOR THE LADIES. Off one side of the strip led short muddy tracks down to collections of bungalows that cluttered on to the beach. Some were built of wood, rather than breeze-blocks, and we chose the first one with a vacancy. An Italian with a shiny pink head who called himself Papa led us to it, a creaky room just inches larger than the bed, carpeted with wallpaper. Rather uncertainly, we headed back up the track through the dark.

'Hello, welcome! Welcome, hello! Hello, welcome!' As we turned the corner and stepped into the neon glare of the strip, about a dozen young Thai women came running flat out at us. They bumped into each other as they pulled up a yard short, some clasping each other's shoulders in feigned astonishment at their own audacity, like teenage girls on a dare. 'Come!' They pointed at a small bar behind them. 'Come!' Twenty yards further down the street this happened again, and then again, and again. Some of the girls wore tight jeans and halterneck tops, and others wore little lycra dresses, but all had long glossy hair, which they tousled from side to side, and laughing, kitten eyes, with which they pleaded. They were stationed at the entrance of every bar, and each time we walked by they spilt off their stools and took a run at us. 'Hello, welcome! Hello! Where you from?'

They did well to make themselves heard at all. Trance and techno blasted from every bar, horns blared and mopeds growled, but still the cries of 'Welcome!' triumphed. Every few yards a new troop of girls would come charging. The torrent was so frothy, so relentless, that we were a good way down the strip before we had even noticed anything else. Westerners were streaming past us, but not the back-packers we'd expected to see, yet they didn't look quite like tourists either. Eventually it dawned that this was because they were all men.

Had we really been in Majorca, these men would all have been about eighteen. Instead, they were about twenty years older, with grey faces, cropped hair and purple smudges under their eyes. At eighteen they would have twitched with light-limbed violence, but these men carried themselves heavily. They wore regulation sports-wear, looked like discreet criminals and filled the pubs and restaurants, drinking slowly and deliberately. On their laps sat Thai bar-girls.

We walked on past bars called Black Jack and O'Malleys showing Premiership football, and past a tattoo parlour – 'Ten years' experience; new needle'. Videos were being shown in every restaurant, their amplified soundtracks pouring out on to the street and curdling into the racket, so it was as though we were walking through a gigantic amusement arcade. Several pharmacies were open, doing a brisk trade despite the late hour. They looked like old-fashioned sweet shops, except that they had posters in the windows. 'Clean wound. Preg test.'

At the bottom of the strip we found a quieter bar where our eye was caught by two men sitting at a nearby table, in their early thirties and unmistakably English. One looked amiable enough – dirty blonde, with a boxer's nose – but the other had bulging red eyes, and his whole face seemed to be chewing itself, sending ripples of sweaty fat down his belly. You wouldn't say he was smiling – his mouth was too busy to form any definite expression – but his whole face was a billboard of enjoyment. Both men were emptying what looked like brown-glass medicine bottles into their mouths – and when I asked what it was, the fat man hurled himself at the conversation.

'Picks you right up when you've 'ad a few, an' you're spinning, like. Down one of these and you're fackin' bang right, innit? Sorts you right out. Look,' and he pointed to the list of ingredients printed in Thai on the label. 'All herbal, innit? Really good for you stuff, healthy, like. Herbs and stuff. Look, it's only point-five amphetamine.'

'So it's not speed, then?'

'Nah,' he said, 'I had about ten last night. Proper good.' His friend with the boxer's nose nodded happily. A few minutes later he mentioned that they hadn't been to sleep for four days.

The fat man was called Gavin. He was from Reigate, and had been in Chaweng for a few weeks. Friends were waiting for him on another island, but bad weather had prevented the ferry from running, so here he was, stuck on Ko Samui – a state of affairs he didn't look unduly troubled by. Eight bar-girls were gathered around his stool.

'You come in 'ere,' he exclaimed, gesturing to the bar, 'and they look after you like a prince. They get a wet towel, they wipe yer face . . .'ERE!' he summoned a barmaid to give Paul a wet towel. 'I tell you, these girls do everyfing for you.' How much did everyfing cost? 'Five 'undred baht and they do *everyfing*. They'll do' – I braced myself – 'your nails, they'll barf you, do your toenails, clean your hotel room. Everyfing! They're diamonds. Mind you, this one here –' he nodded '– she keeps saying, "I love you."' He pulled a disgusted face, shoved her away, and gathered up another girl into a noisy, wet kiss. The girls all beamed.

'This is Sue. She's a nanny from Bangkok, down here on holiday. Well, I wasn't to know that, was I? I say, "How much?" She says, "naffink – I ain't a bar-girl, it's for FREE."' His eyes popped even wider. 'FA-ckin' ree-SULT!' Gavin couldn't keep still for the amazement of it all, and swayed clean off his stool twice, capsized by his own excitement.

Paul bought a round of drinks. A few girls sneaked cocktails on to the order, and Gavin exploded in the fashion of a man never happier than when a friend has been slighted. He pretended to shoot the girls. Gavin affected a proprietorial role towards them, but presently explained that in fact the Thai man at the door looked after them. 'And '*e* won't touch them cos he's BENT. It's ideal, innit?' Gavin was thrilled by the ingenuity of this arrangement, and gazed about him in a daze of joy. His gaze fell on his friend, shadow-boxing in the corner. 'Diamond geezer, diamond geezer. Wouldn't hurt a fly.' Gavin literally couldn't get his words out, so great was his delight.

'Ever been to Goa?' he asked suddenly. 'Now *that*'s cheap, that's fucking cheap. Beer, thirty p! And the Es! Fack me. If you've got the money, get yourself on a plane to Goa, I'm tellin' you. Cheap or fackin' what.' The memory of Goan bargains briefly silenced him, and in the pause Paul said we'd wondered about the ecstasy situation here. Gavin nearly fell over.

'Five hundred, mate! Five fackin' hundred.' Overflowing with happiness, he explained that he had smuggled 500 Es in with him. He'd filled the hollow plastic balls found inside Kinder eggs, 100 to a ball, and secreted them in his rectum. He mimed it for us, panto-miming chronic pain all the way up to his chest and hopping from foot to foot. So was he selling them in clubs here?

'You fink I'm mad? One hit and I'm done, mate. I'll sell the lot to a dealer, and see how long the money lasts. They're wicked, mind. You can have a couple if you like.' He glanced down and noticed the size of the camera on Paul's arm.

'You're not from the papers are you?' he asked. 'You're not from the *Sun*?' and he roared with laughter, then turned and gathered up another girl for an almighty kiss. From where I was standing, it looked as if he'd leant over and eaten her up.

A bar-girl in Ko Samui is employed to attract customers. Almost every bar has at least one girl, and some of the larger bars have up to twenty. You don't see the girls during the day, as this is when they sleep, but by sundown they are back in place on their high stools, ready for another long night. 'Come, come!' they beckon prettily, staying just the right side of insistence, thus ensuring that the effect is girlishly charming rather than sluttish. And come the men do, with faces full of wolfish delight at the joy of this amazing arrangement which allows them to believe that they are sexually appealing.

The overall impression is more Athena than *Asian Babes*, and this is no accident, because 'of course', as everyone will tell you, 'they are not prostitutes'. The girls' official job description is notionally innocent. They are paid a percentage of the price of every drink that is bought by a customer whom they entice and entertain. The longer they can keep the customer happy, the more drinks he will buy and the more the girls will earn. To this end, they fawn and swoon over the men, who can grope and fondle them, sit them on their lap, and bore them to tears with conversation. Wisely, the girls have come up with an inventive deterrent to the latter by playing endless games of Kerplunk or backgammon with them instead.

This is the basic system. That said, if a man would like to take a girl off and have sex with her, all he must do is pay the bar a fine of about four pounds, and agree a price with the girl, which she is allowed to keep. The one-off transaction costs £10 to £20, all in, but a more popular arrangement is what the men laughably refer to as a 'relationship'. Under this agreement, the girl becomes his 'girlfriend' for the duration of his stay – a tirelessly devoted, obliging girlfriend, and a distinct improvement, you might say, on the real thing. In return, the man buys her meals and clothes and petty luxuries, as well as presents for her family – in theory her parents, but in practice usually her children; most bar-girls are single mothers. And so Ko Samui is full of fat and unattractive European men driving around on mopeds with beautiful young women on the back.

There are obvious difficulties in calculating how much a bar-girl earns. A recent Thai university survey put the national monthly average for a 'sex worker' as US$125, but a Patpong bar-girl can earn US$150–200 a month directly from the bar where she works, plus $20 upwards per session for sex with private clients. If she strikes lucky with a generous 'boyfriend', there is no limit to what he might give her. Compared to an official average per capita income in metropolitan Bangkok of US$580 a month, these figures are still relatively modest, but most bar-girls are young and uneducated and come from rural villages where the minimum wage can be as low as US$3 a day. This makes the bar-girl seem wealthy, until you compare her wage to the US$100 average that foreign tourists each spend in Thailand every day.

Tourists in Chaweng hadn't a bad word to say about the bar-girls. How could they, when the girls made everyone feel so good about themselves? The men felt irresistible, and went around with faces stuffed full of self-congratulation. Their mood was so good,

they found themselves behaving nicely to one another, and this
novelty put them in a better mood still. They were positively gallant
towards white women, who in turn were delighted to be spared the
usual advances.

Actually there weren't many white women in the town. Occasionally we would see young European backpackers who had stopped off
en route to other islands, but most of the women were older and
came in big beery gangs with their husbands and boyfriends. They
made a great fuss of getting along with the bar-girls. At night, they
would dance on the tables with them, curl their bodies together, then
fall about in giggles. During the day they could be heard remarking
loudly on how pretty this or that one looked. Being seen to be sisterly
was important, although it was never clear if this was meant to be
read as compassion or as proof that no sexual threat was felt. But
either way, they were thrilled that the girls smiled back, and took the
smiles to mean that they were liked. So everyone felt well disposed
towards the bar-girls.

We first made the mistake of referring to them as prostitutes in a
place called The Club. It was the resort's after-hours venue, tucked
just off the strip, and more tasteful than most, featuring an open-air
terrace dotted with pot-palms and Chinese lanterns. It opened at
around 2 a.m. and within an hour would be jammed and chaotic,
packed with freelance bar-girls dancing hopefully. One night in the
crush to find seats, one of the girls accidentally put her cigarette out
in a Dalmatian's tail; she let out a screech when it yelped, but lost
interest as the dog lay at her feet whimpering and licking the burn.
A minute later, a girl with legs like pipe-cleaners pushed past and
vomited into a pot-plant. The young Englishman sharing our table
didn't notice either mishap, for his eyes were locked on two other
girls dancing on stage in lime-green bikinis.

'Lovely girls,' he murmured dreamily, elbows resting on the table,
chin cupped in his hands.

'What, the prostitutes?' Paul asked. The man turned, sharp-eyed
with shock.

'Prostitutes? They're not prostitutes. They're bar-girls.' And he
looked angry, as if Paul had just insulted him.

This would happen every time anyone said the word prostitute.
Men in Chaweng had the idea that the girls were so lovely, the least
one could do was lie about what they did for a living; it was the girls'
honour this lie was supposed to be protecting, and there was never
any doubt that it was the girls the truth would shame. Their unflagging

loveliness made it easy for everyone to uphold the consensus of deceit; nevertheless, at some level the men did acknowledge the lie, and so liked to feel they were being chivalrous.

Chivalry, though, had its limits. Later that night a scuffle broke out near our table between one of the lime-green-bikini girls and a stocky pink German. He slapped her, she bristled, everyone stared – and then she gave a short, tired shrug and walked away. Nobody intervened on her behalf – and in all the times we were to witness similar scenes, nobody ever did.

Within a few days we had stopped noticing the girls, screening out their screams as you screen out billboards in London. I became increasingly fascinated by the men, though, and took to quizzing them in the street. Paul thought I was mad and left me to it. At first I didn't get far, as I kept meeting Belgians and Germans, who were polite but could offer only pidgin clichés, but one evening I was sitting in a quiet cafe at the far end of the strip when a man leant forward in his seat and waved at me.

'Would you like to join us? You're by yourself.' He had his arms around a bar-girl and was smiling broadly.

Kieran was a handsome, freckled Australian in his mid-thirties with short red hair and the simple, sturdy courtesies of a farmer.

'And is this your girlfriend?'

'Yes, this is Yah,' he agreed, closing his fingers over her forearm as he sat back down. Yah was about his age, soberly dressed, not especially glamorous or beautiful. She gave me a warm smile but said nothing. I asked the usual holiday questions, and Kieran explained that he had come to Ko Samui with ten men from Australia but on the night they were leaving he had met Yah. That was nearly ten weeks ago. 'I would never have stayed if it wasn't for Yah,' he said, squeezing her arm again. He was clearly proud of her, and even prouder of this statement of his love. I smiled brightly.

'Aren't relationships like this compromised from the very beginning?'

'Well, yes,' he agreed quickly. 'You do have to compromise, obviously. I mean, I have to come to terms with . . . you know, overlook her past. And now I'm going to speak very quickly, you understand, so she won't understand what I'm saying to you – there is the intellectual side that's of course a disappointment, maybe a problem, and I have to overlook that so that's another compromise.'

I persisted.

'Well,' he considered, rearranging himself in his chair, 'I expect it raises your hackles, as a Western woman. I feel uncomfortable with Western women now; I do feel their disapproval.'

'And how does that make you feel?'

'It makes me think . . .' He paused to pull a series of weary, injured, irritated faces. 'It makes me think: *Why*? You see, I care about this lady a lot. I care about her. A *lot*.' He took her hand and stroked it. Yah was wearing a pleasant, blank smile, but facing away from the table as though she wasn't actually there. Kieran talked as though she wasn't there, too. He seemed to be enjoying the conversation, measuring his opinions and pausing to admire the sound of each one as it came out.

Had he ever expected to find himself in this situation? 'God no! Never! I would never have condoned it. I mean, I don't condone it. But when you travel, you know, you have to adapt, you have to examine your ideas, you know? And I think, well, if it makes a man happy for a few weeks, well then . . .'

Well then what? 'Well then, that's a good thing, isn't it? And you know what, a lot of the ugliest men here, it turns out they're the nicest men. The really fat, ugly men, they treat their girl so well, they just want to be good to her.'

I asked if he thought Yah would be with him if she was Australian. 'Oh, if she was Australian I would have left her weeks ago!'

'No, I mean would she still choose to be with you if she was an Australian?'

'Ah. Oh, well . . . that's a tough one. I don't know.' He thought for a moment, absentmindedly stroking Yah's black hair. 'You know, she could walk away whenever she wanted. She's as free as I am.'

'You believe all that?'

'Oh *yes*. Y'see, I'd take a good argument over a pretty face any day. I want a wife, not a maid.' Kieran was going back to Australia in two weeks' time. There were as yet no plans to take Yah with him.

Kieran said he hoped that we'd see each other again, and I think he meant it, for he was tremendously pleased with his conversational performance. I found him disproportionately upsetting, though, and avoided him, which was surprisingly easy to do in Chaweng. In spite – or perhaps because – of the town's boundless sexual licence, visitors seemed to need rituals; and one such was the tendency to single out one bar and make it their local.

Paul and I had our own local. Each night, we would escape the techno roar of the strip and drop in at a tiny bamboo bar hidden away inland down a mud track. Covered in garlands of fairylights, it was little more than a shack, with just one bar-girl and seldom any customers. The barman was a young Swedish man called Christian, boyishly sweet and fluent in all Chaweng's cynical delusions. If the bar-girl wanted to have sex for money he shrugged as he sliced lemons, it was nothing to do with him. 'I just want her to eat and be happy. I don't want to feel like a pimp.' When the girl did disappear with a man one night, though, he affected a dizzy bluster and pretended not to know where they'd gone. He said the girls in Chaweng were treated wonderfully, but was embarrassed when asked if they earnt anything when no customers came in. 'That's not my side of the business.' The only time the deal appeared to count as prostitution for Christian was the night a pair of particularly ugly Germans, all clumsy paws and wet lips, took turns mauling the girl at his bar. 'That makes me so angry,' he shuddered. 'Urgh, they're so *big*.'

The girl in his bar was young, with a buck-toothed smile too boisterous to be sexy and podgy legs dimpled like a baby's. Her hotpants were too tight, and her walk was more like a puppy's than a prostitute's. Every night she would beam at us and chatter away. And because of that, and because she looked so ungainly, so unlike the other girls, we couldn't help ourselves. It was amazing, how fast you could forget yourself in Ko Samui. We began to believe she genuinely liked us.

'The girls, you know,' Christian said quietly, in a rare lapse into honesty, 'they are not so nice. They really think about money, you know?' He meant it to be derogatory, but it was the only real compliment we ever heard the girls paid.

CHAPTER 7

Lonely Hearts

Chaweng was not a conventionally dangerous town, but its rhythms were repetitive and insistent, and could drag you under with remarkable ease.

It had begun to rain the night we arrived, and by dawn everywhere was knee-deep in water. Quite amused by the mess, we went out and bought raincoats – bright-pink sheets of plastic with a hole in the middle for your head – and I was delighted by my new outfit, but would have been less so had I known it would be weeks before I could take it off again. In the evenings the rain would case to drizzle, but the deluge returned each morning, not cleansing tropical rain but rather something much dirtier and more malign. It seemed to suffocate the air, and quickly reduced the town to brown liquid-mud; sloshing about up to the knee, it didn't do to think about what might be clinging to bare skin. Also, for much of our stay the town's power was down, so there were no showers or fans, and beneath our pink plastic we began to smell of rancid sweat. This was unpleasant, but in practice unimportant, because the whole strip stank and that was where everybody went. It was a complicated smell, suggesting sewage and lemon grass and chip fat. Not twenty yards away miles of sand stretched empty, but we all stuck to the same septic gutter of concrete.

The routine of life in Chaweng was easy enough to get to grips with. Tourists would start the day in the restaurants, where English breakfast blurred into hamburger lunch, and movies were screened back to back. Diners tended to pick at their food but stare intently at the TV screens; violence was the staple theme, the only alternative being anything with Steve Coogan in it. Afterwards, they would drift into shops along the strip and buy fake Nike trainers and Gucci belts, or they would start drinking again. There wasn't a hint of disappointment about the rain; the weather was neither here nor there. What mattered – in fact the reason why everyone was here – was that life on Ko Samui was cheap.

A man we met in a bar had calculated that his rent was 2.25 pence a night. Soldered on to a barstool, as soon as he heard Paul's Glasgow accent he swivelled round and introduced himself as Larry from Falkirk. He was with five friends. 'This is my gang.' A cheerful polecat of a man, Larry ran a pub in Spain called the Rovers' Return. His friends were all landlords, and spent the winter together in Ko Samui while their Spanish pubs were closed. Most of the gang stayed in the same bungalows as us. 'One of us, though, he's staying at OP Bungalows.' Larry nodded up the beach. 'Bit more expensive.' He looked embarrassed. 'Wife's five months pregnant, you see.'

Larry and his gang were loyal to their local, The Ark, and liked to chuckle over the graffiti scribbled on its bar. 'A stiff cock hath no conscience' was their favourite. We would see them there every day, and the encounters always opened with a brief report from each of how much he had had to drink the previous night. It was like calling a class register. The gang could never seem to get over how joyfully cheap the beer was, though they were knocked sideways one afternoon by a rumour that it was cheaper in Manila.

Besides cheap beer there was also Thailand's legendary pharmaceutical free-for-all. In certain circles Ko Samui's pharmacies are as famous as Amsterdam's coffeeshops, and inspire the same sort of guzzling excitement. Gavin, the fat man with 500 Es, took us to his favourite. The queue stretched to the door, and behind the counter, beneath a blackboard advertising 'Valium, Viagra, Prozac, The Pill', like a pub menu, an elderly Thai lady was spooning pills out of large jars into plastic bags. One man asked about amphetamine pills. Frowning, she said they were banned, then took a scoop of capsules out of a jar under the counter and with a wink slipped them into a bag. He pointed to some purple sleeping pills. 'Very good,' she nodded. 'When you wake up, there is nothing left in your brain.' We bought what looked like half a pound of Valium and a quarter of speed, and got stuck in. Presently both of us began to feel peculiar but we ploughed on regardless, anxious to make the most of this pharmaceutical opportunity. After a week we reached the stage of sleep deprivation when you cannot stop crying, and at this point gave up, but were glad of the insight into what everyone else felt like.

Insomnia turned faces grey and unstitched them at the edges. A group of builders from Leeds moved into the bungalow next door to ours – gangly lads, with skinny legs sticking out of holiday shorts and, at first, an easy charm, but within days they'd developed blank stares, eyes empty of recognition, plates of nothingness. At night they giggled randomly through jaundiced lips, and one of their rare coherent sentences was a boast to the effect that they hadn't slept since we'd met. They acquired a pair of eighteen-year-old Geordie girls in white shorts and pale-peach T-shirts, their puppyish white arms welted with crimson bites. 'Oh yeah,' one said abruptly, after we were introduced, 'I forgot to say. Matt hit a lady-boy last night.' Her voice was neutral, but everyone laughed hysterically. They laughed and laughed, holding their stomachs, until one of the boys said he couldn't remember what was funny. This made them laugh even harder, and they were still laughing when the girl threw up into her lap.

We made friends with a barman in a pub called The Blues Brothers. Steve looked as if he once could have been in Take That, but the bright brown eyes were strained, as though what used to be cockiness had now been stretched too tight. He had arrived on Ko Samui eight months earlier for a Full Moon party on Ko Pha-Ngan, but took so many drugs he missed his flight home, and had been trying to earn enough to get back to Brighton ever since. He was training to sell timeshares and every day we would see him pacing the strip, working himself into a blizzard of agitation about the launch of his career. 'My head's just full of it,' he flapped.

Steve was training with a friend called Angie, a plump peroxide-blonde from Birmingham. 'Ooh, it's a boogger,' she'd agree, and purse her candy-pink lips. Each passing day brought Angie a fresh personal drama to recount, usually a violent late-night fracas from which she'd had to be rescued. She looked pleased to have a story, but would tell it carelessly, as if only half-interested herself. Like landlord Larry's beer report, Angie's dramas seemed necessary in order to prove that she was there. We would see Angie everywhere, for in order to be sure of scoring an ugly scene every night she could never allow herself to go to bed.

Gavin, too, was everywhere – eyes like saucers, face in violent disorder, but still going strong. He liked to tear up and down the strip in an electric blue jeep, beeping at everyone he knew. 'See you tonight!' he would roar, leaning so far through the window that he would have toppled out had he not been so fat. His stock of pills was dwindling fast, the 'one hit' sale having been forgotten in the fun of handing out free Es to bar-girls. There was something touching about Gavin's willingness to believe everything they told him. 'They'd never had an E before they met me!' he boomed, swollen with pride. We passed his local one afternoon and saw him leaning over, kissing a tiny girl who lay slumped on a chair. Her matchstick arm stuck out at an unnatural angle, like the limb of a dead child protruding from the scene of an accident.

The only fly in Gavin's ointment was the behaviour of his friend with the boxer's nose. It was the boxer's first time in Thailand, and to Gavin's disbelief he hadn't had sex with a single bar-girl. We saw him in a tattoo parlour one night, having the lower half of his back inked out, and when he called us in to take his mind off the pain, I asked about Gavin's complaint. He blushed. 'Don't get me wrong. They're lovely girls, I'm not saying nuffink about the girls. Don't get me wrong, I'm not bent or nuffink. It's just –' and he smiled sheepishly '– I've got a girl at home, an' it wouldn't be right.' This drove Gavin completely mad.

There are greedy towns all over the world, but they tend to dress up the greed as ambition. Chaweng was just straightforwardly greedy, and a failure to grab all you could was a personal defect few could sustain. Steve and Angie had a visitor from Brighton, a rather meek character called Tim who seemed to spend his whole holiday testing Steve on timeshare prices and rescuing Angie from fights. We came across him one night alone in a bar, staring into his pint. 'To be quite honest, this wasn't really what I wanted,' he muttered. 'This wasn't how I thought it would be at all. It's such a clique. If you're not staying here for four months and boozing on the cheap, you're not really welcome. My bungalow's a dump, and the roof leaks.'

We ran into him again a week later. 'I'm moving,' he said, much brighter. 'I'm checking into the hospital tonight, a bed's come free. It's got TV, air-con, everything. No, don't laugh, I'm not joking. Everyone does it. The hospital doesn't care. You put it on your insurance, they say you've got dengue fever or something. The place is full, and I don't think there's a real patient in there. There's champagne on the menu, they've got a swimming pool, you get a massage . . . everything.'

And so the days passed in a rainy blur, and once again we found ourselves neglecting the search for ecstasy. With everyone off their heads on over-the-counter drugs, it seemed doubtful that there would be much demand for it anyway, and in the clubs most people looked so muddled up it was impossible to tell what anyone had had. The town's attitude towards illegal drugs appeared to be largely relaxed, although there was one conspicuous exception. It was a local drug called *yabba*, a kind of nuclear-fuelled amphetamine popular with the bar-girls on account of its capacity to keep them awake for ever. *Yabba* came in tiny pills, and if you smoked just one, by all accounts you wouldn't sleep for three days.

People kept warning us that the Thai authorities took an extremely dim view of *yabba*, but they needn't have bothered. I had enough trouble as it was by then just persuading Paul to take an interest in ecstasy. Beer was making a triumphant comeback in his preferences as his patience with Ko Samui's rain and power cuts grew thinner by the day. I could hardly blame him. If I'd been half the accomplished drinker Paul was, I too would have tethered myself to a bar and let Larry and his gang bore me senseless all afternoon while I watched the rain come down. As it was, I went to bed. Memories of these days are hazy, washed away in the downpour.

We finally roused ourselves to the task one afternoon, and set off down the strip to see what we could find. Steve was outside The Blues Brothers, cutting a young Israeli's hair in the rain; hairdressing was one of his sidelines, and after a brief chat it transpired that selling Es was another. 'I've got two MDMA capsules,' he grunted through a mouthful of hairgrips, 'wedged between my bollocks.' I thought he was joking, and he took great offence, huffing that – naturally – they were 'the best' on the island, but he wouldn't hand them over until we'd listened to him practise his timeshare-salesman lines. 'Madam, sir, an excellent morning to you,' he began. His friend Angie arrived, looking a worried orange colour, and the pair chanted together – 'total option on the first twelve months ... Superb contemporary furnishings' – while Steve rummaged one-handed in his underwear for the pills, jabbing absentmindedly at the Israeli's fringe. We tried them that night in The Club, and they were disappointingly ordinary.

Gavin had repeatedly promised five Mitsubishis, never tiring of the sound of his own generosity. We found him the following afternoon in his local, splayed out in a corner armchair, a smirking girl on each knee. After elaborate nodding and winking he and Paul retired to the toilets. Later that night in a club, The Green Mango, we spotted a topless, tattooed figure, more beast than man, clambering on to the stage. As he turned to face the dancefloor, we saw that it was Gavin, looking like a walrus, conducting the crowd with huge flabby arms. Long hair stuck to his back, eyes rolling, E'd up and in full cry, he was a monstrous sight, but I was hit by a great rush of affection. How he had achieved that state was a mystery, though, for we'd been taking his Mitsubishis all night and barely felt a thing.

And so to Christian, the Swedish barman in our local down the muddy track. We found him dancing away to himself there the next evening, and mentioned that we were looking for Es. He beamed. 'Snowballs! Yes, I had one tonight – mwah!' He kissed his fingertips. 'Come to the bar tomorrow night; I will have it all sorted.' He glanced from Paul's face to mine. 'Yes?'

Christian looked like Shane Ritchie, with a touch of leprechaun about him, and could never keep still, forever dancing about as if experiencing minor electric shocks. His bright black eyes darted like a bird's, and his mouth was always on the move, spilling out information: he had been running a bar in Las Palmas when his brother committed suicide, then there was an ugly dispute with licensing authorities, followed by a friend's motorbike accident and a disastrous girlfriend called Maria. Then his great friend Sven phoned to invite him to help run his bar in Ko Samui. 'So here I am! It's going to be great!' Christian wanted to refurbish the bar and call it Orange. He cut an orange in two on the bar, and held up the halves. 'That's the logo! Do you think it will be good?'

When we'd first met Christian he was new to Ko Samui, and solid wih intent to steer clear of drugs and girls, but every day his eyes grew wilder, and his strange dance jerkier. One night Paul revived his favourite fiction that he was a DJ; Christian was enchanted, and would quiz Paul at length for his opinion on Christian's CD collection. Most of it Paul had never even heard of, but Christian never noticed. He became so overcome by 'this great friendship!' that as we left the bar his eyes would often fill with tears. It didn't stop him short-changing us on every round, though.

We returned to our local, as instructed, the following evening and found Sven's wife, Suki, behind the bar. Christian arrived a few minutes later, gymnastic with apologies to Suki for being late. He flapped about chopping fruit for a few minutes – then, as soon as Suki wasn't looking, called us to the bar to tell us in a stage whisper that his dealer wouldn't sell less than twenty Snowballs at a time.

Paul raised an eyebrow. 'Really?'

'Er-er...' Christian giggled lightly. 'Yes.' Paul shrugged, and counted out what began to feel like a rash sum of money. Christian slid it into his back pocket with a wink. With a shout to Suki about going for ice, he jumped on his moped and sped off to fetch the Es, 'OK, I go to Bangkok now!' he laughed, waving over his shoulder. 'See you!'

While we waited, Suki knelt on the bar in her liquid-tight jeans and played cards with Paul. Evidently a bar-girl before marrying Sven, she had a languid, feline beauty and a calculating eye, and the card game she chose was the staple of every bar-girl, a cleverly conceived version of snap full of sexual tension and climax. While they played, two young Australian men at the bar eyed her with cold, hard desire.

Christian returned in a splatter of throttle and mud and excuses. 'The lazy bastard,' he exclaimed as soon as Suki's back was turned. 'He went for a shower. They say wait half an hour, he'll be back, so I wait – and nothing. I'll go back in another half-hour, yeah? That's OK? I still have your money, I didn't go to Bangkok!' We shrugged – 'No rush; that's fine' – and wandered off to get something to eat, but I was mildly uneasy. Christian seemed flushed, wired, and later, on our way back to meet him, I made a bet with Paul that he'd say Suki had had to go off somewhere, preventing him from leaving the bar.

'I'm so sorry,' groaned Christian when we arrived. He clasped a hand to his forehead. 'My boss, she had to go off and do her hair. I can't leave until she is back. But don't worry – he will wait for me.'

And so Paul and I sat at a table under the fairylights and wondered if Christian planned to string us along until he had found a way of keeping our money. 'Doing her *hair*, for God's sake.' Eyeing us from behind the bar, Christian could read our watery smiles and kept up a laborious patter intended to communicate his honesty. Everybody shifted uncomfortably. Just as I could no longer bear it, he announced that – damn it – he would put the bar-girl in charge. Seizing his moped, he dashed off up the track again.

No sooner was he gone than a taxi pulled up and out stepped Suki, her shiny black hair piled into an elaborate new style. 'Where the fuck is Christian?' She scowled like an angry cat at the bar-girl, who slunk back to her stool. We cringed, mortified. Then Christian was back again, all of a fluster, with some risible alibi for her about a toilet emergency. Suki watched him mime his excuse with icy scorn, and stalked away in disgust. At once, he was over to our table, thumbs up but with anxious eyes that wouldn't meet our gaze. 'The man, he had run out of Snowballs. But he has these, Love Hearts, and he says they're really good, really great. If they aren't, well I'll, I'll go back tomorrow and . . .' I gave an empty laugh. Paul closed his hand over the pills, and Christian laughed back, and shrugged.

We took a Love Heart each that night. They turned out to be easily the best pills we'd found so far, and we skittered about the bars and clubs and danced along the strip. At dawn we swam in the ocean, a milky warm bath of relief. But the moment had been soured, and as we fell into bed, salty and exhausted, we both knew it. Worse than the guilt of having doubted Christian was the bleak certainty that we would doubt him again tomorrow. I wasn't sure I liked what we were becoming in Ko Samui.

The rain finally came to an end, and as the resort dried out it slowly recovered its picture-postcard good looks. The sea softened from slate-grey to aquamarine and finally indigo, and miles of golden beach filled up with sunbathers; Thai women laid out mats and performed massages on the sand, Thai boys strolled up and down selling pineapple pieces, and tourists played frisbee. Larry and his gang took up residence on a square of sand behind The Ark, from where they could shout orders to the bar without leaving their sun loungers. Everyone put on sunglasses.

If we walked to the very top of the bay and looked back, it was tempting to doubt our own account of Chaweng. Had the sun shone all along, perhaps we could have felt differently about this place, for the beach was now a dazzlingly beautiful stage and the palm trees behind it a curtain, hiding the ugly mechanics of the strip. But we'd seen those mechanics at work, and it was too late to unsee.

With the rain now over, the ferry to Ko Pha-Ngan was back in service. Although the Full Moon rave was a fortnight away, bar owners on the island had in recent years come up with an enterprising invention, the Half Moon party, thereby licensing themselves to hold three raves a month instead of one. Party-goers had proved relaxed about the finer points of lunar ritual, and up to ten thousand of them flooded the island for each one. With the next Half Moon party a week away, we booked our passage for two days ahead.

The last nights in Chaweng seemed gripped by a kind of madness. Hardmen who go to Ko Samui enjoy the impression that it is rather surprising of them to patronise a nightlife so famously free of violence. (Tough guys like them, coming to such a peaceful spot! Who would have thought it?) But the arrangement can last only as long as they are limitlessly indulged, and the patience of the Thais in Chaweng was wearing thin. Waiters and barmen remained superficially polite, but their smiles were growing brittle, their dark eyes contemptuous. We began to see punch-ups in the street – modest fights, but scorching with temper.

And Christian, poor, sweet Christian, was unravelling before our eyes. Relations with his employers were deteriorating, and he had failed to buy a work visa on the black market. He was involved with a bar-girl who gave him a 'local's discount', but she was begging for more money for her parents and he had run out. We found him alone in The Green Mango, and out tumbled a story about his once being a speed addict and slashing his wrists – 'Look!' He pulled up his cuffs to show his scars. 'But don't tell anyone.' He wept, and clung to Paul. 'I just want to make my life work here, you know?'

On our last night we found him in a shambles, stumbling through the crowds. 'I have been crying all day, all day, like rain,' he whimpered. 'I miss my friend in Sweden, you know, all day I try to call. But he's not there, and so I'm like the rain. First thing this morning, whisky, and all day.' From a doorway a young bar-girl appeared at his side; Christian introduced her as Miaow. It wasn't clear if she was smiling or angry.

'This is your girlfriend?'

'Yes. No. She's my . . . she's my . . . I don't know what she is,' Christian sobbed. 'I'm so, so . . . lonely.' He swung towards her, angry and needy, but she shrank away, and he turned back to us.

'I need something to pick me up, you know, a little something to make me happy. You have the Love Hearts?' He checked himself, and shook his head. 'No, it's OK. I should stop, yeah? It's not what I need. I should go home.' Laughing maniacally, he spun around to embrace Miaow, and in the crush we edged away.

CHAPTER 8

The Beach

Anyone who has read *The Beach* has a picture in their mind of the beach. It is the strip of gold at the end of every traveller's rainbow; it is the perfect beach. Naturally, the problem for the movie-makers when they came to film the book was that they couldn't find this beach. Each new curve of sand was another faulty imitation, and the beach we eventually saw on our screens was like an old-fashioned special effect, over-egged and almost funny. Yet the thousands keep pouring in, looking for an idea – and washing up on Ko Pha-Ngan.

The upper deck of the ferry was jammed tight as a Mediterranean resort with backpackers, fresh in from Bangkok and heading straight through. A pair with braided hair leant on the peeling safety-rail and cracked Essex-girl-style jokes about Ko Samui as they tossed fag ends into the water, but most said nothing at all. They put on sunglasses, did crosswords, and lay down to sleep. Even when the mountains and white sands of Ko Pha-Ngan came into view, mockingly beautiful, like a Bounty-Bar advert, nobody seemed to notice. Sunglasses and Walkmans stayed on as we docked in a turquoise cove, and rucksacks were set down in silence on the rickety wooden jetty. Then, along a dirt track leading inland bounced a dozen or so pick-up trucks; the drivers jumped out, called 'Taxi!' and everyone exploded into life.

'A hundred baht? Each? For ten of us?' Young men who five minutes earlier had been fast asleep now swarmed around the drivers, waving bronzed arms in a pantomime of disgust. '*How* much?' 'You must be joking, mate.' 'A hundred? Fuck off.' Rucksacks were thrown on to a truck, then snatched back if the price wasn't lowered. 'Ten times a hundred – that makes a thousand baht!' a young Israeli screamed. He was tall and sinewy, wrapped in a caftan, and the muscles in his neck stood taut with rage. He bent right down into the driver's face. 'A thousand baht! That's a lot of money *for you.*' At 60 baht to the pound, 1,000 baht made £16.60.

We hung back on the jetty, slightly amazed. I couldn't imagine where so much passion had come from – and they really did care, there was no question about it. The dispute was over a matter of 20 baht a head, approximately 30p. We decided to walk.

The boat had docked on the western side of a peninsula, and the town of Had Rin lay on the other side, ten minutes away. The track across this finger of island was a narrow, sandy footpath, at first through nothing but shrubs and boulders but soon lined with primitive wooden shacks. Some were bars, but most either flip-flop shops or Internet cafes, often both at the same time. 'Mosquito net', read a sign outside one store, then, 'Fast screen, 17-inch, non-radiation'. It was a soundless walk, no traffic or tarmac or bar-girls, just a peaceful haze, and even when we reached the town only a moped broke the silence. Had Rin isn't really a town, only a thickening of the flip-flop huts and a muddle of bamboo bars and makeshift restaurants leading down the beach. Framed by boulders and surf, speckled with tanned bodies playing frisbee, it is a cliché of backpackers' paradise. Wooden huts on stilts are built into the cliff above, painted apricot and topaz and crimson, the veranda of each one strung with a hammock, like a necklace.

'Something, isn't it?' A man called down from one, and waved. 'Yeah, you've got to be here, right. It'll go off here for sure. Best beach party in the world. Gotta be here. Unless you go to Goa, mind – you could be there, it'll go off in Goa too. But it goes off here all right, goes off every night.' He tipped a bottle of beer in welcome, and his friends waved hello. 'M'names Neesy, we're from New Zealand. Between us we've got fourteen years' travelling experience, and forty-three years' drinking experience. I think that's enough.' His friends nodded their dreadlocks. 'Yep, hardcore. But we're still working on it, for sure?'

Neesy was hardcore all right. His nose was so badly burned it was falling off. We would see him sauntering up the beach every day, commanding awe among more junior travellers, although also a little secret alarm. They would gaze in admiration as he passed, then hiss: '*Christ*, did you see his nose?' when he was gone.

★　　★　　★

Backpackers look nothing like tourists. At first glance, though, they do all look like each other. Everyone looks good, in the way young people do when they have lost a stone and grown used to wearing hardly any clothes. They are also scuffed with bites and bruises, but these imperfections are all part of the look and so tend not to be noticeable. Italians have good skin and wild hair, the Dutch have tattoos, and Americans come in rather serious thirtysomething couples, or as galumphing college boys, but initially this is as much variety as you notice. To the naked eye, the Ko Pha-Ngan dress-code looks entirely relaxed.

It took a day or so to grasp the full anatomy of style rules. A sensible Netherlands sandal was unsexy; but an obviously sexy shoe was out of the question, so anything involving straps or heels was unwise. A flip-flop worked best, implying frugality as well as beach bum/mountain goat agility. It was also important to have a tan deep enough to convey that you took being a backpacker seriously. The correct position of the knot in one's sarong was a minefield; we watched one girl discreetly tie and re-tie hers in the reflection of a window for fifteen minutes. Bikinis were strictly of the stringy sort, thongs being too *Baywatch* and underwired cups too C&A, and ethnic jewellery was essential, although overkill betrayed amateurish enthusiasm. Combat shorts were all right for boys, if worn topless with a good tan, and the classier girl traveller rolled the waistband of her skirt down into a hipster. Here and there you would spy pale-skinned boys who had been thoughtless enough to come to Thailand wearing long trousers and Ben Sherman shirts. They stood about awkwardly, studying everyone else's outfits with dismay.

Ko Pha-Ngan's code of conduct is similarly deceptive. To the casual observer, backpackers are a sociable bunch who spend their days playing beach volleyball or frisbee. They swing barefoot in shady hammocks in the afternoon, and at dusk gather on the rocks above the beach to strum softly on guitars. In the noon heat you see them lying stretched out asleep on bungalow verandas like cats. They learn to juggle with brightly coloured little cushions, and in the evenings leave their shoes at the door of the bamboo restaurants, and sit crosslegged on the floor, eating rice. At sunset they meander along the beach in threes and fours – a real community of leisure, you might think, without a care in the world.

This carelessly languid first impression is misleading. The back-packers' social code permits acts of random friendliness like Neesy's only if you also have his incinerated nose, otherwise it is taken to indicate inexperience, and considered shamefully gauche. Travellers were awkwardly nervous of each other, reluctant to make social advances for fear of looking foolish, and the threes and fours tended to remain just that, in their self-protecting little huddles. It was safer to send emails than risk talking to strangers, and this is what people spent a great deal of their time doing. Fortunately, the Internet cafes were so crowded it was easy to spy on people's mail, and this revealed quite as much about travellers as we established face to face. A high percentage of emails began 'Subject: Hangover', and a surprising number gave rather arch and worldly accounts of the Bangkok sex industry. Middle-class boys sat in front of screens all day long composing wry emails to their fathers ('went to see women perform interesting acts with ping-pong balls'), and sauce to their mothers ('was offered sex for 200 baht!!!'), followed by similarly breezy but more graphic accounts to their friends of what happened when they accepted.

Apparently few male backpackers had made it through Bangkok without at least paying to watch women eject ping-pong balls from their vaginas. Most of them were young men who were highly unlikely to visit a stripper or prostitute at home, let alone tell their parents; but Patpong was part of their global itinerary, a morally neutral must-see. But there were no emails about eating dog, another Thai tradition, nor about any other adventure into cultural relativism. Just a lot about bargain sex.

When backpackers got drunk they were more talkative, but they didn't talk about this interesting anomaly. As far as we could gather, the social code imposed a strict embargo on any discussion that could be considered controversial; what hippies would once have called 'heavy' was now discredited as inappropriate, and girls in particular made quite a performance out of rolling their eyes at the first sign of conversational trouble. Boys liked to boast about how little they knew of what was going on in the world, for to be caught with any know-ledge of current affairs was worse than tying your sarong the wrong way. Instead, the favourite conversation – if not the only conversation, or at least the only safe one – would always begin with the same line. 'Such and such a place,' someone would volunteer, 'is supposed to be *really* cheap.' And then everybody would sit up and listen.

'Ocean Blue Bungalows is supposed to be really cheap.' In a bar on our first day on the island we were discussing where to stay when a French girl offered this advice. At once, two tall English blondes were at her table firing questions – how cheap? Where? What were they like? – and soon the four of us were making our way to Ocean Blue together. We found the elderly Thai owner on a veranda, being shouted at by a beautiful Italian about her bill. 'Look around us! Look at where we are!' Her arm swept across the bay. 'And we are talking about *money*?' The problem seemed to be that Ocean Blue had put up its rate by a few baht because of the Half Moon party. As backpackers outnumbered beds on the island each time there was a party, this was standard practice among the guesthouses. We took a bungalow. The two girls from London refused, 'on principle', and shared a supportive cigarette with the Italian. 'How *dare* he?' they sulked, kicking the sand. We agreed to look after their bags while the pair looked elsewhere.

'It's disgusting,' they stormed each time they returned with more bad news about another place hiking its prices by thirty pence a night. 'They shouldn't be allowed to get away with it.' Kate and Suzie were halfway round the world, and indignation seemed to be a theme of their tour. Time and again, Kate complained, they arrived somewhere new only to discover that the prices were *way* higher than anything they had been told to expect. Suzie wished they had gone straight to India now. Thais were just too greedy. Thailand was *finished*.

Kate and Suzie ended up sleeping on our floor. During the day they dozed on the beach, or practised their new hobby of juggling, or did sums in the flyleaves of their paperbacks to calculate how much they had spent. Their world tour was going to take them twelve months, but it seemed that most of this time would be spent trying to save money, a pursuit they invested with moral significance. 'Don't buy that!' Suzie would chide strangers in shops. 'They're selling it for ten baht less over there.' Suzie and Kate liked to show off their concave midriffs, not out of conventional vanity but as a boast of how little they'd managed to spend on food. They would sit up until the early hours trading tips with other backpackers on where in the world one could best avoid spending money.

Kate and Suzie were graduates from Kent; on their return home, they expected to become lawyers. In the meantime, however, having volunteered to survive on £8 a day, they chose to think of themselves as poor people. 'Look, I've only got eight pounds a day, all right?' Suzie would remind anyone she felt was failing to make every possible concession to her self-imposed poverty. Thais should give her a break, Suzie thought, and she was forever losing her temper with another shopkeeper who didn't seem to understand that she was *on a budget*. 'Fucking rip-off merchants,' she would hiss to Kate, handing over her coins with a poisonous scowl. Both girls had extremely pretty faces, but they were twisted into a permanent fix of disappointment, a parody of long-suffering housewives.

In truth £8, or 500 baht, was not a lot to get by on in Thailand. A beer cost 60 baht, a meal maybe 200, and our bungalow in Chaweng had been 450 a night. But if Kate and Suzie were therefore facing a measure of austerity, it was as nothing compared to what the Thais had suffered as a result of the 1997 crash. Since that summer, when the baht lost almost half its value and the economy practically collapsed, unemployment had more than doubled. Inflation was running at 7 per cent, and the rate of growth had reversed to minus 8.5 per cent. The crisis had hit the poorest sections of the population worst – but for a time it had also represented a jackpot for backpackers, with the devalued baht making Thailand a tropical bargain to rival even Goa. Word spread that for a fiver a day you could live like a king.

Happily for Thailand, this had ceased to be true, but backpackers seemed to treat this turn of events like a broken promise. When I suggested to Suzie one evening that if she had come away for less time, she could have had a bigger budget and would not have had to spend her journey talking about money she looked confused. 'But you have to have a year. I mean, that's what you get, isn't it?' To Suzie, the year out was less a rite of passage than the constitutional right of all young professionals, and it was the Third World's duty to keep her within budget.

Paul was going round the bend. After a few days I said we should kick the girls out, but by now he was beyond that, and spent a morning trawling the beach with a face like thunder, scouting for suggestions of alternatives to Had Rin. Various people told him about a guesthouse tucked away up the coast in the jungle. It could be reached only by boat, but there, it was suggested, he would find a different kind of traveller, closer to the old-school spirit of Thai travel. 'If you like that kind of thing, mate.'

The Sanctuary was a cluster of pretty wooden platforms on stilts in the cliffs of a deserted cove, backing on to a shelf of jungle. It styled itself as a retreat for the higher class of traveller who had come to experience a culture, as distinct from a discount economy. Low tables, embroidered cushions and hand-woven hammocks were dotted about the platforms; ethnic trance music lulled in the background, and the waves lapped below. A board behind the curved stone bar was reserved for a 'Thought for the Day', and the thought when we arrived was: 'Once you realise God knows everything, you are truly free.' Another sign suggested: 'Try to realise you are a divine traveller. You are only here for a little while, then depart for a dissimilar and fascinating world.' Cats were stretched out over cushions, in between Europeans sitting crosslegged and stiffly erect.

A longtail boat dropped us off in the surf late that afternoon, and we waded ashore, to be greeted by a woman in a low, dreamy voice who appeared to float, rather than walk, as though the gravity had been turned down wherever she went. The guests tried to copy her, and greeted our arrival with slow-motion nods and whispery half-smiles. There were about a dozen of them all reading in silence or gazing out to sea – except for a young American man with braids and a goatee who urged us to try a book about the mystical significance of birthdays. When the sun sank behind the mountain, perfumed candles were lit. Paper lanterns swung in the breeze.

We were still trying to decide if we had stumbled into some sort of cult when a young blonde woman joined our table and began talking. She had fractured her ankle ten days earlier, she confided, and had been confined to her hammock here ever since. She was using the time to write a book, but was as yet undecided on the title. It was a choice between *That's the Way the Cookie Crumbles* and *What's It All About?*

'The weird thing is, when I'm here, at The Sanctuary, my ankle's OK. But as soon as I go somewhere – uh-oh. In Ko Samui it hurt like hell. So maybe, who knows, it's some mystical thing or something. I can never leave now. Maybe; I don't know.' She winked, and flashed her enigmatic smile.

'It must have spoilt your plans,' Paul suggested.

'Plans? Plans? I have no plans. Hey, that's supposed to be the name of the game, isn't it? No plans. If this happens, and I'm stuck here, then I guess that was just meant to be.' She was travelling in Thailand for three months.

'And after that?'

'Oh, I have big plans! I'm going to New York. To a performing-arts school!'

Steffi, twenty-three, came from Berlin. She was a performer, she said, and suddenly she was holding our bottle of water and singing into it. She had tried and tried to get into drama school, and then finally – 'Yes!' – she was in. But they threw her out, saying she had the wrong personality. 'The wrong personality! I tried and tried to have the right one. I would say to the drama teacher, "What method should I try? Should I use this method, or that method, or what?" And then she says, "Acting is just about being, just about being." And I think, yeah, but I just want to be on the stage.'

Steffi had small features and worried blue eyes, and moved as though she thought she was being photographed. She hoped a quick injection of Oriental serenity might be the life-method she was looking for. Did we agree? Wasn't that what travelling was about?

'It's so hard. Because all the time I'm thinking, I want to live the right life. And I think, am I doing it right? I'm trying with the Eastern philosophy now, the idea that everything that happens is right; whatever happens, it's the right thing because it happened. Stop torturing myself, you know? It's hard, but I've got three months to learn. That should be enough, shouldn't it? And the yoga, I think that will be really good for my jazz classes in New York, and for my step . . .'

After supper we had to say 'Paul and Decca' to the waitress. No money changed hands until it was time to check out, and our tab was filed under our names instead of our room number. 'When you stay at The Sanctuary,' staff would chant to any guest who still needed it spelt out, 'You are not a number, you are an indiv . . .' and so on. It was at least a relief to go a whole day without hearing anyone mention money – but it was prudent of the owners to operate such a system, for their prices were at least double the going rate everywhere else. The Sanctuary belonged to a European, and its staff (excluding the cleaners and cooks) were all Westerners. They sold The Sanctuary as an experience of pure, authentic Thailand, yet in contriving not only to overcharge backpackers but also to get them to pay without complaining, were alone among any Thai business we'd come across.

The guests were mainly British. They worked in the arts or media, liked yoga and boiled rice, tied their sarongs in inventive new twists, and were conspicuously possessive about The Sanctuary. They sighed about 'other' backpackers – and, in an interesting inversion of tradition, took great pride in paying Sanctuary prices, as though by spending more rather than less, they could prove their authenticity as travellers.

In the next bay lived a Thai housewife in a Robinson Crusoe-style shack. She spoke no English, but would rustle up an omelette for 30 baht – a fraction of The Sanctuary's price. The path to her bay was steep, in places only a narrow ravine carved out of rock, buried in undergrowth, but it cleared at the last to reveal a milky white sweep of sand. A curl of blue smoke rose at the far end of the beach, and there the woman squatted at her fire.

On the morning before the Half Moon party we had breakfast there, and while the woman cooked, her children played nearby – three toddlers in rags, tugging a rusty toy tank across the sand by a piece of string. A young man with a straggly blonde pony-tail appeared from inside the shack, yawned, stretched, and settled down in a hammock. We smiled hello, and he smiled back with crinkly blue eyes. Easing into a Che Guevara T-shirt, the traveller lit up a joint.

He was a farmer from Israel. This was his third visit, and he always stayed here on this beach; he didn't pay for his sleeping platform in the woman's shack, but bought all his meals and ganja from her. Why did he come? He blinked, bemused.

'Well . . . for the smoking, the beach.' He waved his arm. 'All this.' It should be answer enough. He wouldn't be going to the Half Moon party that night; that kind of thing appalled him.

'To be honest,' he volunteered presently, 'I don't really like most of the travellers I meet. Not in Thailand. In India, yes, it's different. Here, in Thailand, it is too touristy, everyone is drinking. I don't like that. That is why I stay here, away from it all, on my beach.' He liked to live with local families – that was *real* travelling. He joked gently with the woman, in English, and smiled at her ragged children.

'What lucky children to be growing up here.'

The young farmer was worried about people in Had Rin coming and spoiling his beach.

'Don't say the name of the beach, don't say where it is. If you write about it, just say, "a beach". It is so precious.' He settled back in his hammock in a sleepy haze of smoke, while the Thai woman's family went to work in the undergrowth, hacking out a path with machetes for backpackers so the lucky children could afford to eat.

CHAPTER 9

Only a Laugh

Had Rin looked like a sunny Glastonbury when we returned late that afternoon, a teeming circus of rucksacks and juggling balls and dreadlocks. By the time we had found a room we were a mile from the beach, and in the soft, sudden gloom between sunset and darkness I unpacked and discovered I had left Christian's Love Hearts behind at The Sanctuary, hidden in a pot of aspirin. Paul took the news surprisingly well. 'That is a fucking disaster. But hey, everything that happens is right, yeah; it was meant to happen. Isn't that the idea?' We walked back through the dark to Had Rin.

And so this was the famous Ko Pha-Ngan party. The beach had been refashioned into a late-eighties warehouse party, with fairylights glowing in the cliffs and strobes raking the sand, catching luminous crescent moons of silk staked along the beach. The effect was spooky, and unexpectedly pretty – although perhaps not as unexpected as the lengths to which the thousands had gone to dress up for the occasion. Girls wore spray-tight trousers in amusingly lurid patterns, boys came as ironic tramps in woolly hats, and both wore gigantic trainers. They strode up and down in tight little groups, faces hardened by expectation.

There was no ecstasy to buy, of course, because the alternatives were cheaper. People drank beer, and took speed and magic mushrooms, and – apart from the unlucky ones whose hallucinogenics made them scowl by themselves at the sand – they danced. Like everywhere else in Thailand, the music was a hardcore fusion of techno and Asian trance, but the dancing took me a moment to place. It looked like a small child's impersonation of a mentally handicapped person, incoherent and demented; round and round everyone span, all the way down the beach, most narrowly managing to miss the beat and some apparently dancing to a different record altogether. And then I remembered. It was the dance from Manchester student raves almost a decade earlier.

Clubbing has reinvented itself so many times in its brief life that to catch sight of a previous incarnation is like seeing a ghost, yet surrounding me here were scenes from an old university rave. And *the same people were still dancing*: shy white boys who had fallen on a fashion that made them formally cool providing they bought the correct trainers and drugs. And the poor girls, pretty, damaged anorexics, fresh out of boarding school, who had found their nerve in a pill, and would sparkle all night, then mess up each other's heads at the chill-out afterwards and wind up weeping in the bathroom. Every drug casualty I have known came from that set, and their parents would always express amazement – and blame the drugs.

And now, after all this time, here they were again – younger versions, perhaps, but otherwise unaltered. It is not in the nature of clubbing for anything to endure. In 1990 the students had been doing their own imitating – of the original warehouse scene of 1988's Summer of Love – for mainstream nightlife then was unacceptably common to them, still rooted in the traditions of pop and stilettos and sex. By contrast, the rave scene, although predominantly working class, had the irresistible appeal of counterculture – and so warehouse parties in the early nineties became strange social hybrids where the man dancing next to you was either called Dwayne or Rupert.

Back then, ecstasy club culture was still on the margins of mainstream social structures; it was a subcultural, basically underground phenomenon. Traditional nightclubs weren't interested in it, the assumption being that there was little money to be made from unisex ravers who drank only water all night. Ravers, in turn, had no interest in shiny high street venues. But when the Conservative government passed the Criminal Justice Act in 1994, large-scale underground events were made illegal. Outdoor raves and warehouse parties were no longer viable, and Summer of Love-style clubbing had run its course.

Tastes were changing as well as laws. In the early nineties, gay clubs began their conversion from traditional disco/hi-energy to house as the preferred choice of soundtrack. Very quickly the ecstasy aesthetic was completely reinvented, the asexual tracksuit-and-trainers look replaced by a fabulous glitter of feather boas, and industrial techno abandoned in favour of gospel house divas and big piano tunes. Before long, clubs like Flesh in Manchester were heavily over-subscribed by straight clubbers, impersonating gays in their bid to get in. Straight, unisex raving was out of fashion.

The new gay model had commercial potential, glamour being a more lucrative commodity than its predecessor. Traditional club pro-moters were suddenly interested. Their only task was to appropriate the genre from the gay scene, and in the mid-nineties this was success-fully undertaken by high street clubs all over the country. Done out in gorgeous velvet and gilt, clubs like The Hanover Grand and Miss Moneypenny's sold gay clubbing to the straight market with instant results. On the understanding that the whole caper was ironic, girls returned to the make-up boxes, boys bought shiny trousers – and they resumed getting off with each other.

The pink-furry-bra phase lasted for two or three years. But the irony alibi had been stretched beyond breaking point by around 1998, and clubs – or 'clubland' as they had become collectively known – faced a credibility problem. Ministry of Sound clubbers were now indistinguishable from those at The Ritzy, the common look being up-for-it *Blind Date* contestant. House had softened into a girlish subgenre called handbag that was practically pop; 'Dreamer' by Livin' Joy was on *Top of the Pops*; superclubs like Cream were corporations not unlike Rank Leisure. The solution clubland opted for was a shift in music policy back towards hard house, considered more 'credible', and the introduction of trance, a swirly version of ethnic techno. By the end of the decade a blind man would have mistaken most dance clubs for old-fashioned raves. A deaf man would have thought they were old-fashioned discos.

The complete history of ecstasy and clubbing is more complicated than that, and local sub-plots were woven through the decade, but the consistent and enduring pattern has been one of reinvention. You could not count all the explanations clubbers have volunteered for this. For example, there have been theories based on the natural limitations of house music's structure. The music industry has been accused of never having overcome its antagonism to dance music, and of wilfully marketing it as a fad in order to destroy it. But most common of all are the theories about the *wrong people*. In effect, goes the theory, clubbing produces something great, and then along come the wrong people and ruin it.

The parallels between clubbers and travellers are striking. They are thinner, better-looking and more battered than other people. Both have inflated a hobby into a lifestyle for a time they know to be both precious and finite, thus their encounters share the same accelerated intimacy and sadness. Above all, travellers have a familiar range of theories to account for the ruin of this or that destination. Did it go too commercial? Did the unfashionable masses invade? Resentful of corporate predators, they regard hotel chains with the same suspicion levelled by clubbers at superclubs; and hotel chains and superclubs offer the same defence. Both claim to be 'democratic': giving value for money and making travel/clubbing accessible. The argument is endless, and the parallels would be as well were it not for one critical distinction. Whatever went 'wrong' with, say, speed garage, there was nothing fundamentally wrong with it – or indeed with any other club scene – in the beginning. But the idea that travelling in Thailand has been ruined presupposes that there was nothing wrong with it in the first place.

As the night wore on, the dancing thinned, and thousands of people lay back in the sand on their elbows, smoking cigarettes and gazing about them in wonder. 'Wicked,' they nodded, grinning at each other. 'Wicked.' Drifting among them, I overheard conversations familiar from old raves, when everyone used to laugh about discos and girls who wore make-up. Only here, it was Ko Samui being mocked – tatty, tarty Ko Samui, lavishly scorned with the same lazy pleasure all the way along the beach. One group in particular seemed unable to let the matter go, and as the night wore on became thoroughly worked up about protecting Ko Pha-Ngan from the vulgarians across the water. Everyone, they agreed, had a duty to keep out the beer-bellies and credit cards.

In the dark we lay back and pictured the horror that would greet Ko Samui Gavin's arrival. The only difference I could identify between him and everyone here, though, was that Gavin paid up for his pleasures without complaint. As it grew colder, before dawn, the disagreeable thought occurred that there was also little difference between them and *us*. We had taken it for granted that the Thais were happier to have us there than the travellers, because we weren't rude. But the backpackers assumed prostitutes preferred to sleep with them, rather than Gavin, because they weren't ugly – and we thought they flattered themselves.

What had Paul and I done to be so pleased about? All any of us did in Thailand was buy things. Travelling like this is a euphemism for shopping, an endless spree, and whether we buy breakfast or sex

94

it's only because it's cheap. Paul and I had smiled about the couple in the hotel bar in Bangkok, thinking it funny and slightly tragic that they'd come all this way for a fake handbag and believed themselves to be on an exotic adventure, but it hadn't occurred to us that we might be the same. The debate about which type of traveller is to blame for spoiling Thailand is, ultimately, quite meaningless. We all are, and in the process we spoil ourselves a little too.

The tourists on Ko Samui are at least candid about their greedy exploitation. I used to wonder why university friends who'd survived their Asian gap year on a triumphantly tiny budget showed no compassion at all for the poor in their street, let alone any insight into how they might feel. But the explanation became suddenly obvious. Despite backpackers' fond belief in their own poverty, what they actually take away with them from Thailand is the experience of being immensely rich. They behave accordingly, just as careless and bored and discontented as rich people anywhere else, with so much time and no purpose but their own amusement. Guarding their money like millionaires, they greet every Thai with flinty-eyed suspicion and mix only among their own. And to think some of them hoped to find themselves here.

Long-haul travel on this scale is scarcely a generation old. It began in the seventies, in overland lorries to Khatmandu, and it was only in the eighties that round-the-world tickets became commonplace. The phrase 'gap year' wasn't heard outside public schools until the nineties. Yet already it is accepted without question that a long stint spent somewhere like Thailand is an essential and improving experience. And so here we all were, on a beach, faithfully observing the convention, impersonating the time of our lives.

The sun rose over the beach to reveal a rubbish tip of empty bottles and cigarette boxes and raddled dancers. The basic dance-move had evolved into a hunched stomp by now, like the flinch of an old woman who has heard a mugger approaching from behind. Boys peed in the ocean, girls lay sobbing on the sand, wretched as the drugs wore off, and here and there teenagers summoned the energy to pick fights with each another. Three Scousers were shouting at a shopkeeper in a shack about the price of a plastic cup of vodka.

'*How* much?'

'Fucking bitch.'

Taxi drivers at the far end of the beach were herding unsteady bodies on to pick-up trucks. We threaded our way through the casualties, and, after some bleary confusion over which truck went where, ten of us sat facing each other in two rows over the wheel arches. The pick-up was about to pull away when a skinny young man stumbled up and threw himself in, face-first, over the tailgate.

'I just wanna wind them up, like,' he slurred from under our feet in a thick South Wales accent. 'Say I won't pay more than thirty baht.'

The driver walked to the back of the truck, leant and said quietly that the fare was sixty baht. The Welshman took a swig from a bottle of whisky, levered himself on to his elbows and told him to fuck off. A laugh and cheer went up in the truck. Suddenly we were all out of the pick-up, then somehow all in again, minus the Welshman, and agreeing to pay the fare. But the driver wanted it up front, and as we were paying the Welshman came flying in, head-first again, only this time backwards, landing between our legs with the whisky bottle held safe in an outstretched arm. Again, the driver leant in to ask calmly for the fare.

'Fuck off,' spat the Welshman.

'Just pay him,' Paul muttered.

'No, I like to wind them up.'

'Mate, please pay him the fare.'

'Shut up, it's a laugh.'

'For fuck's sake, PAY HIM,' Paul made to fly at him. Other passengers stared in astonishment, and the two other girls on board slid supportive hands on to the Welshman's shoulder. Still the driver waited, silently impassive. At the front, two Swedish skinheads lost their temper.

'Drive the car! Drive the car!' The pair looked like Hitler Youth members, hairless pink faces twisted into fury, stamping their feet on the floor.

'Fuck-ing drive the fuck-ing car! Drive! The! CAR!' Then everyone was shouting at the driver, and in the uproar someone paid for the Welshman and we were off, bumping through the jungle on a red-raw sunshine morning. For a second, the surprise of being under way silenced everyone.

The bundle at our feet stirred. Pulling himself upright, he rubbed his eyes, took another swig and offered the bottle around. 'It's only a laaahf, stupid,' he grinned at me. 'It's only a *laaahf*. They're thieving bastards anyway.'

'How much do you earn?'

'Grand and a half a month. So what?'

'What do you think the driver earns?'

'I don't want to be lectured. I'm travelling.'

'It doesn't give you a licence to act like a cunt.'

Hot shock jolted through the truck, and hostile eyes settled on me. The two girls stroked the Welshman's neck. A man at the back shook his head slowly and let out a low whistle. The Hitler Youth squared their shoulders, and one coughed.

'I think you'd better mind your manners, young lady, don't you? There's no need to be rude.'

We had just enough time to go back to The Sanctuary for the forgotten Love Hearts before the ferry left for Ko Samui. The woman in charge summoned a shy, faltering Thai girl from the kitchen. Had anything been left behind in our room? The girl nodded. Did she know where it was now? Another tiny nod. The girl was dispatched to fetch it, and while we waited a low grumble murmured around the bar. These girls, they were always 'keeping' things, taking them back to their bungalow, couldn't be trusted. Paul suggested she'd probably mistaken it for rubbish and thrown it away, but the woman clicked her teeth and shook her head. When the girl reappeared with the aspirin pot, now full of ants and rubbish, rescued from the dustbins, Paul tried to thank her but she was ordered back to the kitchen. The woman was annoyed now, and we turned to leave.

'Hello. Do you have any rooms?'

A pale English man was standing at the back door. He could only have arrived by walking ten miles through from Had Rin, but was airily composed, a smile dancing around his mouth. The woman stared, startled into a half-scowl.

'Well, what kind of thing were you looking for?'

'Oh, I don't know. Five-star luxury, air-con, TV, hot and cold water, room service. That sort of thing.' The woman shifted suspiciously at the joke.

'Well, how much were you looking to spend?'

'I don't care. I'm on holiday.'

All the way back to Ko Samui, we hugged the words, laughing like lunatics. 'I don't care – I'm on holiday.'

We found Gavin in his local in Chaweng.

'You know my mate?' he beamed, slapping an arm around Paul and calling for drinks. 'Going on like a right pansy, not shagging nuffing? Not any more!' He gave a triumphant nod. 'That's right. Got him on the old Viagra, didn't we? Can't get enough. Told you we'd sort 'im out, didn't I?'

Was he not going home to his girlfriend for Christmas, then? 'You are joking, ain't you? My boy ain't goin' no-where.' We looked for Christian later that evening, but his bar had been demolished.

In Bangkok we finally went to see the Kao San Road. Superficially chaotic, it nonetheless efficiently farms the migrant backpacker herds; the pavements are clogged with stalls selling regulation gear to pale-skinned new arrivals, and the tailor shops brim with backpackers about to depart. A hand-made suit is one of Thailand's famous bargains, and the stores do a brisk trade running up job interview suits for travellers on their way home. To advertise, the tailors plaster their shop windows with polaroids of customers modelling their new outfits. The figures stand awkwardly, ruddy with sunburn, like farmers dressed up for a hunt ball.

I remembered the pills we bought on our first night in Bangkok. Curious to know what they were, we found a smart-looking pharmacy and waited while a pair of grey-faced Geordies stocked up on tranquillisers. When our turn came I handed the two little red pills to the man behind the counter, and asked him to identify them. He took the pills in his palm, peered closely, then looked up at us, studying my face and then Paul's while he fingered the pills. He'd spoken fluent English to the Geordies, but as the silence stretched I thought perhaps he hadn't understood the question. I'd begun to repeat it when he let out an ear-splitting scream.

Smashing his hand on the counter, he screeched something in Thai. Two younger assistants came rushing out from the back store. The man shouted again, pointed at us and thrust the pills in their faces. One scuttled to the telephone and began to dial. The other slid out from behind the counter and made a dash towards the exit. Grabbing my hand, Paul barged the assistant out of the way and we escaped out the door and down the street, dodging tuk-tuks and bicycles and taxis and food carts until we'd covered half a dozen blocks.

'*Jesus*,' Paul gasped. We stood doubled over at a corner, fighting for breath.

'What the *fuck* was that about?' I shrugged, sank on to the pavement – then leapt up as I felt a hand close on my shoulder.

''Ello darlings. You all right?'

Steve and Angie, the timeshare trainees from Ko Samui, were grinning down at us.

'Everything OK, love?' Steve offered me a hand. 'Fancy a beer?'

We hid in a bar and Paul told them what had happened. Angie let out a great hoot.

'You daft bloody boogger, you. Them was *yabba* pills you had, wasn't it? Didn't anyone tell you about them? They'll get you into right trouble, they will. Police hate 'em. Want another beer?'

Steve was in Bangkok to renew his visa; Angie was looking for a doctor.

'You didn't hear what happened to me, then? Ooh, I ended up in hospital. I'd been drinking all day, and had a sleeping pill or something.'

'Her eyes were like this.' Steve widened his in fright. 'We took her home and we thought she'd be out for the count, but we locked her door anyway, just in case she woke up.'

'Well, I kicked the door down, didn't I?' Angie shrugged carelessly. 'And passed out in The Club. They had to take me to hospital. They said I had diabetes.'

'Boh-llocks.'

'Yeah. Well, actually, it runs in the family. I do have all the symptoms, it sort of fits. But at the hospital they were trying to sell us all these drugs, and so I thought, bollocks to it.'

'Yeah, and the guy we met in the taxi back, they'd said exactly the same thing to him. I think it's just their stock line. Bollocks.'

'Yeah. I dunno. We're going to try and chill out in Malaysia while we sort out Steve's visa. Sure you don't fancy coming too?'

We were flying out to South Africa that evening.

'Oh well. Nice meeting you.' Angie kissed us and they stumbled off.

EMPTY PROMISE

CHAPTER 10

Christmas Crackers

Cape Town is in fact a small city. Its geography, however, divides it into districts so separate and distinct that the overall impression is of somewhere altogether larger. Such a diversity of quarters would invite the label 'melting pot' elsewhere in the world, but, this being South Africa, Cape Town is more what you might call a pick-and-try-not-to-mix counter.

The city centre faces northeast, towards the old harbour. Near the docks you find the usual urban hinterland of flyovers and bus depots and street markets, where the faces tend not to be white. Behind the docks are the wide streets and high-rise offices of any Western city, where white men in suits buy sandwiches in the lunchtime sun, and black men in T-shirts watch their cars for them. Then there are the elegant colonial buildings of Long Street, with their wrought-iron balconies, vegetarian cafes and fashionably scruffy young. Nearby are the cool green gardens of Government Park, peopled by bronze statues of dead white heroes. Behind all this stands Table Mountain, towering over the city, gazing out to Robben Island.

If you were to stand on Table Mountain and turn to face southwest, you would look out on to Cape Town's riviera. Directly below lies Camps Bay, an exclusive seaside playground of bars and sports cars and bikinis. From the beach, you can follow the line of the coast north, passing the still more glamorous beaches of Clifton and the slightly dowdier promenade of Sea Point. The coastal stretch is cut off from the city centre to the east by a flank of mountain called Signal Hill, but if you follow the shoreline through Green Point, all the way to the northern tip, you reach the Waterfront, a luxurious new development of shops and restaurants pitched heavily at foreign tourists, rather like Covent Garden. Beyond the Waterfront, you are back to the old docks.

Inland to the south and east are Cape Town's spacious and exclusive suburbs, curling back from Table Mountain through a fold of lush green. The signs on the gates in Constantia and Newlands read like a Haiku of Africa's colonial history – Xanadu, Fairview, Kooblakhan, Dunroamin – and beyond them driveways sweep through sculptured gardens, up to doorsteps scrubbed by black maids in starched white. Some of the suburbs to the north of the city are plainer, and some, like Woodstock, are hipper, but between them they accommodate the middle classes in considerable comfort. At the point where they peter out into open country, you might say that Cape Town ends, but it is beyond, on the sandy, windswept land to the east, that the majority of the population lives. This barren sheet is known as the Cape Flats, and is home to townships housing more than a million blacks and coloureds. Under apartheid, the townships were carefully located so that anyone arriving at the airport could drive all the way into town without knowing they were there. Since majority rule, the corrugated-iron and packing-case homes have been allowed to creep closer to the motorways and are now clearly visible, if you choose to look. Speeding past in a flash of locked steel is the closest most white Capetonians have ever come to them.

Apartheid's architects were fortunate to have had nature provide their segregation programme with such assistance in Cape Town. The politics have now changed, but the topography continues to create the illusion of order, helping to keep everyone in their place. More deceptive still is the extraordinary light, so bright that it makes the city look dry-cleaned, stripped of all ambiguity. The clarity is blinding, giving every outline razor-sharp definition and producing an effect of hyper-reality – like looking through glasses for the first time and seeing a world without blur. Every blade of grass is an exaggeration of itself, and when the sun goes down the stars over Cape Town literally twinkle. A full moon throws a great pool of light across the ocean, gleaming bright as the sun.

Our delusion of clarity lasted for less than twenty-four hours. We flew in on the morning of Christmas Eve and proceeded to Sea Point, where we had booked ahead into a guesthouse. From the outside it looked promising – a picturesque, balconied wooden house shaded by trees, two streets back from the seafront. A middle-aged white woman appeared at the door. Tall, angular, and rashly made-up, she looked like a painted pigeon, and the force of her welcome took us slightly by surprise. Squawking with delight, she flapped her wings as though we were children returning home.

Drusilla fluttered us in out of the burning heat. Inside, the house was cool. It looked rather like a London Victorian terrace, with stripped wooden floorboards and doors, and heavy chintz drapes. Flannel-covered toilet seats, satin-covered tissue boxes, and matching-pink vanity units all dreamt of a long-forgotten Britain. Drusilla pointed out each feature with breathless pride, then apologised for its short-comings, so that by the time Paul and I were at last alone in our room, we had been obliged to declare every inch of the house quite the most beautiful sight in the world.

We spent the afternoon arranging a hire-car. Drusilla stationed herself in the tiny lounge, firing off faxes for us and filling us in on her twenty-seven-year marriage between pages. Married at nineteen, she had three children, but her husband had left her seven years ago. She seldom saw her children. 'You make a nice couple, actually,' she said, staring hard, eating us up with her eyes. Whenever we left the room she would retreat to the kitchen, but would come scuttling back out as soon as she heard our approach. We began taking the hall at a brisk dash, but she was always quicker and would intercept us under the grandfather clock, eyes bright and wings outstretched, to usher us back into the lounge for some more sad and erratic confidences.

It was late by the time we escaped Drusilla's welcome and slipped out to the car. The night was warm, and we joined Main, a well-lit four-lane boulevard dotted with guesthouses and bars and the occasional prostitute, leading north around the coastline towards the city centre. Traffic was light, and the pavements almost empty. Just as Paul was remarking how strangely quiet it all looked, a bomb went off.

I heard myself scream. The car shuddered and swerved into the next lane. Paul clung to the wheel, and for a moment we drove on in shock – then turned a bend and found the road ahead blocked by a frantic white figure in a chef's outfit. He was shouting something in Afrikaans, throwing his arms in the air, and seemed to be ordering us back. In an instant, the road was a river of wailing blue light, and police cars came hurtling from every direction.

We drove back a hundred yards and parked. At the scene, police were already taping off the road, and ambulance crews were carry-ing bodies away on stretchers. Crowds had emptied out of nearby restaurants to press up against the tape; they were shouted back by the police, but kept pushing forward. A small police van stood parked in front of an Italian restaurant, and the windows of both were blown out; glass lay shattered across the road.

The crowd quickly swelled to hundreds, most in T-shirts and shorts, out for a Christmas Eve drink. The mood was almost festive; jokes and cigarettes were traded between the gawking and pushing, and a middle-aged blonde man in a navy blazer was particularly enjoying himself.

'I heard the blast,' he broadcast to his friends, 'and I thought, oh well, I won't be getting any sleep – I might as well come down and see the fun.' Then, at the top of his voice, to no one in particular, 'This country is falling apart! They don't know how to govern this country any more! And when people leave, Mandela doesn't care!' He fell back to chatting with his pals, but every now and again would scream, 'This country is falling apart!' – looking absolutely delighted.

Through the crowd similar mutterings began to stir. One white man lost his head completely; 'Fuck this FUCKING country! I've had enough of these fucking drug lords! The police are corrupt! They are all corrupt! FUCK this fucking country.' Spitting and shaking with rage, he marched up, leant over the tape and treated us to the surreal spectacle of a white South African bellowing at a black policeman: 'The police in this country are fucking OUT OF CONTROL.'

The police didn't look out of control so much as shambolic. In due course one officer produced a loud speaker. 'This is a polite request,' he began falteringly, 'that, er, that everyone make their way to their, er, places. That's right, er, please leave now.' But nobody moved, and in the end he gave up, put the megaphone back in a van, and had a cigarette. Among the crowd there was strangely little interest in exactly what had happened; people tended to look surprised if we asked. A knot of reporters had gathered on the central reservation to hear the police commissioner's statement, but were too busy on mobile phones ('I'm RIGHT here at the SCENE!') to listen.

'At ten-twenty this evening the police station at Sea Point received a call,' the officer began, but it wasn't clear whether this call had been a bomb threat or a report from a member of the public about a suspicious package. Either way, a police van was dispatched to the restaurant, and as it arrived a bomb exploded in a rubbish bin. The commissioner searched at length for the word 'detonate', but couldn't find it, and eventually hurried on. The police might or might not have seen a 'suspicious-looking man' drive off, and seven – or was it nine – officers were now in hospital. The statement was over.

It had made no sense at all, and none of the reporters could conceivably have understood what had occurred. But they seemed happy enough, and got back on to their mobiles to begin filing the story. To this day I don't know who planted the bomb or why – but neither does anyone else, and nor do they expect to. The Christmas Eve bomb was our introduction to the state of profound confusion we would grow to consider perfectly normal.

We had come to South Africa looking for a club scene where ecstasy was new. In a city like Manchester, the old formula of chemicals and clubs can be reworked over and again, but the freshly minted astonishment of happiness cannot be recaptured – at least not by this generation. Without the surprise, ecstasy can offer only pleasure; it can make you feel good, probably better than most, but this is private gratification, not collective wonder. In the early days of Strangeways, the sound system had been so ropey that if too many people danced on the pool tables at the back of the club the music would cut out, and everyone would sing the record themselves while the DJ looked for the screwdriver. We were in South Africa looking for ecstasy in its infancy, the magical time before clubbers get to thinking of themselves as consumers.

The quest could have led us to any number of different cities. Moscow was one option, as were most of the former Soviet bloc capitals, and there was talk of a house explosion in the clubs of Buenos Aires and Rio. But the whole of South Africa would be new, we thought, fizzing with post-apartheid reinvention; a brand-new nation, with ecstasy the icing on the cake. Clubbing would be fresh and innocent, we expected. And on Christmas Day, it looked for a while as if we might be right.

Unity was promising a holiday special of 1999 anthems. It was Cape Town's only superclub, and we were expecting something like the Ministry of Sound – but when we reached Buitensingel, we found something more like the Notting Hill Carnival. Two rows of Scorpion military trucks and police vans were parked at either end, fencing in a road jammed solid with clubbers. Hundreds were dancing on the pavements, with more balanced on car roofs, and still more lining garden walls, all dancing like crazy. Sweating and laughing, they waved and called to each other in the hot night air, above the torrent of hard house blaring from car stereos. As we pushed through the crowd a truck screamed up in reverse, screeched to a halt, and about fifty clubbers jumped in the back and broke into dance, like extras in a Coca-Cola advert.

'Just another bomb scare,' shouted a young white man dancing on a car boot. 'Third week running for this club; fuck knows who's behind it. Everyone was inside when the music went off. We thought it was a raid, so everyone took all the drugs they had on them. Now everyone's completely off their head.' He laughed, pointing to the police. 'They take our club, we take their streets, yah?'

In London the temper would have been foul – 'Can't they sort their fackin' security out, then?' The clubbers here looked like Londoners – black, white and coloured, in tight sleeveless tops and designer combats – but the mood was unrecognisable. Pairs skipped to a nearby garage for more chewing gum, cigarette boys handed round Camels, and there were amicable whoops at the police, who leant, arm in arm, on bulletproof trucks and watched with bemused good humour. Some were black, and others the white officers from a thousand newsreels – squared heads, clipped blonde moustaches – except that they too had apparently mistaken themselves for Coca-Cola extras.

The bomb scare was a false alarm. After an hour or so the police and soldiers clambered into trucks and pulled away, waved off by cheeky goodbyes until the last vehicle was gone. But there was a problem. The queue wasn't being allowed re-entry. Everyone had been locked out for almost two hours, now, yet still nobody really appeared to mind – though a querulous ripple began to flicker through the crowd. A promoter in a Unity T-shirt strode by.

'Right,' he shouted, looking tense. 'We've got a real fucking problem on our hands now. Darren's gone missing, and no one knows how to turn the fucking sound back on. Where the fuck is Darren?'

And so Cape Town's only superclub waited on the pavement and danced to car stereos while lots of people looked for Darren. Eventually the promoter climbed on to a car and could be heard shrieking above the noise, 'Daaaaaa-renn?' Darren was presumably found, for minutes later a bassline juddered to life and the queue began to move. I thought I might faint at the charm of it all.

Drusilla was hovering in the hall when we got home. 'Come and have a little chat,' she wheedled, elbowing us into the lounge. 'Just you two and little old me.' She patted the place next to her on the sofa. When she heard about the bomb scare she flushed beneath her make-up, and began pulling angrily at her rings.

'Oh! Well. You see, it wasn't like that *before*, oh no. The crowds – it is black, black, black, everywhere. And the whites have nowhere to go. It's not that we don't want to mix. It's just that it's so *rough*. The cultures don't mix, you see. You can't just chill out. They take *over*. You understand? They *take over*.' We didn't see what this had to do with the bombing and Paul asked her what the bombs were about, but it was as if she couldn't hear the question.

'The blacks, you see, they're here all the time in Sea Point! Ten years ago, my darling, I would walk around. You could jog down to the beach at two in the morning. Not any more. Oh no. It's all *gummy* with these African street stores, and the street kids – the *crowds* of them, there are *crowds*. They are fighting, and drug-smuggling. It's rough, you know? And they are constantly pleading poverty. You look in the papers, now it is only black people, black people all the time, and their poverty. But you should see the cars they drive! And if you go and shop where they shop, go to the hypermarket, they shop better than us! Two, three trolleys. They are not poor, not poor like you think. They live better than me.'

Wasn't she at least glad, I tried, to be living in a democracy? She gave a humourless laugh. 'No, not really. I don't give a shit about democracy. Listen, I am God's child, I'm not interested in politics. I don't care about having a vote.' Flushing deeper still, she became random. 'And now, now they show Robben Island, and say how Mandela was mishandled. But look, he had a cell. He had facilities. He lived like a king. He ate better than we did! Yes! Really.' She fell silent for a moment.

'I lived with the blacks once, in the Transvaal. Their floor was made of dung, the walls were made of mud. And it was spotless. Plates – white, like that! And white lace. Brilliant! I speak their lingo, I'm not scared. I don't hate them. Lots of people do, but not me. I understand their culture.' Another pause.

'The blacks, they get houses now, and they think they don't have to pay rent. They have schools built for them, and then they go and burn them down. What more do they want? You know, what more do they *want*?' In the long silence Paul and I stared helplessly at each other. When Drusilla stirred, she looked surprised to see us there.

'Ah! Oh well, my darlings, I suppose I should be seeing to the maid.' She kissed us each on the cheek, and left the room. And we sat there, a pair of innocents, thinking that was surely the most extraordinary outburst we would hear in South Africa.

CHAPTER 11

The Sun is Shining

If we were supposed to be examining cultural constructs of happiness, Cape Town was obviously an excellent case study. Would blacks and whites in the new South Africa club together? In London this had seemed like a terribly good question, for one of ecstasy's big surprises in Britain in the beginning was its impact on previously entrenched prejudice. In the late eighties, style magazines were astonished to report that white Wythenshawe scallies and black Moss Side gangsters had been spotted sharing bottles of water in the Hacienda. Famously, rival football fans in Manchester took Es on the terraces, and stopped trying to hit each other. Clubbers were moved to speak highly of their former enemies, and the definition of a good night was adjusted from one that ended in a fight to one that ended with a new friend. The delight, I think, came less from the new friends' loveliness than the novel thrill of no longer hating them.

The simple answer to our question was yes. An embryonic multiracial dance scene was emerging in Cape Town, pioneered by clubs like Unity, and it should have been what we explored – only there was one problem. Their DJs played only hard house and techno, and here Paul put his foot down. That was that, and I wasn't sorry, but the techno ban necessarily confined us to the more culturally questionable social circles of Camps Bay.

Camps Bay is a kind of seaside Knightsbridge. Tucked between the ocean and the rear face of Table Mountain, it is a tiny resort but wildly opulent, attracting fashionable whites from all over South Africa. For the holiday season, two open-air clubs had been built on the cricket field opposite the beach, and their DJs played astonishingly beautiful house.

Both bars did a roaring trade. From mid-afternoon until the early hours they were jammed with Cape Town's young rich, and the overall impression up close was of a *Baywatch* party. During the day, topless men in surfer shorts and women in neon bikinis drank bottled beer and shrieked with laughter. At night, the girls changed into miniature skirts and strappy sandals, and backless tops tied together with ribbons, which they checked carefully every few minutes. The men wore tight white tops and liked to smoke fat cigars, and everyone's dancing was faultless, as polished an accomplishment as the rest of their appearance, giving the scene the flawless choreography of a pop video. In the corner of one bar was a pair of jacuzzi tubs, and these were particularly popular. All day and night, you would see people dancing waist deep in the foam, a mobile phone in one hand and an ice bucket in the other.

Evidently everyone spent a tremendous amount of their time in the gym; alas, they were all so perfectly beautiful that they tended to cancel each other out. The men in particular looked faintly unreal – like action superheroes in boys' comics, with inflatable bodies and upside-down-triangle heads, spiky yellow hair, pink lips and wrap-around sunglasses. They didn't actually outnumber the women, but they gave that impression and dominated the space. Between back-slapping and joshing among themselves they would eye up the women sensatinally blatantly. Towards one another, though, the single women were icy, and fiercely competitive.

On our first night in Camps Bay we fell into conversation with a couple at the bar. Mark was in his late twenties, here from Johannes-burg for the holiday with his terribly pretty blonde girlfriend, Sophie. It was a 'trial honeymoon', he joked; they were getting married next year. Sophie was hysterically excited about our newlywed status. 'You guys must start reproducing at once! What are you waiting for?' Sophie could answer only two questions with ease. When are you getting married? What star sign are you? (The second was in response to her asking ours. Sophie was genuinely troubled by an anecdote Paul told about an end of the pier astrologer in Brighton who read our charts and found us calamitously incompatible. She listened sympathetically, and looked alarmed.)

I asked Sophie what she did for a living. 'Well, Mark's an account-ant,' she announced with pride, but then fizzled out. What she did for a living, I think, was encourage Mark to marry her – and she was doing a brilliant job. She straddled him, fawning and cooing delightfully.

We had a few more drinks, and began to warm to the scene.

Everyone's favourite tune in Camps Bay that Christmas was a remix of Bob Marley's 'The Sun is Shining'; it sent them wild, and they danced along without a trace of irony. When it came on I put down my drink to dance but as I turned, I happened to glance across the street towards the beach, and spotted a young black woman dancing alone in the dark. She moved with shy delight, hands longingly out-stretched towards the music; I nudged Paul, and Mark and Sophie saw us turn and look, but they appeared unable to see her.

The two-way mirror effect is a fixture of the smarter parts of town. Blacks and coloureds linger in the shade watching whites enjoy themselves in cafes and convertibles and clubs, but the whites are frequently blind to the dark faces eyeing them from just feet away. Even on Long Street in the most bohemian bars, the artless young liberals seem not to notice that the staff collecting their glasses at 4 a.m. are old black women in frilly maid's uniforms. In time we grew accustomed to the blindness, but it made the study of race and clubbing a non-starter for ecstasy is in no danger of making riviera lovelies get down with their brethren. What rich young white South Africans like to do when they take it is undress in front of each other, for a bouncing riot of muscle tone.

Gender was a more surprising study than race. White women never, ever went out in groups together, let alone by themselves, but instead soldered themselves at all times to the gigantic arm of a man. They were smaller than the men in every way, and you had the feeling that were all the men in a room to leave at once the women would simply deflate. One afternoon when we forgot our mobile number I asked a man in a Camps Bay cafe if I could call his phone to see our number come up. The woman beside him tugged laughingly on his arm, and shook her glossy mane from side to side. 'She's just after your number, Stefan!' She flashed me a thin, dangerous smile. 'Good strategy! I'll try that myself some time.'

At times it felt as if we'd flown back to the 1950s. There are no sunloungers or parasols for hire, so everyone brings their own, making a patchwork of multicoloured deckchairs, and giving the seafront the look of an old postcard. Along the peninsula south of the city, in the pretty seaside villages with their strict speed-limits, twee horticulture and oppressive community rules, it is easier to believe yourself in Guernsey than Africa. Late in the day, the verges along the coast road become dotted with hampers and wine coolers and deckchairs as Enid Blyton families assemble to watch the sunset.

The shops in Cape Town have their own distinctive atmosphere, unnerving for anyone raised in the slick, sullen retail world of Top Shop. Apart from the new Waterfront complex, there are practically no chainstores in the city, and instead you find stores that would make *Are You Being Served?* look dangerously modern. Shop assistants are faultlessly attentive, call their customers madam and sir, and refer to each other as Mr This or Mrs That. But South African culture has become a muddle of new and old, the peculiar economics of apartheid delivering unimaginable luxuries without producing the usual high-street standards of a consumer society. For example, we could find virtually no bookshops, and certainly none that sold much besides Maeve Binchy and cookery books. The supermarkets are a dowdy shambles, like Britain's in the seventies, selling cleaning products from an age of carbolic soda. As white women never had to do the housework, what would have been the point of improving the products?

Drugs, on the other hand, are fantastically easy to buy. The sixties more or less skipped white South Africa, but majority rule in the nineties has produced one of the most liberal constitutions in the world, so next door to the prim fifties dating culture of Camps Bay are Green Point's new sex shops, brothels and gay bars. On Boxing Day we were sitting on a garage wall watching the comings and goings outside a club called Detour when Paul noticed a group of coloured gay men fumble with something. One handed it to another, and with a wince he swallowed it.

'Hello.' Paul marched straight up. 'I'm from London and I'm trying to buy drugs. Do you know where we can get any ecstasy?'

'Of course,' said one. 'How much do you want? Hold on a sec and I'll go and get some.' He disappeared into the bar.

While he was gone we chatted with the others. One was just back from London; another had been working on a farm in Telford until Christmas. Another was home from Johannesburg for the holiday. 'Cape Town. Yeuch,' he sniffed. 'It's so provincial, so lah-di-dah, so let's-do-it-tomorrow, why worry? And they have no *sass*. They have no style.'

The first man reappeared with pills, and we bought two. He looked more Asian than African, with high cheekbones and flashing eyes, and had the delightfully straightforward attitude to drugs often found on the gay scene.

'Here's my number, I'm Faisal. If you want more, give me a ring. The dealer's a good friend.' A police car idled by just as he was handing over the pills. 'Oh,' everybody shrugged, unfazed. 'The puh-lice.'

The pills turned out to be brilliant, and we saw a lot of Faisal over the next few days, as we sampled Es with the forensic dedication of lab technicians. With New Year's Eve only days away, we were leaving nothing to chance – much to the amusement of Faisal's dealer, who was reported as thinking ours a 'very British' approach.

The ecstasy hunt was going splendidly, but Drusilla was becoming an issue. Her role at the guesthouse was only as hired help; the owner was an older woman, Sylvia, an immaculately groomed tyrant who appeared to do nothing but go to church. They had a peculiarly toxic relationship, and poor Drusilla was eager to involve us in its resentful rhythms. In a recent act of caprice, Sylvia had taken away Drusilla's mattress. Drusilla reported this latest indignity with studied cheeriness, as though oblivious to her own tragedy. 'But I have a life beyond this gate,' she quivered, suddenly afraid we might be taken in by her brave face. 'A lonely life, maybe, but I still want a life beyond this gate.' Whenever Sylvia appeared, she would shrink into herself and twist her fingers behind her back, but towards Grace, the black maid, she was unnervingly sharp and loud.

Every morning, heavy with hangovers, we would drag ourselves out apartment-hunting. The heat was ferocious, for Christmas is the height of Cape Town's summer; vacancies were scarce, and landlords unenthusiastic. There is a general air of profound sleepiness about many white Capetonians. It is hugely appealing, but tends to make them sound vague, placidly indulgent, as though nothing much could really trouble them. You could say that nothing much does. Staff see to life's drudgery, and all the pressures of a normal modern economy have yet to make themselves felt. The leisured abundance is another echo of the fifties – except that now apartheid is over, far from never having had it so good, this is for many the worst it has ever been. It's a mindboggling thought.

A fortnight before we arrived, forty people had been injured in an explosion in a Camps Bay pizza parlour. The newspapers were agog with rumour and allegation, but no organisation had claimed responsibility; and following the Christmas Eve blast the city grew palpably edgy, holding its collective breath in the stifling heat as it awaited the next. Police and military trucks patrolled the city centre, grey, lumpen, geriatric hulks cruising the streets as though they had driven straight there from Londonderry *circa* 1972. A row of them stood stationed behind the beach in Camps Bay, honey-limbed teenagers playing frisbee in their shade while soldiers trained their gaze on girls' bikinis.

All over the city, in every shop, club and bar, brusque security guards searched bags and scanned bodies with metal detectors. Buying a bar of chocolate had become as complicated as getting on an aeroplane.

The mystery bombing campaign's one dividend was a late rush of cancellations from frightened tourists. After a week, a room became available to rent in a large, airy house at the other end of Sea Point from Drusilla's guesthouse. We were packed and out in under an hour.

It must have been late in the seventies when the thought first occurred to me that I would be alive at the turn of a millennium. Awed by the discovery, I did some quick maths, only to find I would be twenty-bloody-nine and obviously way too old to enjoy it.

Twenty-nine had grown miraculously younger by the mid-nineties, when I began to speculate on the exciting possibilities ahead. I couldn't say precisely when this view was in turn revised, but by the time Paul and I left London the fact that we would be out of the country for New Year's Eve had become a good enough reason to justify the whole journey. Thank God, we told each other, we would be missing all *that*. We did realise that by merely relocating we could not expect to opt out altogether, but other people's hype, like other people's housework, is always more manageable than one's own.

So it was a surprise to arrive in Cape Town at Christmas and find a city just waking up to the idea that the thirty-first might be a big night. Asked about their plans, people we met generally looked puzzled and said they hadn't given it a thought. Before even leaving London we'd arranged press passes to the city's two major club events, yet just a week before lift-off most clubs hadn't even started selling tickets; newspapers were only just starting to talk about traffic jams, as if biblical chaos was a brand new idea. Of all unlikely developments, we found ourselves recast at the last as the excitable ingenues.

This presented the inevitable dilemma. Because nothing the traveller does is ever strictly necessary, there's no excuse for anything to be less than brilliant. If everything is a once-in-a-lifetime opportunity, to squander a second on the wrong choice is unconscionable – and so you live in constant fear of underachievement, and agonise over every choice. This is one of the great problems of travel – onerous enough at the best of times, but completely disabling with New Year's Eve 1999. We had tickets for Synergy, a house extravaganza in a country club, and passes for the main club event in Camps Bay. With two days to go, though, we began to worry that whichever one we chose, it would be the wrong choice.

It was then that Paul had the idea of spending midnight in a club in a township. *Cool or what?* I thought it was a stroke of genius. We would forget about Camps Bay and country clubs, and hang out on the Cape Flats. Brilliant! A bold and original choice. The only difficulty, as far as I could see, would be finding one. Even today, the townships are rather like great swathes of nineteenth-century Africa; the whites know they're there, but are hazy on the location details. You can buy a map that details every city-centre paving-stone, but the Flats are typically illustrated as a shaded grey block. As far as much of white Cape Town is concerned, when the blacks' minibuses leave town they are driving off the edge of the world.

We decided our best hope for a suggestion lay in a bar near our house in Sea Point. It sat above a sex shop on the scruffiest stretch of Main, and at weekends the balcony was crowded with black and coloured faces. We had wondered about going in before; Sea Point is more mixed than most of the city centre, but the bars still tended to be either white or not, and we weren't sure how welcome we would be. When we presented ourselves at the door later that night, a mountain of a bouncer studied us in silence. He seemed to think about it – then, with a brief nod, motioned us up the stairs.

At the top of the unlit flight we found ourselves in what could have been an after-hours local in East London. Smelling of ashtrays, it had wooden floors, an ancient jukebox, a pool table and, behind the bar, a photograph of Princess Diana. The only white was the landlord, a Dudley Moore figure from Enfield who'd moved here four years earlier. He'd intended his bar to be mixed, but it hadn't worked out that way.

'Don't matter, mind. Got myself a nice house, drive a BM. It's all right, innit?' Bobby was giggly, almost camp, and very much the Londoner. 'Nah, I ain't learnt the lingo.' A woman tried to buy her bottle of beer in small change. 'Don't bring your parking change to me; I want real money. If you have to ask how much it costs you shouldn't be 'ere.' But it was a smiley bark, and he was enjoying his performance.

Bobby couldn't decide between boasting about the charms of his adopted home and frightening us off. 'Life's cheap here, I'm telling you. Go down to the townships? Why would you want to do that?'

Was it all right for us to be in a non-white bar?

'Put it this way. This is a black bar, so you're going to be out of place. But you won't have any trouble. If you have any trouble, there'll be trouble,' and he jabbed a finger at his chest. 'Believe me.'

In fact nobody paid us any attention at all. Young men played pool or sat alone, brooding on barstools, smoking cigarettes in the gloom. According to Bobby, the handful of women were all prostitutes, though you might not have guessed. Unfortunately, as most of his customers were migrant workers from central Africa and spoke no English, we made little progress with advice on township clubs. The night was drawing on and our hopes were fading when three coloured men entered the bar together. The first man was gaunt and bald, the second a twin of Daley Thompson. The third was goofy and spectacled, his hair gelled tight like a permed pub-singer from Liverpool. They were brothers, highly articulate, and eager to talk.

The bald brother was David. Daley Thompson was called Alex, the goofy one, Matthew, and they had been active in the ANC since childhood. They talked of their country with desperate pride, and wanted our impressions of everything. 'In order to live it,' David urged solemnly, 'you have to slum it.' Before leaving, the brothers agreed to take us to a club in the townships, and show us 'the real South Africa'. We skittered home, drunk and delighted, and phoned half of London to boast about our night in the badlands with the ANC. Oh, were we ever on the edge.

The following day brought a series of phone calls from Alex about footwear. He was firm and specific: we were not to wear sandals. Paul took this to mean that it would be muddy, and maybe dangerously crowded. It took a long time to get ready that evening, as he kept making me put on more layers. Eventually satisfied, we set off dressed for a winter barn dance in the Scottish highlands.

Our rendezvous instructions had been pleasingly mysterious. As we pulled in on a motorway bridge out of town at nine, moments later a car drew up behind us bearing the agreed licence plate. I was slightly concerned to notice Alex and Matthew wearing ironed shirts, polished shoes and slacks. We tailed them north through several miles of what looked like suburban America, passing 7/11 stores and KFCs, until we reached what they called a *shebeen*. The *shebeen* turned out to be a normal off-licence, quite legal and well stocked, like a branch of Oddbins. Slightly surprised, and hoping to hide our disappointment, we bought a bottle of Smirnoff.

David lived in a largish bungalow in a tidy, upper-working-class neighbourhood that had once been whites only. He greeted us warmly at the door, arms around two handsome children and his quietly smiling wife. Inside, we arranged ourselves in the living room on matching black sofas beside a sleek stack-stereo system, while David's wife passed around glass bowls of peanuts and crisps. Her long chiffon dress swirled as she moved, and I wondered helplessly how to explain why her guests had come looking like tramps.

Everyone smiled at each other, dimpled with awkward enthusiasm, like families on a foreign-exchange programme. David was a supervisor for a mining company, but he talked about growing up on a rural farm, where the shop had a fence dividing the white side from the black. Bananas on the white side were always golden yellow, and blackened on the black. He became politically active in his teens, and described leading his school out on strike with white-knuckle pride; he was prouder still of his government building homes with electricity and toilets. Thinking of our ghetto badland hopes I glanced at Paul, and got a faint but very firm shake of the head.

David and Alex wanted to know what everything looked like to us. The *shebeen* – how did it seem? The neighbourhood – what did we think? David's house – what did it look like? At first we were baffled, but as the night wore on it became apparent that David and Alex's imaginative relationship with the rest of the world was an intense, grand passion. For the white South Africans we'd met, the outside world barely existed, but for the brothers it was the soulmate of their struggle, and they longed to show it South African beauty. We were the first Westerners they'd ever taken home – and I felt a vague sense of shame.

After midnight Alex told David to change into smart pants, and we set off to a US-style mall, and a neat, redbrick venue called The G-Spot. The neighbourhood was Epping, and we really could have been in Essex, for The G-Spot looked like a home-counties Harvester. A Liverpool FC scarf hung behind the bar, beermats were strung like bunting across the ceiling, and the menu announced lasagne and chips. With the women in tight trousers and sheer blouses, and the men in sports tops and slacks, there was a terrific clunking of gold jewellery and a fog of perfume. Paul and I looked like militant sociology students. We were the only whites, and our entrance attracted some curious looks – but I think this was largely due to what we were wearing.

The scene departed from the general Harvester theme only on the dancefloor – but not towards ghetto fabulous; more in the direction of *Come Dancing*. Arm in arm, young couples crushed the floor, their feet and hips making invisible patterns like liquid; and although the music was a kind of swingbeat, the dancing was more like ballroom jazz, deadly serious, but carried off lightly, with brilliant, careless smiles. It was quite, quite beautiful – and the absolute opposite of everything we were looking for.

'This is Cape Town jazz!' David shouted in my ear, his eyes shining. 'This is typical coloured Cape Town jazz. The world has never seen it. And now you see it!' I pointed to my open mouth.

'Amazing!'

'What do you think?' the brothers kept asking, beaming from ear to ear with pride. 'Is it how you expected?'

In the end it was a grand night. I peeled off most of my layers in the ladies' and someone lent me her lipstick, after which people stared less. Paul got drunk, and Matthew attempted to teach me some Cape jazz dance steps – a charming gesture, if ambitious, given the twin obstacles of his stutter and my mountain boots. Neither Paul nor I felt able to explain that we had been hoping for something slightly grittier, and when we awoke the next morning it was New Year's Eve, and we were back to square one.

CHAPTER 12

Pride and Prejudice

It was just a simple question of finding a club. Faisal met us in a cafe on Long Street for lunch, to drop off our final selection of ecstasy – first-rate pills, the best of the trip so far – but he had no suggestions. 'Have you heard about Synergy?' After he left we had one final debate, and reluctantly agreed to abandon the idea. Paul went to pay – and returned from the bar with a triumphant grin, flourishing a piece of paper. It was a leaflet advertising township music tours. He rang the number, and found himself speaking to a young man called Barney who agreed to come and meet us.

'Ten minutes, yuh? Ciao.'

Barney turned out to be from Hemel Hempstead. He had a fluffy beard and round spectacles, and ran a company that took tourists into the townships to hear live African music. Barney didn't like the idea of sending us anywhere unaccompanied one bit. His leaflet warned against wandering off from the group, 'under *any circumstances*,' but Paul bullied him into surrendering a suggestion. If we really wanted – and on our heads be it, yuh? – we could try a club called Tiger's Place, in Langa.

'I've got nothing to do with this, right?'

'Absolutely.'

'OK, then. You take care. Good luck. Ciao.'

'Ciao, Barney.'

He walked away shaking his head.

It was about ten o'clock in the evening when we pulled into Tiger's Place, the moon casting the only light as we threaded our way into the township. Langa is a small black settlement in the near reaches of the Cape Flats, and the approach road was lined with the classic patchwork of corrugated-iron shacks, with bony livestock grazing among the flotsam in the gutter. Deeper into the township, the houses became modest concrete squares, most in disrepair and some dilapidated but others approaching a degree of suburban orderliness. But the roads, were an unlit labyrinth, rutted with poverty, and for all our bravado we were starting to lose our nerve. From out of the shadows, dark faces stared at us through the car windows, and with each new bend further into the maze this ingenious idea of ours lost a fraction more of its appeal.

Not a bar or club in the conventional sense, Tiger's Place was more a back yard on a corner, sheltered by a lean-to roof and lit by a single bulb, with drink sold through a hatch in the wall. Our arrival was met by frank stares. Men sat on upturned crates, resting their backs against the warm bricks, nursing bottles of beer, eyeing us warily. Nearby, a group of children froze, open-mouthed, like cartoon characters. Smiling vaguely, we strolled up and took our place in the queue for drink. 'I think,' whispered Paul from the corner of his mouth, 'we might have made a serious mistake.'

There can't have been more than thirty people gathered in the yard drinking, plus a mill of comings and goings. Most people in the queue were buying drink to take away; they would stare sharply at first, then pretend not to see us. We kept smiling, foolish, middle-distance grins, and began to wonder where we would put ourselves once we had our drinks. I was still trying to read the situation when from behind me in the queue a young woman tapped my shoulder, then introduced herself and her brother. They were tipsy, fizzy with smiles, and soon Paul and I were included with them in a circle of young men.

'Where are you from?' asked one, in tattered jeans and a vest. 'London? Oh, London! I was there last week, in Hyde Park. I stayed in Kensington. Yeah, I work for South African Airways. I'm an air steward.' He chatted about Chelsea FC, and Arsenal, and the weather. His friend asked about the Ministry of Sound, and we found ourselves involved in a conversation about the merits of various London DJs. A tall, skinny young man hovering at Paul's shoulder butted in with the announcement that he worked for Ogilvy & Mather – in town, he said, in market research. He was starting up his own business as a consultant to multinationals, offering them help with marketing their products to black consumers – and within minutes was boring us to tears with share ownership and product-placement plans.

'So, guys,' Paul asked desperately. 'What are your plans for tonight? Where will you be going?' Everyone looked at him in surprise.

'Oh, The Waterfront, definitely The Waterfront. We're all going there, it's the best place. Aren't you?'

'Isn't anything happening here? We thought maybe we'd stay in Langa for midnight.'

'What? Are you joking? Nothing's going on here. Like I say, everyone's going to The Waterfront.' They studied us kindly. 'You do know where that is, don't you? You have heard of The Waterfront?'

'Doesn't anything happen here at all?'

'Not really. We have live music here on Wednesdays, when tourists come. But the band is playing at The Waterfront tonight. After that I think it's doing some party at a country club.'

By eleven o'clock the only people left in Tiger's Place were Paul and myself. The hatch had closed and overloaded cars had roared off towards the N2, bound for The Waterfront. Scarcely able to believe we had come to the badlands and been bored about marketing by a man from Ogilvy & Mather, then abandoned for The Waterfront, we now had less than an hour to go and no idea what to do.

Only one option remained – and, looking back, it was of course where we should have chosen to go all along. Speeding back into town, we raced up Kloofnek to the foothills of Table Mountain above the city. We were too late to queue for the cable cars ferrying parties to the mountain's summit; but where the road forks left to the cable station there is a turning on the right for the road to the peak of its sister flank, Signal Hill. Police had blocked the way for cars, but allowed us to park. At twenty to twelve, we began to climb into the darkness.

The black lane wrapped around the edge of Signal Hill was silent, and freezing. As we climbed, it grew colder still, a night wind whipping across the mountainside. As we ran we took an E, and with each steep twist grew more breathless, urged on by stragglers sprinting up behind us in the dark. The road seemed to go on for ever, but with just minutes to spare we turned a final bend and at last reached the summit of Signal Hill. We were among a great crowd perched on the edge of the hillside, waiting for midnight.

Cape Town had become a carpet of fairylights. Harbour lights cut into the black of the ocean, embers of helicopter tail-lights glowed above, and in the distance fireworks from Robben Island were showering red and gold sparks over the bay. On the face of Table Mountain green lasers projected a giant ticking clock, and a single beam shone out from the foothills all the way to Robben Island, a perfect neon arc across the water. Strains of music and cheers drifted up from the city below – and as we stood and stared it seemed suddenly astonishing that we had thought of being anywhere else. We could have gazed down on any city at that moment and marvelled, I know, but Cape Town at the close of the twentieth century was moving beyond all words.

Midnight struck. Whistles and shouts began to ring out across the hillside, echoing back from Table Mountain until they swelled to a roar, and the cool dark mountainside erupted into a stadium of cheers. Fireworks exploded in the harbour, and ships' horns rang out in the night. The top of Table Mountain burst into camera flashlight, like a horizontal sparkler, and below, on the mountain face, the date 2000 shone out in neon green. Crowds shrieked and hugged and kissed and cheered, and fireworks burst on, showering the bay with Technicolor glitter.

By the time we reached our car we were clean off our heads, warm and giddy, and laughing. Down in Camps Bay the thousands were in full cry, clutching champagne bottles and spilling out of marquees, a whirl of Gucci and white teeth in the moonlight as we drew up. At the gates, house poured out on a wave of laughter and warmth, sweeping us in. It was New Year's Day, and we were going to dance.

'Happy?'

Paul nodded. 'Very happy.'

'Want another E?' He nodded again, laughing.

'Oh. Oh God.' I searched my pockets frantically. 'Oh fucking hell. I think I must have dropped them on Signal Hill.'

And so the first hours of the new millennium were spent on our hands and knees in the cold on Signal Hill, hunting for a little bag of pills. By some miracle we found it, but it was late when we returned to Camps Bay, and the first dawn of the year would soon be breaking over the valley. The crowds had scarcely thinned, but the party was unrecognisable from the glittery dazzle we had left an hour or so earlier.

No club looks brilliant by daybreak. Most, though, have a loose-limbed cheery anarchy – and it was plain that Camps Bay did not. A scatter of young lads were charming; trying to dance, they could manage only a wriggle, lost in their own amazement at the night. A few older men looked as if they hadn't done this before, either, and were crashing around like golden retrievers, unable to believe they were still up. But overall, despite a prodigious consumption of drugs, the party had splintered into factions who were circling one another warily.

Up close, all the women over twenty-five looked like old hags. They hadn't eaten for at least ten years, and wore tight dresses, high heels and tiaras, but somehow managed to give the impression of belonging on the scrapheap. They stared at each other with a candid mixture of resentment and hostility, and were thrown into a spin, unable to drag their eyes away, whenever one passed by in an outfit substantially different to their own.

Each marquee played different music, but the women had just two dance moves. One was a parody of what they must have taken for sexy femininity, a kind of lap-dancer routine of shoulders and come-get-me eyes. The other involved pointing a forefinger and stomping about, hard-eyed, with a fist in the air – an odd sight to see, in a pink slinky dress and kitten heels. It was meant to suggest feistiness, I think but looked like angry loneliness. There were also younger, thinner women, in short dresses and cowboy hats and clompy knee-length boots. These boots probably started the night looking quite glamorous, but as the morning wore on their owners began to look more and more bird-like, until they were just cold, underfed, tiny little girls, hugging their shoulders and starving for a pair of jeans and a meal.

And then there were the men. One half were thirtysomethings in black jeans and little gold-rimmed glasses, the others bodybuilders in Lycra and sunglasses, all fooling about together on the dancefloors. Towards the women, though, they were coldly casual, sneering at the longing in their emaciated eyes. They seemed to toy with their power, but couldn't quite be bothered to exercise it.

Like everyone else, the bodybuilders had taken a bucket of ecstasy. They carried themselves with severe self-control, though, and gazed pityingly at the shambling younger lads – yet their rigid little dance moves betrayed them. All the glorified self-confidence of Camps Bay bars had been stripped away in the night, and had we sneaked up to one and whispered that he looked ridiculous, we would only have confirmed his darkest suspicion.

As the sun rose, the marquees slowly emptied, scattering clubbers across the grass to watch the dawn. Dancing by herself nearby was a woman of about thirty with the body of an eleven-year-old, in trousers rolled down as hipsters and a tassled bra top tied together with string. With thick, golden, waist-length hair and big brown eyes, she was truly beautiful, a willowy blend of Bridget Bardot and Twiggy.

A grotesquely bloated, topless bodybuilder watched her. Presently he made his approach, and she arranged herself into a helpless pose of shrunken shoulders and big eyes. He bent down and said something. She smiled neatly.

She began dancing keenly now, a sway of limbs and hair, making her face fall into a strange expression where her eyes would go empty and dead as her limbs twisted around her. Assured of his interest, she made her way to the small stage in the corner of the field, climbed up and danced. The others on stage were all men, and I doubt she would have joined them unless certain of an observer, for fear of looking unwanted. But the stage raised her premium, for the bodybuilder would now see other men watching her.

The trick, which she accomplished nicely, was then to dance as though she hadn't noticed he was watching. Observing the rules, he watched from a distance, then closed in to stand just a few feet away. From there he proceeded to dance at her. She continued to pretend not to see him, while he did his classic bodybuilder dance. It's a limited move, just a flick of the lower right arm across the groin and a flex of the upper-body muscles. You see bodybuilders doing it in clubs all over the world, and it looks like wanking. With each beat he would flick and flex again, another great, repulsive wank, and his efforts were duly rewarded with a smile. When the next record began, the blonde stepped down from the stage and together they left, arm in arm.

We must have cut a curious figure, Paul and I, wandering around that field at dawn, staring at people with morbid fascination, like displaced social anthropologists. I think white South Africans are so extraordinarily mesmerising because at a glance they are so instantly recognisable – affluent global clubbers, who dress and dance and speak as people do in London or New York. The outward appearance of social life in a Camps Bay party is familiarly reassuring – not exotic or arcane in the least – without any warning signs to alert you to the truth of its extreme other-ness. It is a measure of just how 'other' it is that, even with all the house and ecstasy in the world, Cape Town clubbers are locked in rituals as anthropologically alien to us as anything to be found in Africa.

They may have looked like clubbers, but they behaved more like characters in a Jane Austen novel, acting out the roles of young gentlemen and ladies at a ball. It felt as though we were watching a period drama in reverse, with the characters played by actors from history, dressed as people of the future. The spectacle only became less disorientating when the realisation slowly dawned that this was, of course, what a party would look like if feminism hadn't happened. Having always grumbled about how little feminism has altered our lives at home, it came as quite a shock to see a snapshot of what social life would be like without a hint of it. And it wasn't social life at all, but prodigiously hard work. One of the prices white South Africa paid for apartheid was a de facto ban on the sexual revolution, a political trade-off that might once have looked attractive but has proved to be at a desperately high cost. At dawn in Camps Bay on New Year's Day, Paul and I appeared to be the only two people not working flat out.

Paul led the way down to the beach. In the shade of a tree, we lay down and reflected on the sad strangeness of the night. It had seemed to go on for ever, and still it wasn't quite over; South Africa's supply of the bizarre and unreal is quite limitless. As we were almost drifting to sleep, two middle-aged white men clattered down beside us from nowhere, as though they'd just fallen out of the sky.

'How long are you guys staying here?' His sunburnt face was scabbed and bloody and wild. 'We just want someone to watch our stuff. We just want to sleep. We missed the whole year. We just need to sleep, but no one will watch our things.' He nodded to two carrier bags. His friend folded into the sand without a word. The speaker's words came out in hoarse gasps.

'We're just back from the war. Up in the borders, Sierre Leone. We're mercenaries. Nobody knows what's going on up there. Nobody cares. So many are dying up there.' He began to ramble.

'The Americans, they lost a chopper, all dead. I've seen so much, it's haunting me.' He paused. 'You'll have noticed about me, I never speak Afrikaans. I hate them, the Boers. They signed me up to kill the black man. But I love the black man. He's my brother.

'I've done so many bad things. We're mercenaries – that's all we can do now. But we haven't been paid yet. Not a penny. We're on sixteen days' leave, and I'm finding it hard to relate to society . . .

'I was kicked out of the police for dealing steroids. I used to deal ecstasy in California – then I fell in love with a beautiful woman. The most beautiful woman – she was Cindy Crawford, only without the beauty spot. And a bit shorter. Slightly lighter hair, maybe. But apart from that, the same woman. She was a cocaine addict – and after that, so was I. Then one day, she couldn't get another gram, so she took a gun and shot herself in front of me, through the head.

'So many bad things, so many, right back to my childhood, which I don't want to talk about right now, if that's all right.' He shook his head. 'We're just so tired. I'm sorry about all the blood, all the blood . . .' He tailed off again into silence.

Then, abruptly: 'I'm a qualified nutritionist. I did seven years as a pharmacist, nearly got my doctorate. I told Jean-Claude Van Damme, "Your diet sucks". I bodyguarded for Dolph Lundgren. Arnold Schwarznegger is a personal friend; I can call him up and say, "Hey, Arnie, how y' doing?" '

We smiled.

'You know what?' he said suddenly. 'Thank you. Thank you for being you. Sir, you look after her. Ma'am, you look after him. You're special, you know?' We got up, drove home, and slept for three days.

BROKEN PROMISE

CHAPTER 13

People Against Gangsterism and Drugs

The heat intensified in January, melting tarmac and blistering skin. Beaches choked, and in the city, workers wrapped towels packed with ice around their heads. Every day the temperature inched higher, scorching the record books, burning Cape Town to a crisp. At night we would surround the bed with basins of ice, and still wake, sodden with sweat, hours before dawn.

Perhaps wherever we were by then we would have tired of clubbing; whatever the case, neither of us could face another night out in Cape Town. More than the stultifying heat, the peculiar cruelty of the city's social rules had defeated us; ecstasy was easy to come by, but the chance of finding anything like happiness in these lonely clubs was remote, and by then we'd grown too antagonistic to keep looking. I didn't really care, for our attention had shifted elsewhere.

More interesting than assessing the effects of ecstasy on South Africans was the wider question of what drugs were doing to South Africa. The bombing campaign haunting Cape Town that Christmas was said to be the work of a vigilante organisation called People Against Gangsterism and Drugs. Pagad had not claimed responsibility for the recent blasts, nor for the other explosions that had rocked the city during the previous two years, but police were confident of the link, and every day the newspapers carried new allegations based on rumour and suspicion. Pagad was a relatively new outfit, founded in 1996. As with most of the problems faced by the new South Africa, however, the origins of gangsterism and drugs stretch a long way back in apartheid's history.

Under the apartheid regime, the population had been formally divided into three classifications of colour – white, black and coloured. Historically, Cape Town had a large coloured population, but in the late sixties, under the terms of the Group Areas Act, this population was forcibly removed from its homes in the city and dumped into townships on the bleak sandy plains of the Cape Flats. In these shattered communities crime spread quickly, and gangs began to form. One of the largest and most notorious coloured townships was Manenberg, and its gang activities soon earnt it the reputation of 'Murdererburg' and 'Kill Me Quick Town'.

Of the number of gangs to form, the most prominent was the Hard Livings, founded by twin brothers Rashaad and Rashid Staggie. But South Africa in the early seventies was an efficient police state, and the Staggies were soon imprisoned along with most other coloured gang-leaders. In the mid-eighties, however, just when ANC-led civic uprisings began breaking out across the townships, the leaders were released. The timing of their release was no coincidence. The state hoped that their old gangs would reactivate and provide an attraction for township youths to rival that of the ANC; in some cases the police even paid the newly released leaders to terrorise anti-apartheid activists. It was the old principle of divide and rule, and made for a cosy relationship in which coloured gangsters bought their freedom with acts of violence on behalf of apartheid, and police duly turned a blind eye to their other criminal activities. By the time the apartheid regime had collapsed, the gangs had been allowed to flower from crude thieving outfits into heavily armed criminal empires.

South Africa in the early nineties became a gangster's dream opportunity, a real once-in-a-lifetime conjunction of circumstances ripe for organised crime. The end of apartheid led to the opening of the country's borders, which facilitated the wholesale trafficking of guns and drugs. At the same time, stricter controls were being imposed on points of entry into the USA and Europe, making South Africa an attractive new trading post for global drug routes. Sophisticated gangs were also expanding in the former Soviet Bloc, looking for new international partnerships – and so, perhaps inevitably, South Africa's gangs were rapidly transformed into organised crime syndicates. With the Staggies once more in charge of the Hard Livings, they declared they were no longer a crude gang but rather an 'organisation'. Other gangs quickly learnt the new language of 'seeking a mandate from its members', and 'letting the community decide', enabling the Cape Flats gangs to refashion themselves as the righteous voice of their communities.

And what could the South African police do to stop them? The transition from any police state to democracy is always characterised by a weakening of law-enforcement structures – look at the former Soviet Union, for example. In South Africa, uncertainty within the police force about its changing future – and in some cases blunt resistance – created splendid openings for enterprising criminals. Policing was in chaos. The force still had to learn the novel skills of detection and investigation, since the old method of extracting 'confessions', on which they'd always relied, was no longer acceptable.

On top of all of which, the gangsters believed they had an official justification for their illegal activities. They'd seen a political agreement chiselled out between the parties that included the idea of amnesty for political offences, and in their estimation this was a formal licence to commit a crime and get away with it. If political leaders were 'getting away' with their crimes, then, by their logic, so could they.

By 1994, the Hard Livings had established itself as the biggest and most powerful gang in the Western Cape. It was efficient, organised, well armed and heavily involved in the drug trade from top to bottom. It had contacts with the Sicilian mafia and the Chinese triads, was smuggling cocaine via Colombian drug cartels, and selling Mandrax on the street to teenagers. Further, and more importantly, it occupied the dominant power-base at the heart of its community. The Hard Livings operated mobile shops and gave out food on credit; they distributed money to the unemployed; they introduced a loan scheme for the needy. Protection was provided to *shebeen* owners, taxi drivers and other township businesses. Even more importantly still, the Staggie twins cultivated an awesome cult of personality around themselves.

In the words of a former Hard Livings leader, 'Rashid Staggie is the one. He is the Chosen One. Everything that we do today is not about and for ourselves. He is that guy. He is the leader.' Revered and feared in the townships for their random acts of outrageous violence or generosity, the twins would drive through Manenberg like royalty, showering coins from their car. As their power and notoriety grew, they expanded their territory to include the city centre, where they took over the whole of Sea Point, running prostitution rings and protection rackets and drug deals right there in the heart of the once exclusive, whites-only riviera. Staggie became a household name in Cape Town, and Cape Town in turn became known as the gang capital of South Africa. By the mid-nineties, the World

Economic Forum had rated South Africa's organised crime problem third in the world, behind only those of Colombia and Russia.

In 1996, Pagad came to public attention. Originating from the same coloured townships as the gangs, its leaders claimed to speak on behalf of the communities sickened by the violence and drugs, and they declared war on the gangsters. At first, Pagad enjoyed a euphoria of public favour. The media, police and government all pledged enthusiastic support for its stated goal of eradicating gangsterism. This euphoria died down very quickly, however, when Pagad demonstrated what it meant by 'eradicating gangsterism'.

In August 1996, the media were invited to a Pagad rally. It began in a mosque with an address to a crowd of 4,000, and the ensuing scenes were filmed and broadcast live on news bulletins to the nation. 'The legal process has collapsed!' screamed the speaker. 'There is nothing the police can do about the gangsters. Enough is enough!' A chant broke out, led by men in masks: 'Are the drug merchants and the gangsters your enemies? Yes! Are they the enemies of the community? Yes! So what must we do? Kill them!' The crowd poured out of the mosque in a convoy, and descended upon the home of Rashaad Staggie. In full view of the cameras and a massive police deployment, the chanting mob swarmed around the house.

Rashaad Staggie appeared moments later, and a masked man shot him through the head. Staggie fell to the ground, pouring with blood. An ambulance man rushed to help him, but another masked man got there first, doused Staggie in petrol and set him on fire. As Staggie stumbled and lurched, wrapped in flames, the crowd bayed: 'God is great! God is great!' While he lay dying on the pavement, seventy-five more bullets entered his body, and men thronged around his charred corpse, kicking and beating his head. A helpless medical crew cowered in their ambulance as the mob hammered on the vehicle's windows, screaming: 'Fuck off or we shoot you, too! Fuck off or you die!'

Staggie's televised murder was followed by the killing of more than thirty other senior gang-leaders in drive-by shootings. The government took fright and sought to contain the group's violence, at which point the state itself appeared to become its new target, and Pagad's anti-gangster statements assumed an Islamic-fundamentalist tone. Police stations were attacked and robbed of weapons; businessmen who refused to pay protection money had their premises pipe-bombed. A detective assigned to investigate the organisation was assassinated, and in August 1998 a bomb went off in The Waterfront, killing two and injuring twenty-five – all civilians. Another bomb struck The Waterfront on New Year's Day 1999, and the year ended with the Camps Bay and Christmas Eve blasts.

By the end of 2000, more than one hundred Pagad members were in prison awaiting trial for urban terrorism, but there hadn't been a single significant conviction. On the other side of the battle, Rashid Staggie remained the Hard Livings' leader and was at this time on bail, charged with stealing weapons from a police station. He had recently made a surprise conversion to Christianity, and was being ushered about like a prize trophy under the protective wing of the Church. Few believed for a minute that the gangster had found God, and his conversion served only to confirm a general picture of thumb-nosed contempt for the forces of law and order.

The war between Pagad and the gangs had been fought for more than three years when Paul and I picked up the threads. After little police success on either side, it was suddenly announced that a Pagad leader had been arrested and charged with the murder of Rashaad Staggie. The papers were agog, and we were intrigued. With Abdu-Salaam Ebrahim scheduled to appear in court the following day, we decided on a holiday from clubbing and a detour into journalism. Strictly speaking, the story had little to do with the perfect E – although, incidentally, it brought us very close to finding it – but it was the vivid story of Cape Town and drugs in the new South Africa.

Cape Town magistrates court is a gracious redbrick building not far from Government Park. Milling around outside in the early-morning sunshine were hawkers, and groups of young black men sprawled on the grass in the shade. Parking was the usual city-centre arrangement: a smiley, toothless African waved us into a space and told us to ignore the meter. 'You give me four rand, and then if a traffic warden comes I buy him a Coke and that will do. My name is Michael. I watch your car.' Beside the court house a stall sold fruit and chewing gum – a sort of justice tuck-shop – and as we approached, another man tried to sell us a piece of plastic tubing in an old carrier bag. 'It's, well, a kind of air freshener,' he suggested. The police cars lining the street were battered, rusty heaps missing numberplates and bumpers. In an effort to raise revenue, the fleet carried adverts for estate agents on their bodywork – an unseemly association for the police, you might think, but one of even more questionable advantage to the advertisers.

The Ebrahim bail hearing wasn't due for another hour, so we took a wander through the building. The court rooms were spare and cool, and inside them translators were busy on their feet; although some judges were white and others coloured, all of the defendants were black. The Cape coloureds' language is usually Afrikaans, and generally the whites speak English, but most of the blacks speak an African language called isiXhosa, famous for its extraordinary clicks. When someone speaks isiXhosa it sounds as though halfway through a word they crack bubblegum, or imitate the noise of a ping-pong ball hitting a table, and the clicks crackled through the courts. In one court room, though, there was a desperate silence. Two teenagers stood accused of burgling a white woman's house, but they appeared to have no legal representation – and when the woman had finished giving evidence, the judge invited the pair to cross-examine her themselves. Neither could think of a thing to say.

Back outside in the sunshine, a court official announced to reporters on the steps that the Ebrahim bail hearing had been postponed. The pack galloped to the side exit from where the prisoner would be led out, and we sprinted with them, but there was no sign yet of the Pagad leader. Cameras and tripods were laid back down, cigarettes were lit, the waiting game resumed. We chatted to reporters, sultry and lethargic in the scorching heat, until a noise was heard above our heads. The pack fell silent and listened.

High above in the redbrick wall, through a slender, barred window, came a soft lone voice – a man's voice, gently ululating, a distant, haunting song. As we listened, a crowd of middle-aged Muslim women began to gather around us on the pavement beneath the window. They wore traditional dress and headscarves, but also sunglasses and smart handbags, and though their faces were stern, occasionally one would spot another and blow a kiss. Soon thirty or forty were gazing up at the barred window, listening intently.

The man's voice came again, and the women joined him, singing a low, melancholic lament. Silence fell. The voice from the window began again to sing. The women listened, faces upturned to the window, straining to pick up the melody. When silence fell for a second time, a cry rang out from the window in Afrikaans, and the crowd of women echoed it with a chant. Another cry, another chant. It went on, back and forth, louder and louder, increasingly insistent, fists now pounding the air, until I turned and saw that the crowd had swelled to a throng. A man on the pavement wearing a Pagad baseball cap struck up a chant in English.

'One gangster!'

'One bullet!' the crowd roared back.

'One merchant!' (Drug dealer.)

'One bullet!'

'Are we organised?'

'Yes!'

'Are we disciplined?'

'Yes!'

'Are we scared of gangsters?'

'No!'

'Who are we?'

'We are People Against Gangsterism and Drugs!'

'VIVA PAGAD!!' Everybody cheered, and lumpy grandmothers in headscarves punched the air.

In a fury, one heavy, elderly Muslim woman suddenly turned on the pack.

'You reporters,' she bawled, 'you should come and see where we live! Everywhere skollies skollies, skollies [gangsters]. You cannot walk anywhere. You should see! And not one gangster is treated the way the police treat our people. Wonderful South Africa!' She was becoming hysterical and the mood of the crowd growing ugly when Ebrahim was suddenly bustled out of the building and into an armour-plated van. Shaking his fist through the window, he sped away, the crowd hammering on the side of the van and screaming for Allah.

A Reuters cameraman took us for coffee. He had been covering the Pagad story for months, and rolled his eyes and spread his arms as if to say who the hell knew what it was all about. But if we liked, he said, he could arrange for a contact of his to take us into Manenberg to meet some of the gang leaders. We exchanged numbers, and later on that afternoon he called to say it was arranged. We were to meet his contact, Armien, in a cafe on Long Street at five o'clock.

Armien was sipping coffee in the window when we arrived. A slight, wiry coloured man in his late thirties, he was softly spoken and slightly twitchy. Sure, he said, eyes darting over our shoulders and scanning the cafe. No problem, he could take us to gangsters, show us the really bad stuff, maybe even set up a meeting with Rashid Staggie. He reeled off a list of foreign media teams he'd worked with – CNN, BBC, ABC and so on. It would cost us 500 rand (£50) a day, he said, and we could make a start tomorrow. We shook on it.

On the way out, he mentioned that an American news team had recently been in town to film a story about the gangs. They were given Armien's name as a contact, and in no time had summoned him to their hotel for urgent assistance. He duly arrived, to find that what they wanted was this: could he get hold of any decent cocaine or ecstasy?

Paul laughed. 'And did you?' Armien looked offended.

'Oh yes, my friend. The very best.'

Armien hadn't been in the car many minutes the following morning before I began to have my doubts. He said he'd joined the Hard Livings at seventeen, and remained a member to this day – but then he also claimed to freelance for the *Cape Times* and to dabble in photo-journalism. A fee of 500 rand seemed too modest a sum for a senior gang-member to concern himself with, yet he described himself as the late Rashaad Staggie's right-hand man. When he pointed out the window and cried: 'Look! That is the Table Mountain cable car!' the possibility occurred that we had hired nothing more than an unusually expensive tourist guide.

Manenberg is a fair drive out on to the Cape Flats, where the land becomes a rubbish-strewn tract of wasteland and the whining wind blows dust in your mouth. The buildings are stacked in rows, like barracks – long, thin pairs of grey three-storey blocks of flats facing each other, with lines of washing strung between them, dancing like cartoon ghosts. It looks like the worst council housing you might find in the East End of London, and is surrounded by people doing nothing. Women squat on rusting fire escapes, cradling babies; men hunch in groups on the kerb, and children tug go-carts fashioned out of packing cases through the copper-coloured dirt. The heat is venomous.

Heads jerked up when we drew up on a corner and got out of the car. Waving vaguely at odd faces, Armien took the lead, and we walked up and down a few streets. Along one was a row of charred shells, burnt-out shopfronts petrol-bombed during one or another gang dispute. There were no other shops. A thick film of dust clogged every surface, henna-brown, like the earth, and the initials of different gangs were sprayed liberally everywhere, in doorways and across rooftops – JFK, HLK, CK. Tattered strips of fabric fluttered helplessly in the windows as the wind tore through cracked and broken panes. Only gigantic murals on the gable ends of every block broke the monotony of poverty – ghoulishly meticulous, like Ulster's sectarian murals, portraying gangsters in suits carrying guns. 'THUG LIFE' was printed in bold white capitals, five feet high, across one.

But there are worse spectres of poverty in the world, and this thought must have shown in our eyes for Armien became somewhat put out. 'You should see inside!' he exclaimed. 'Just one bare room. No hot water!' He led us around the corner and showed us a corrugated-iron extension built on to a block of flats. This was the famous Hok, the *shebeen* where the Hard Livings used to drink, and where rival gangs would from time to time carry out drive-by shootings. Armien walked us through an incident – 'I was there, Rashid was where Paul's standing' – in the manner of a *Crimewatch* reconstruction. We did our best to look impressed, but really it was just Armien, standing outside a shed, playing air-guitar on an imaginary AK-47.

The sun was beating down on us now. Armien disappeared into a block of flats to look for a 'big gangster', but reappeared alone. He tried another flat, this time emerging with a story that the man he was after had been picked up by the police – for murder, that very morning, not an hour ago! Paul began to whistle at his feet, and Armien became increasingly embarrassed. 'I don't know where they all are,' he muttered, kicking the ground irritably. Then, suddenly: 'Oh yes, *I* know what the trouble is. It's Thursday, of course, and a lot of them will be away to the prison – it's visiting day. They'll be very busy getting drugs to take with them. That's what it is.' Paul bit his lip.

We walked on to look at some more murals, but Armien couldn't find any. 'They were everywhere, dammit,' cursed Armien in despair. 'Everywhere! Oh, you should have seen them. But they've all been whitewashed over. Just recently.'

Armien was at a loss, when across the street he spotted a big tall man in a red and white football shirt. He darted over to say hello, and chatted for a moment, grinning lavishly with relief, before beckoning us over.

'This is Behr; he will talk to you.' He stepped back, leaving me on the pavement looking up at a mountain of a man.

'Go on, go on!' He hissed from behind me. 'You can ask him questions, anything you like.'

Behr looked down, thoroughly puzzled, and I smiled up helplessly, skirt flapping in the wind, thinking that Armien might have given me a little bit more to go on. As we launched into a stumbling interview, children gathered to stare, squealing with laughter as my notepad blew away. Behr couldn't speak much English. What he could say I couldn't understand, and we'd got as far as him working for a supermarket after he left school when a shiny blue Golf GTI drove past. Behr looked up. So did the children. So did Armien. The car came to a halt, and out stepped Rashid Staggie.

CHAPTER 14

Hard Living

Rashid Staggie, South Africa's most famous skollie, looked like an Israeli businessman on holiday. A slim man in his mid-forties, with a neatly trimmed beard and tidy, discreet movements, he had none of the flashy swagger of a stereotypical gangster. He wore clean, smart jeans and sandals, a pleated belt and designer sunglasses. Apart from a trim rim of gold in his mouth where his upper teeth should have been, he looked resoundingly innocuous.

Yet, from nowhere, people began to gather. They didn't flock so much as gravitate, until Staggie was surrounded by a swarm of children and young men, the youngest squatting at his feet in the dust. The older boys affected a casual nonchalance, shoulders shrugged, thumbs hooked into pockets, heads half-turned away, but for all that they visibly tingled, like interns around a president. Staggie leant on the car bonnet and began speaking to them, very softly, in Afrikaans. There was no commotion, and yet every single person on the street, hanging off fire escapes and squatting on kerbs, was aware that Rashid Staggie had come among them.

Armien was ecstatic. Standing beside me in the shade at a slight distance, watching Rashid address the boys, he kept up a breathless stream of whispered praise.

'He looks after everyone, solves their problems, brings peace. You see? Rashid, he *never* forced anyone to be in his gang. He *never* encouraged gangsterism. He was just a great leader. The Hard Livings never robbed here. *Never!* They went outside, places where people had money. It was the law, Rashid's law . . .

'There's always kids around him. Kids just love him. Because he buys them things. Gives them sweets, that kind of shit. He used to throw money. Yes! He loves that shit. He is a *good* man, he just wants peace. People have him all wrong.'

'What are they talking about?' I nodded to Rashid and the boys.

'Oh, that? Dealing drugs.'

Presently, Armien sidled up to Rashid, whispered in his ear, then beckoned us. Would Rashid mind answering a few questions? He studied us coolly through his sunglasses, lordly with non-cooperation. When he spoke it was a cold voice, heavily accented with Afrikaans.

'There's a lot of angry people inside our neighbourhood,' he said slowly. 'There's people living in poverty. When I was in the war, I was with the Devil. Now I'm with the pastor. The Devil is no longer in me. Come to the church next Thursday, eight o'clock. You will see.' The audience was over. We made our rather courtly goodbyes and walked away.

'He came, you see! He came!' Back in the car, Armien exploded. 'He came! I sent word for him to, but didn't know if he would, but he came for me. There's a lot of journalists in Cape Town won't believe you met Rashid. Rashid Staggie! That is really something.'

We were driving to meet another gangster, a man called Gansie Uys. According to Armien, Gansie was a senior Hard Livings member who had just been released from prison. He was staying away from Manenberg for a while, south of the city in a place called Ocean View. All efforts to extract more information were a waste of time. Armien sank into the back seat, lost in a daze over Rashid Staggie.

It was becoming harder and harder to keep up with Armien's account of Staggie. He had a rather melodramatic style of delivery, a low, rapid-fire rasp, like a TV-movie baddie, and his statements managed to be both enigmatic and emphatic. It was never clear whether he was privy to insider information or just spinning gangster-groupie fantasy. One minute Rashid wasn't a gangster at all, but the saintly leader of a benign organisation, devoted only to helping the poor and creating peace. When I suggested the police were sceptical of Staggie's godly conversion, Armien spat back: 'They don't believe anything!' and slumped into sulky indignation. Only a minute later, he was boasting about Rashid's unspeakable badness. 'People are fucking scared of him, I'm telling you.'

Ocean View's name seemed like a spiteful joke, for there was no view of the ocean – or of anything else. Hot, dusty and tormented by wind, it was another shabby housing settlement for impoverished coloureds.

This presented a language problem, and one I'd not anticipated. Armien spoke excellent English, but in a place like Ocean View the residents' English ranged from non-existent to very hit and miss. This made us entirely dependent on Armien as our translator – a role he fulfilled fitfully and not always, I suspected, entirely truthfully. It wasn't at all clear, when we arrived, whether Gansie was expecting us or had any idea what we were doing there.

The cramped ground-floor flat smelt of stale sweat and cheap cooking oil. Following Gansie, we squeezed our way through a poky kitchen, past a woman frying an egg over a portable gas ring, and into a tiny living room – a brick box furnished with a mattress, two sagging chairs and a threadbare carpet. Armien nodded us into the chairs. Big black flies swarmed over everything in the sweaty gloom, crawling across my face and my mouth until I had to sit on my hands to stop myself brushing them off. Still standing, hands in pockets, looking awkward, Gansie mumbled something in Afrikaans. Armien translated. 'He says, this looks like somewhere poor people live. He doesn't want you thinking this is his home. He is very happy to meet you.'

Gansie Uys was thirty-six, but looked older. Tall, but stooped, with a slight paunch, he had no front teeth, which gave him the puckered face and jutting chin of a village idiot. It is a popular fashion statement amongst Cape coloureds to have their front teeth removed, a task typically carried out by a friend with a pair of pliers. When Gansie smiled, he looked terrifyingly stupid. But his English was quite good, and he was not, as Armien boasted afterwards, half as stupid as he looked.

'How you liking Cape Town?' In a thick accent, his words slopped out in a gummy slur.

'Very much.'

'Cape Town is very nice,' he gurgled, flopping on to the mattress. 'No crime. No crime in Cape Town, heh-heh-heh!' And his shoulders heaved up and down as he laughed at his joke.

Another woman, stony-faced and with no front teeth, appeared from the kitchen and handed round bottles of beer. Others edged into the doorway, and children, spindly gaggles, shy and smiley, crept in one by one and sat on the floor. More men appeared in the doorway, toothless and shirtless, staring and silent. Paul and I perched in our seats, sipped beer and smiled politely at everyone, waiting for Armien to say something. But he was lost in a world of his own, sprawled next to Gansie on the mattress, picking at a hole in the cover, apparently feeling no need to let us know was happening.

There must have been more than twenty people crowded into the room, and still the silence lengthened.

Then in struggled a tremendously fat man carrying a television set. Lumbering out again, he presently returned with a video recorder. A woman rummaged in a cupboard for a video cassette. Fresh beers were handed round, the children crossed their legs expectantly, the screen flickered into life – and we found ourselves watching a BBC safari programme. Armien sat up and sighed happily. 'This is my favourite programme on television. I fucking love that safari shit.'

I stared at him in amazement, wondering why he'd brought us here. Then the fat man produced a remote control, and up on the screen appeared the opening credits for a documentary film about Pagad and the Hard Livings gang. For the next thirty minutes, we all sat and drank and smoked, and watched Gansie on the television – an all-action extravaganza featuring Gansie selling drugs, Gansie smoking drugs, Gansie loading guns. The gangster watched his performance lovingly, his face inches from the screen. At the scene with the guns, the children all clapped their hands and squealed, and Gansie beamed. 'Big skollie, heh-heh-heh! Big skollie.'

After the show, any doubts about his credentials had been dispatched. Gansie was the real thing, all right, and now that we had admired his television stardom he seemed more relaxed about getting down to business. With an amiable growl he cleared the room, and settled down with a fresh beer to talk about his life as a drug lord.

'When the Hard Livings first moved into town we hit Sea Point. There were no gangs – just one or two dealers, maybe. We chase them all away and start to sell drugs. Oh, and prostitution too. Good money. We would take the street kids, and give them shelter, and get them to sell drugs. And we sold the drugs to our prostitutes. Yes, we looked after our girls. You see, they were our customers, *and* our daily bread.' He chuckled.

'Then came the extortion. It was just normal. First we will have the argument with the bouncer. Then we start the fight. We frighten the bouncer away. If they won't pay, then the club closes, simple. And then we sell the drugs inside. Ecstasy, Mandrax, *dagga* [marijuana], cocaine, crack . . . The community liked us. Soon, twenty, thirty shop owners there, they would come and smoke crack with us. The police liked us too, no trouble. We pay them good money. They don't earn a lot. They are always hungry. No cigarettes. And ninety per cent are big boozers. That makes it nice for us. Heh-heh-heh.' How many people had he killed?

'Ooh, I don't know. Ten or twelve. Not a lot.'

Gansie Uys was a model interviewee on the subject of his life's work. ('You see?' whispered Armien. 'He doesn't give a fuck.') He grew less straightforward the further he strayed from the factual towards the philosophical. What, for example, was Gansie's opinion of Rashid Staggie's conversion to God?

'Heh-heh-heh! If I had the money he's got, I would find God too.'

'Aren't you offended when he says that as a gangster he had the Devil in him?'

'I also have the Devil in me.'

But then, moments later: 'It's better like us, though. Gangsters, we help the community. The community likes us. Me, now, I'm not a gangster. I joined Hard Livings at fourteen, but I'm a community guider now. If I had known then what I know now, I would not have been a gangster.'

'What do you know now?'

He gave a dark look. 'There's nothing I don't know now.'

Gansie had just spent three months in prison, on remand for armed robbery, but the case had been dropped after witnesses mysteriously withdrew their evidence. The Hard Livings, he explained, had seen to that. Now he was lying low in Ocean View. Was he hiding from Pagad? He snorted. 'They've never been a threat to gangsters. I'm not scared. If you give me a chance to stay alive, your whole family will go. I kill everybody. Your big mistake.' No, he said he was in Ocean View to keep away from crack. 'Put this,' he announced abruptly, pointing at my notepad. 'I was a big drug addict before, in Sea Point. Gave up. Simple. It's all in the brain, we don't believe in drug rehabilitation. You are not a drug addict, you are a drug glutton.'

That is more or less the official Cape Town gangster position on drugs. Where Pagad accuse them of ruining lives, they retort that addiction is a myth. Drugs do not 'enslave' anyone. Oddly enough, I'd heard a similar argument made by an American professor at a conference on ecstasy some months earlier, but whether Gansie was trying to make a serious point or just talking off the top of his head I couldn't guess. I asked if he thought the police should do anything to try and stop them selling drugs. Gansie nodded vigorously, and mimed placing his neck in a noose.

'Oh yes, definitely. Death penalty, bring it back. That would help. If you know you are going to hang, then maybe you think twice. Now, you see, you do not care about the police, because if they catch you, you are only going away for a holiday. You get everything in prison! What you see here,' and he pointed around the room, 'you see there. Ooh, and you make a lot of money in prison. It is nice.' He giggled. 'And that's why we go there for the holidays.'

Gansie didn't think much of Ocean View. 'No skollies,' he spat, gesturing outside through the window in disgust. 'People here, they drink. They smoke. No guns. And, furthermore, they have sex. I tell you, they live for sex; that is all they do.' His gaze fell on a clutch of children who had crept back into the room and were huddled along the wall. '*And* . . . they start very young. Like here – a small example!' He jumped up and grabbed a pretty young girl, slender and pale, manhandling her to her feet. She stared at the carpet, stricken.

'How old do you think she is?' Gansie demanded.

'Nine?' Paul tried.

'Four-teeeen!' roared Gansie, triumphantly. 'And she has already been pregnant! Haven't you? Come on!' He shook the girl roughly, his great arm wrapped around her tiny waist. She looked dumbstruck.

'Come on!' he yelled. 'They want to talk to you about if you like the sex.' He turned to us. 'I tell you, they know everything, these kids. Well, go on then. Ask her if she likes the sex!'

Paul looked horrified. Very softly, he knelt and leant towards the girl.

'Have you had a baby?'

'Yes,' she whispered, still staring at the floor. Gansie's arm remained tightly gripped around her, but she was frozen rigid. There was an agonising pause.

'A girl or a boy?' The girl stared harder still at the floor, and a tear dropped on to her shoe.

'I . . . I lost it,' she whispered.

'She's made history in Ocean View!' bawled Gansie delightedly, releasing her arm and shoving her towards the door. 'The youngest ever!'

Gansie's good humour was developing a life of its own. He trooped us outside and down an alleyway between two blocks of flats, to show us teenage boys smoking Mandrax. 'I show you everything, my friends! Everything.' The four boys looked slightly taken aback to see us, but a sharp glance from Gansie told them to get on with it. Crouching out of the wind in a doorway, they filled the bowl of a small pipe with a crushed-up white tablet, packed it down with *dagga*, then lit the bowl and took turns to draw on it, sucking long, thirsty gasps. Seconds later they were slouched across each other's laps on the doorstep, comprehensively wasted. Delighted, Gansie sent Paul off to fetch his cameras, and a crowd of children and old women gathered round to witness the unlikely spectacle of Gansie telling Paul how to take pictures of the slumped boys. Fuelled by his audience, Gansie became unstoppable. He grabbed one old woman and clutched her roughly to his side.

'They like the guys! You see? They love us!' Like an out-of-control tabloid editor, he made Paul photograph the women and children surrounding him like Page 3 models. They squirmed in his grip as on his instruction they made a Hard Livings symbol in the air with their fingers.

'Peace in our community!' he bellowed. 'Hard Livings! Peace in our community!'

I glanced at Paul and saw that he was slightly worried. The situation was beginning to feel out of hand. Armien was drunk, the smokers catatonic, and the more raucously joyful Gansie became, the more his mood threatened volatility. Further men had gathered silently in doorways to watch the peculiar commotion, and teenagers were eyeing Paul's cameras hungrily. Nudging me forward first, Paul managed to steer the four of us back inside, where he settled Gansie down in a chair and asked if he would mind posing for some photographs. Gansie gurgled happily, cracked open a fresh beer, and stripped off his shirt to reveal a battleground of gangster tattoos – Hard Livings symbols and slogans alongside amateurish images of guns and women. Perching on the edge of the mattress, Gansie began to pose. Then a thought occurred to him.

'I should have my gun!'

'No, it's fine –' Paul began, but already Armien had unhooked his own gun from his belt and tossed it to Gansie.

'Use mine.'

Paul was crouching at the far end of the room, near the window, holding his camera. I was sitting in a chair. A younger man, Peter, had entered the room, and now sat beside Gansie. The pair were on the edge of the mattress, our knees less than three feet apart. Armien squatted on the floor a few feet to my right, leaning against the door to the kitchen. There was nobody else in the room.

Gansie caught the gun with one hand. Laughing, he pointed it at Peter's head. Peter grinned easily; I tittered nervously. Smiling softly, Gansie fingered the black casing for a moment, then spun the gun around and looked directly at me. Chuckling gently to himself, he lifted it and pointed the barrel straight at my head. I stared, frozen. Everything was suddenly very quiet. His finger started to pull back the trigger.

'STOP!' Armien was on his feet, wide-eyed, arm outstretched, pointing at the gun. 'Stop!'

Gansie's finger froze, and he turned to Armien in surprise. 'Don't worry, it's empty.'

'No. It. *Isn't.*'

'Yes it is. Look, I am an expert,' Gansie chuckled. Shrugging, he turned back to face me, raised the gun and again began to squeeze the trigger.

Armien lunged. His elbow collided with Gansie's hand, and the gun went spinning across the room towards Paul, rattled against the wall and finally came to land beneath the window. Paul and I stared at it, paralysed and speechless. Armien stalked over, picked up the gun, and with a quick flick unloaded the magazine on to the mattress.

'See?' he huffed.

Gansie cocked an eyebrow in mild surprise. 'Oh. Oh yeah.'

We couldn't get out of the flat and away fast enough. Paul had gone white, and I was trembling as I shook Gansie's hand when we said goodbye in the kitchen. Armien looked mildly embarrassed. Gansie was terribly sorry to see us go, though, and keen to set up a night out together in town.

'We don't pay to get in, they don't search us. We don't pay for our drinks, they are our friends. You will love it!' He followed us outside to the car, and when Paul started the engine he tapped on the window. I wound it down.

'I've just thought of something. Can you say ex-gangster?' he shouted above the wail of the wind. 'But then again,' he yelled, as Paul turned the car, 'if you are Hard Livings, you can never be ex! You see, Hard Livings was never a gang. It was a way of life!'

CHAPTER 15

Gangsters in Wonderland

If Gansie had shot us by mistake, I don't imagine he really would have minded, although he would rather have taken us clubbing. He would certainly have had no trouble justifying it to himself. Gansie inhabited a world of endlessly moving goalposts, and could knock up a moral defence in a flash. But the further we dug into the labyrinthine world of the drug barons, the less sense anything made, until I could barely remember what it was we were trying to find out; and ultimately the Alice in Wonderland logic Gansie spun was no more perverse than anyone else's. Everywhere we turned, we found fresh trails of conspiracy and contradiction. For out-and-out rubbish, though, nobody matched Pastor Martins.

The pastor was next on Armien's list of people for us to meet. He used to be a minor gangster, and his name featured regularly in the papers. During a spell in prison he had professed to have found God, and on his release had returned to the Cape Flats to found a church, ostensibly ministering to a flock of gangsters. For a time he was regarded as just one more dubious local eccentric. But when Pagad declared bloody war on the gangs in 1996, he leapt to fame as the founder of an organisation for gangsters. It was supposed to be the democratic expression of their commitment to peace, and at its height several thousand gangsters marched on parliament under its banner. There was even talk of gangsters standing for parliament, and for a brief spell Pastor Martins was hailed as a peace-loving miracle-worker who had found goodness in these devils. Before long the organisation fell apart, amid accusations that Pastor Martins was not so much a spiritual leader as an accomplice. The gangs, it was said, were buying his charade of respectability with fat wads of drug money.

Undeterred, Pastor Martins continued to minister from his church on the Flats. A coloured man in his late thirties, immaculately groomed in a three-piece suit, he greeted us with an oily welcome and ushered us into his office. It was a small room, militarily tidy, and he eased himself into the slot behind his desk with a great sigh of satisfaction. He smiled brightly, opened his mouth to begin – and that was the last time he drew breath for about half an hour. Pastor Martins was a great admirer of the sound of his voice, and lavished it on us generously, punctuating every thought of his own with a lengthy quote from the bible. Unfortunately, he was incapable of making a statement without contradicting himself in the next. He also had some difficulty in remembering to refer to gangsters as 'they', and kept lapsing into 'we'.

To begin with, Pastor Martins attributed all of Cape Town's troubles to the wicked drug barons. 'They have got more rights than anyone, too many rights,' he thundered. 'Police can't use their guns any more, and gangsters talk to police with no respect. The constitution gives them too many rights – we've got a gangsters' constitution.' In this analysis, it was the police who were the victims of misguided liberal anarchy.

'Look at the old apartheid regime. Take their legal system. That was when you kissed the policeman's shoes. Yes! That time was better. We walk on our streets, nobody afraid to go to the police to press charges. Now no one governs in South Africa, everyone steals. The old regime, they took policemen by size, not by education. They gave you one slap, and you respected them. That was law and order! When you said, "Yes, boss. Yes, chief."'

A moment later, though, it was coloured gangsters who were the victims. 'If you see the way we get treated now by this government, especially gangsters on the Western Cape, we are going through the oppression now that the black man went through. Only coloured people get exposed in court as drug lords. But coloureds have respect for law and order. It is not fair. We have respect, but we are the ones being sent to prison.' Despite this, however, Pastor Martins thought that Pagad vigilantes – also coloured – were getting away with murder.

'Our government are so afraid of Pagad, they treat them with kid gloves, destroying our law-and-order system. That Pagad leader, Abdu-Salaam, will come out of that court case with nothing, you watch. Pagad are threatening the government, and the gangsters are the scapegoats! Where is the justice?!'

By now Pastor Martins was on his feet, banging the table. Sweat poured on to his starched white shirt and his eyes bulged. Suddenly, mid-sentence, he sat down.

'I'm not receiving any money from a gang,' he said dully, as though being interviewed by police. 'I am not part of a gang. You must make the point that we are not sponsored by gangs or drug money.'

As he was speaking, an assistant slipped into the room and coughed politely.

'You are not taking any dirty monies, Pastor,' he interjected firmly. 'Your income is purely clean.'

'Right.' The pastor composed himself. 'Quite right. Thank you, James.' The pastor motioned to James, his 'legal man', to join us. James slid on to the desk and took over.

'Pastor Martins,' he began softly. 'Pastor Martins is the *real* victim.' The press had 'victimised' the poor man; it was a terrible injustice. James explained that he'd come to the pastor's aid as a 'private entrepreneur', and that the pair were now involved in a complicated property-development scheme. As far as I could see, it was a money-laundering arrangement in which James cleaned up the Pastor's dirty money in return for a slice.

'As a person,' James continued, 'I just wanted to give something. You know, give something back to the community.'

I smiled. 'Let me get this straight. Your involvement in this property development – it is one hundred per cent altruism, nothing else? You do it out of the goodness of your heart?' James was thrilled to hear it put so eloquently.

'Yes, yes, yes! Absolutely!'

On the way out, Armien pointed out that Pastor Martins's car was an inexplicably large, shiny brand-new BMW. 'Charlatan!' he spat. '*Man of God.* Yeah right.' Which, coming from Armien, struck me as a bit rich.

Another allegedly neutral faction in the war on the Cape Flats were the Neighbourhood Watches. We met one in Manenberg, a group of young Muslim men who were thrilled to be interviewed and who led us on a tour of the local streets.

'We are just concerned citizens from the community,' the watch leader explained. 'People that have stood up and said, yes, we have a problem here with gangsterism and drugs. We are trying to get rid of that in our area.' The group had registered with the police, received licences to carry guns and went on nightly foot patrols. 'The community is very supportive,' he claimed. 'Very co-operative.' And nobody minds? 'Not at all. Funnily enough, in fact, since we got guns and became a Neighbourhood Watch, the people really start to respect us.'

He was rather sweet, but his tale sounded improbable, for the people who were the problem were the gangsters, and what possible civic co-operation could a Neighbourhood Watch command from them? While Paul took their pictures, Armien became apoplectic.

'They are fucking Pagad,' he whispered angrily in my ear. 'I'm telling you. They only form a watch so they can get a licence for firearms. Then they go shooting our people for Pagad. It's a fucking front, I'm telling you.' When the watch leader produced his gun for the camera, Armien was beside himself. 'Call that a gun? That's not a gun, that's a peashooter. It only shoots six bullets! My gun, it shoots twenty-two – and if I had it modified it could shoot even more.'

Back at the car, he pulled a face when he saw me unlock the door. 'I just don't do that,' he sniffed grandly. 'I never lock my car. *Never.*'

'Yeah,' I agreed, 'I really know what you mean.' And I rambled on about how lately I'd been thinking maybe it was an act of faith to leave it unlocked, maybe there was something dehumanising about endless keys . . . Armien looked extremely put out by this unexpected conversational turn.

'No, listen,' he interrupted crossly. '*I* don't lock my car because nobody – *nobody* – fucks with my car. Right? Nobody would *dare* fuck with my car. I leave the doors open. Big stereo system. No-bo-dy fucks with my car.'

The following night, we returned to Manenberg in the hope of meeting Rashid Staggie at his church. 'He *will* be there,' Armien kept repeating from the back seat. 'He will be there. If he says he's going to kill you, he will kill you. If he says he is going to bring you food, he will bring you food.' He realised what he'd said.

'If he's *not* there, there will be a very good reason. *Very* good. It would be something very important. His kid sick, or something.' Armien nodded emphatically.

We stopped off en route to pick up Armien's journalist girlfriend ('The best journalist in Cape Town! She knows *all* the gangsters'). I wasn't sure what to expect, but it was nothing like the tall, handsome Afrikaner brunette who clambered into the car with an open smile and a big booming voice. Articulate and engagingly forthright, Judith felt like a blast of sanity – but within minutes was off on a riff every bit as bewildering as her boyfriend's.

'Oh, so many gangsters have been killed, Pagad are murdering bastards,' she shuddered. 'It really hurts when another gangster is killed, I can't bear it.' Then, cheerily, moments later: 'I don't know what we'd do for a living without Pagad. They're great, they keep us in business. So much work!'

Manenberg in the dark was an altogether more forbidding prospect than by day, deserted save for hooded figures lingering in the shadows. We drew up outside the Hok, an ex-*shebeen* that since Rashid's conversion had been functioning as a church, and spotted the gang leader in a parked VW van, sitting beside the Hok's minister, Pastor Wood. Armien mumbled that they were praying, but it looked more like the two men were having a drink. After another courtly dance of uncertain greetings, the pastor said he would see us in the Hok.

Forty or so women in satin dresses and stiff wedding hats were sitting in rows facing a makeshift lectern, behind which a young man in a pale blue shellsuit was doing an excellent impression of a nightclub MC. A microphone cupped in both hands, he paced up and down, hammering out a torrent of words that came fast and furious – and incomprehensible, apart from the occasional 'PRAISE Jesus'. The congregation joined in from time to time with yelps of divine reverence, until the rapper ran out of breath, at which point they erupted into hallelujah, stood up and hugged the person next to them.

We had slid in unnoticed, but once the rapping was over a young man took me firmly by the hand. For a horrible moment I thought we were going to be involved in the service, but he led us to the front row and sat us among dozens of children in pyjamas. Suddenly, music burst out over the PA, and the whole room was on its feet and off, singing something between deep gospel house and disco, arms in the air, heads thrown back, eyes half-shut, for all the world like clubbers at a rave. I glanced round and, right at the back, dancing and praising the Lord, stood Rashid Staggie.

When the pastor reappeared he beckoned us into a side room. A caramel-coloured man, twinkly and plump like a teddy bear, his manner was warm, and plausibly clerical, until we were all seated. Then he launched into the most unexpected appeal.

Rashid Staggie, he began solemnly, was not long in the fold. Sometimes he did not use the right words, and then the media took them out of turn and twisted them. As his pastor, it was his job to guide him. He was his shepherd.

'Now, Rashid is no longer the man that Armien knew.' He nodded to Armien. 'Armien will tell you that. But he is only human, and it is a long journey. Now, he has to support his lifestyle – not the same lifestyle, obviously, but he has to live. And you journalists, you come here and take, and you don't give anything back. Rashid gives everything – and what does he get in return? Nothing. So, as his pastor, I am here to guide him, and make sure that he can live his new life. So it would help if you understand that, obviously it's not like the old days, when he would charge 20,000 rand from the media, but nonetheless, he needs something . . .' The words trailed away. Pastor Wood scanned us all and the smile slid away. He stared belligerently as I coughed.

'I don't mean to be funny, but how come he drives a shiny new Golf GTI, then?'

The pastor glared. 'Its not actually his car.' He paused. 'It's, er, a loan-car. I mean, a hire-car.'

Armien stood up abruptly and pushed back his chair. 'We do not *pay* for interviews,' he hissed.

'Is that so?' Pastor Wood replied. 'I see. In that case, I see no need for you to stay.' He rose to his feet, icily stiff. But before showing us the door he made me read aloud my shorthand notes, like a naughty schoolgirl.

'That fucking pastor!' Outside, Armien was hopping mad. 'As if Rashid needs to beg! How dare he? His *shepherd*. Can you believe he called himself Rashid's shepherd?' He smoked a cigarette furiously, but by the time we were back in the car had cooled off and was reflecting with satisfaction on his day's work. Earlier he had told Paul he planned to buy some Es, and as we passed the murals he shouted to stop the car.

'There's Ronnie!' Armien pointed to a figure on the corner. 'Rashid . . . um, Rashid told me to send him to the church.' Jumping out, he jogged over to him.

Ronnie was Rashid's right-hand man, a lay preacher and the keystone of Staggie's new faith. We watched him disappear up a fire escape into a flat with Armien, and then re-emerge transmitting the unmistakable signs of a man who's just completed a drug deal. It's a particular blend of cocky nonchalance, loose-limbed and shifty-eyed, the same the world over. Armien had clearly just bought ecstasy from Ronnie the preacher.

Driving back to Cape Town, I tried to draw Judith out on the delicate matter of Rashid's conversion. Judith was a great fan, but needed only minor encouragement to concede that he was lying through his teeth. Armien kept interjecting with 'allegedly' until she said 'everyone knew', when he changed tack without a blush and agreed that this was so.

'I'm pissed off with this church shit,' he sulked. 'When there's peace, there's no handouts. I tell Rashid – and I'm the only one who can tell him, when he talks this church shit – I say, that's bullshit! Your pockets are full. But when there's peace' – he spat the word – 'there's nothing for the others. Look at those men in Manenberg; they are fucked. No drugs to sell, no handout. It's totally fucked up!'

All right, then, said Paul. Perhaps we could be of some assistance in the current economic slump by buying some Es. Armien was delighted to sort this out for us. But what did they think Rashid *meant*, I pressed, when he said he wanted peace but was clearly still a gangster?

'I don't know,' huffed Armien. 'All I know is, when he calls for me next to do some bad shit, I'll be there for him.' Judith just laughed, easily, with her head thrown back. 'No, I don't know what Rashid means. Nobody does.' And she really didn't mind. South Africans' graceful accommodation of confusion is a complex and amazing phenomenon, although it has nothing to do with post-modern theories about the illusory nature of 'truth'. It seems to be more a matter of finding virtue in necessity.

A young boy on a bicycle gave Armien a casual thumbs-up. 'That is a general's salute!' he squealed delightedly, bouncing on the back seat. 'Look, a general's salute. Not everybody gets a salute like that. It is a special sign. It means he will make sure everything is OK.' And now he was happy.

The last piece in the jigsaw of Cape Town's drug war was the police force. Armien reluctantly conceded that in this one line of enquiry he was probably not the man to help us, but the police press-liaison officer we called was disarmingly obliging. British journalists? Interested in the policing of gangs? We must come in and meet him at once.

The city's police headquarters is a grey, imposing building near the court house. It would be difficult to escape a shudder at what took place within its walls under apartheid, but the corridors have now been painted turquoise and purple, with gold leaf around the doors. On the fifth floor, Captain Rod Beer bounded over to greet us. He looked like a caricature of a Boer policeman, with the square face vaguely suggestive of Down's syndrome, the broad teeth and fuzzy moustache, but his manner was closer to that of a showbusiness agent, spilling generous intimacy. We settled into comfortable chairs around a low table decorated with an ornamental candle. There cannot be many organisations in the world with a greater image problem than that of the South African Police Service, but Captain Beer was going to change all that if it killed him.

It would be his pleasure to send us out for a night with the Flying Squad. Anywhere in particular we wanted to go? The Cape Flats! Great choice – no problem – of *course*! There was just one *tiny* thing. He coughed, embarrassed to even mention it.

'We do have a little problem with morale, as you may know. People are sometimes demoralised, and sometimes – *sometimes* – that means they do things they shouldn't. Now that's no excuse! And we have press freedom here. But if you do go on the vehicles, and see something that might not show us in an *entirely* positive light ... well, perhaps we might have a gentleman's agreement that you will show me what you've seen.' He almost blushed. 'We are undergoing so much transition, you know. And we need to change within ourselves before we can move on.'

We could hardly believe our luck. With police corruption an ongoing and almighty scandal, access like this was a remarkable leap of PR faith. At one point in 1996, one in four of Johannesburg's entire force had been under investigation for a criminal offence, and stories of drunkenness and negligence circulated daily. Only a few days before our meeting, a Cape Town politician had phoned a township station to report a crime but after twenty minutes nobody had answered the phone. When she drove to the station, she found long queues waiting at the counter, several phones ringing – and the entire staff gathered round a TV, engrossed in an episode of *The Bold and the Beautiful*.

Grinning from ear to ear, Rod Beer showed us out, promising to call as soon as everything was arranged.

In the following days we had time to ourselves, and drifted around the city. There were times when Sea Point felt as quaint as an English seaside town, fresh with the familiarly spiky smell of the Atlantic. Every morning the clipped green lawns along the promenade would be clogged with white people jogging, or walking their dogs. Joggers in San Francisco had carried all sorts of hi-tech jiggery pokery –

weights, heart monitors, stop watches – but here they wore old-fashioned whites, as though off to play tennis with Dan Maskell.

But for all the trimmed lawns and tennis whites, a century of prim Anglo efforts to build a new Basingstoke hasn't succeeded in taming the Cape. By now, the city was in the grip of a full-scale heatwave, a ferocious furnace that sent cigarette lighters on cafe tables exploding into flames. Forest fires were raging on the outskirts of the city; fanned by the wind, they tore through winelands, destroying houses and sending stockbrokers scrambling for safety. Day after day, the news showed firefighters battling helplessly against the inferno as the flames licked closer to the city. Thick black smoke gathered overhead like storm clouds.

The city's narrative had an angrily primitive drama. One day the sea would be softly mewing, and the next it would whip the sea wall, shattering into vicious spray. Early one evening we found a crowd gathered along the water's edge, drawn in silence by disaster. Heads peered into the inky dark, spellbound by the swoop of a searchlight from a rescue helicopter overhead. An elderly man had gone for a sunset swim, and had been sucked away in the waves. There were days when the cloud over Table Mountain would tumble like an avalanche down the rock face, and on others a perfect double rainbow would form across the bay, pale bands of sugary confection. Sunset could look like a nuclear explosion on the horizon, the last shafts of light catching the corner of our house, bleaching our faces like a floodlight.

Outside virtually every home in Cape Town hung a sign that said something like 'Armed Response' or 'Sniper Security'. These indicated that the home was protected by an armed private security firm, whose gunslingers would come charging like the cavalry should an alarm be disturbed. Private security guards outnumber police officers by more than four to one, and South Africans spend 12 billion rand every year on the dream that they can insulate themselves from the menace of assault and robbery. Houses are barred and grilled like mini dungeons; even inside them, anxious women fit sliding metal grilles known as 'rape gates' across the door to every room.

But nobody escapes the smell of danger, for the peculiar violence of Cape Town goes deeper than cold statistics of crime figures. It hangs in the air, heavy and brooding, licking its lips in the forest-fire flames or in the lapping of the waves. It was tempting to think this a ludicrously fanciful notion – nervy neurosis, the product of reading too many newspaper stories about hikers on Signal Hill murdered for 20 rand. But there were times when it felt as if violence had been branded into the soul of the city. It's amazing how soon you start to think like this in South Africa – and it makes the designer riviera a dislocatingly indolent world to awake to every morning.

The other tenant in our house was a young woman from Johannesburg called Tanya. Tanya was the lazy sitcom writer's idea of a grasping blonde wannabe – a cliché so perfect I had never dreamt such a creature could exist. Her initial cohabitation strategy had been to ignore us, but when she found out that Paul was a photographer she opened up like a flower.

'I've decided,' she confided, 'this is The Year. I'm getting into modelling seriously, and starting acting – really trying to get into the movies. I don't want to get to thirty and think, Why didn't I do it? You know?' Every day a red-faced Tanya would return from a casting or audition to report a fresh indignity she'd been forced to endure. How DARE anybody treat her like that? Tanya was clean blown away by the sheer volume of *injustice* out there. The final insult came the night Paul Oakenfold DJ'ed at a club in town. Tanya went dressed to kill ('He. Is. AWE-SOME'), but was home only hours later in a black sulk.

'Well,' she fumed, kicking off her heels and throwing herself on to the sofa. 'The music was good, I'll give him that. But you know, we had VIP tickets, and when we got there, they were actually letting *normal people* through in front of us. Yah! And then we got upstairs to the VIP area, and you know, there was nothing special. No free drinks, no promotions. Nothing. Do you know what I felt like? I ac-tually felt like I was just – like I was just . . . "*up-stairs*".'

CHAPTER 16

So I Shot Him

The call from Captain Rod Beer came the following Friday, summoning us to the police radio-control base at seven that evening. A sprawling redbrick building on what looked like an industrial estate it lacked ostentatious security and waiting in the foyer was a plump, coloured captain prone to great gusts of unexplained chuckles. He looked so pleased to see us, I half-expected a hug. Bustling us into his office, he pointed out the window at a duck pond, newly installed next to the car park. 'All part of the change, you understand?' He beamed at the ducks.

The captain apologised for making us sign indemnity forms – 'Just a formality, in case anything should, er. Yes, well . . . Here we are. Lovely!' – and spread out a map of Cape Town. 'Take your pick.' We chose Manenberg, were issued with bulletproof vests, and dispatched to a squad car and the care of Sergeants Peter Cleophas and Mervin Jackson.

As Flying Squad officers, it was Peter and Mervin's job to drive around Manenberg and the surrounding areas, waiting for the radio to summon them to an emergency – a crime in progress. 'A shooting, usually,' Peter explained, 'or a drug deal. Maybe a rape.' A gang member had been killed that morning, he said, so tonight there would be retaliations. 'Oh yes,' he assured us, smiling grimly. 'You'll see plenty of action, all right.' Inevitably, within the hour both officers were marvelling at the astonishing quietness of the radio.

Dusk fell, and we idled along empty unlit streets, passing housing ranging from iron-barred bungalows to shanty-town shacks. This was a part of Manenberg we hadn't seen before, more organically squalid and ramshackle than the barrack-style blocks Armien had shown us. The streets were still, so we drove on to the black townships of Guguletu and Phillipi. More desolate than the coloured settlements, they were pitted with tracts of wasteland, literally covered in rubbish, like fields growing crops of litter. In one house in Phillipi, an entire family had died of Aids in the course of a recent weekend. As we drove through the area, we passed not a single car on the road, but saw horse-drawn carts piled high with junk, and a pony pulling a shopping trolley. Men loomed out of doorways, drunk and cackling, and toddlers in rags stared. Still the radio stayed silent. For hours, the biggest drama came when Armien phoned our mobile to check how many Es we wanted, which made for a slightly awkward conversation.

Both sergeants were coloured reservists, unpaid part-time volunteers who had signed up during the transition to democracy. Peter was like a model citizen of Utopia – handsome, articulate, and quietly honourable – and as he drove us through the Flats he volunteered a sympathetic commentary on his patch. He said he felt sorry for the criminals, the conditions they lived in, the joblessness and emptiness. He didn't dare join up full time for fear of having the humanity stripped of him. With flawless English, he was a diligent translator for us throughout the night.

Mervin, on the other hand, was a weaselly, God-bothering pedant who thought there was no excuse for breaking the law. He offloaded his prejudices in an irksome riff – 'See that child there, look how young he is! He should be in bed . . .' – and when he wasn't wittering about wickedness and God's work, he pointed out bus routes. He drove a bus for his day job, and he harboured a sad, if comic, obsession with buses. 'Look, Paul, there is a bus!' he exclaimed all night. Or, 'Look – over there! A bus depot.'

At around eleven o'clock a man flagged us down. Crouching at the window, he whispered a tip-off to Peter about an illegal firearm in a nearby house, then slipped away into the shadows. The address was too close to Mervin's own home for us to attend, but a radio call to local officers was unsuccessful, so Peter made contact with an Operation Good Hope patrol. Good Hope was a special police taskforce – high profile, commando-style, bristling with armoury – drafted in some months earlier to combat Pagad, but not yet distinguished by conspicuous success.

Minutes later we pulled into a brightly lit petrol station on a main road. Two unmarked cars drew up behind us, and out of them piled a dozen or so coloured and black men and a very fat white woman sporting a crewcut. Within seconds they were hauling AK-47s out of the boot and slotting pistols into holsters strapped around their thighs. 'No pictures,' the fat woman barked at Paul. 'Undercover.' But the performance took place in the glare of the forecourt, and by the time they were tooled up like Rambo and ready to go, at least fifty people must have seen them. Half the men were wearing Operation Good Hope polo shirts, which didn't seem very undercover either.

We drove in convoy to the corner of the street where the house stood, and parked in the shadows. But then Mervin had to get out and show the Operation Good Hope crew which house it was. All hope of discretion had long since evaporated; people were out of their houses and standing in the street to watch the fun, and then, to cap it all, up strolled the informant. Peter jumped out the car and pretended to frisk him, but the pretence looked woefully lame – especially when the pair sauntered off together.

Unfortunately we missed the action, as at the last second Mervin took it upon himself to drive the car a block away and hide. We waited, heard nothing, and soon the radio summoned us back to the petrol station. Everyone was shouting angrily at each other, stomping about the forecourt unstrapping guns and loading them back into car boots in disgust. Peter translated the gist of the disappointment, which was that by the time they'd burst into the house it was full of nothing but children and there wasn't a weapon in sight. When the four of us pulled away, the car was terse with dejection.

We cruised on into what was known – and this is quite a distinction on the Cape Flats – as the disaster area. A tornado had ripped through the district, destroying acres of homes, and the destitute population had been rehoused on a scrubby wasteground in tiny garden sheds, known as Wendy Houses, or in aluminium shacks like Portaloos. Mervin was expounding an elaborate theory about why God was actually right to make such things happen, when suddenly the radio burst into life. There had been a shooting.

We screamed north, lights blazing and sirens wailing. I have no idea how Peter knew where we were going, as the streets were a dark and cluttered tangle, unsigned and unnamed, but soon we drew up outside a squat little bungalow in a coloured district. Two police cars were already parked outside, and neighbours, mostly teenage girls in bathrobes and curlers, were converging on the garden. Craning on tip-toes to see inside the house, they looked more excited than distraught.

Following Peter and Mervin, we squeezed into the living room. It was a tiny space, but tidy, with photographs of babies on the walls and a sideboard crammed with trinkets. In an armchair just inside the door sat a man about Paul's age, his top off and his long, lean back bent forward, elbows slumped between his knees. An older woman wiped his face with a damp cloth, and a man knelt, holding the man's head up with both hands, gripping the jawbone so hard his knuckles were white. '*Stay awake*,' he urged. But the sunken eyes were hanging and lifeless; and though his lower jaw trembled, the man made no sound. In his back, near the kidney area, was a dark-red bullethole.

I looked around the room. Four other men, shaven-headed and whippet thin, were pacing the floor, urging him to stay conscious. There was urgency on their faces, but no shock, as if the sight of their friend dying before their eyes were a foregone conclusion. Junky Funky gang tattoos covered the man's torso, and his face wore a look of pain too close to death to be recognisable. He had gone out for cigarettes and been gunned down by passing members of a rival gang.

More coloured officers squeezed in to gather round and stare. There were four police cars outside now, but still no ambulance. Peter murmured that people only ever called the police, because they did not know the telephone number for an ambulance. Often they didn't even know the toll-free number for the police, and would walk all the way to the station – or they would phone the station, not understanding that from there a call would then have to be made to central control. With a dying man in front of us, still nobody knew how to phone for an ambulance. The crowd in the garden was swelling, noisier and angrier now; but the atmosphere of shock sounded muted, irreconcilable with the catastrophe of a young man gunned down.

Still more police arrived, but they were not allowed to drive an injured person to hospital; apparently they weren't insured. Peter offered anyway, but the injured man's friends shook their heads angrily. 'He's not going to De Joost.' De Joost was Manenberg's emergency trauma clinic, but gang victims were afraid to go for fear of being followed by their attackers and finished off on the ward. And so the man sat there, a bullet burning inside him, sinking towards death – and it was only when a fifth police car arrived, bringing a Disaster Management officer, that an ambulance was at last called. 'He knows how to call,' Peter whispered inexplicably. 'He is allowed.' During the wait, a burly young woman thrashed her way into the room, wailing and gnashing, apparently the injured man's girlfriend. Catching sight of Paul's cameras, though, she cut off the hysteria mid-shriek, and began to pose, hands on hips, like a calendar girl. One of the men barked at her, and Peter gently steered us out to the car.

When the ambulance arrived an hour later, we followed it to Mitchells Plain hospital in a neighbouring district. More like a prison than a hospital, armed security men guarded its gates, and a sign on the sentry-box read: 'No weapons. Please hand them in at reception.' The entrance itself was blocked by an iron grille, a metal detector and two more armed guards. Visitors were not allowed inside, and had to sit and wait on benches in the car park; they were coloured teenagers, joking and smoking as though waiting for kebabs, a normal way to wind up a Friday night.

Inside, the hospital was shabby and threadbare. At the trauma-ward door, a staff nurse ticked off the evening's score – fifteen stabbings and three gunshot wounds by midnight. She nodded us through. The only doctor on duty, a young Bulgarian bleary with exhaustion, stood surrounded by blood-splattered young men on stretchers. One had a knife wound on his right shoulderblade, cut so deep into the muscle that it formed a perfect eye, pink and wet; when he stood and began to walk, the blood slip-slopped with his every step. The doctor hadn't treated the young man we'd seen shot earlier, he told Peter. He had died in the ambulance, less than a mile from hospital.

The radio summoned us to Kensington, to a scene that looked as though it had been lifted from a bad movie. A wall of police vans blocked both ends of the street, and between them blazed a mayhem of shouting and blue light and AK-47s. The 100-yard strip was swarming with officers, coloured and white, uniformed and plain clothes, all bearing down on a tatty little house at the far end. As we watched, several dozen stormed over the garden wall and through the yard, kicked down the door and dragged a young man shrieking and kicking out of the house. Two slammed him face-down on to the bonnet of a police van, and a third pounded his face with one hand, shoving the other between the man's legs, twisting higher and higher, until the screaming man was flapping like a fish. Other policemen clustered round and kicked. A tall, bony plain-clothes officer, taut with fury, thrust his rifle to a colleague, took out a pistol, and whipped it over and over the man's head.

After two more suspects had been dragged out, beaten and thrown in the van, the frenzy subsided. Officers stood around and smoked and laughed, waves of adrenaline cooling in the night breeze. There were one or two sharp looks at Paul's cameras. 'Yah,' Peter mumbled, slightly uncomfortable. 'They are very frustrated, and sometimes they, um, let their frustration run over.'

The police had shot a fourth man in the house before we arrived, and we joined the flashing blue convoy escorting his ambulance through empty streets to Groote Schuur, a city-centre hospital. On the way, Peter explained that the incident had started with a routine raid, nothing out of the ordinary. Two officers had visited the house in Kensington earlier that evening to look for drugs. But one of them was beaten in the face with a chain, Peter said, so he shot his attacker on the spot – and the chaotic violence had skeltered from there. Barely a mile from the hospital, another gunfight broke out in the streets, bullets flying across four lanes of traffic and gangsters diving between cars like stuntmen. The police all spoke in Afrikaans, so we couldn't tell who was in charge, but the operation seemed to have careered out of all control. Ducking behind the car as bullets whistled past, it became faintly surreal.

As we pulled into Groote Schuur's car park, the wounded man was being stretchered in from the ambulance, followed by a clatter of police galloping down the corridor, rifles bouncing over their arms. It was a smart hospital, and in the trauma ward implacable staff set to work unclothing the man and laying him out. The police crowded round the bed to stare. The man was the leader of the Scorpion gang, and as he was stripped naked the officers milled closer to get a better look. He had bullet wounds in his arm and his side, but the police were giggling, pointing towards something else. Across the brown mound of belly, rising from the groin towards the chest, was a tattoo of an ejaculating penis. Nudging his colleagues and sniggering, an officer stuck out his finger and poked it.

In the corridor outside the ward we came across the policeman who had shot him. He was a white man, out of breath, still flaring with adrenaline but plainly not someone who had been beaten in the face. 'He just came at me,' he complained belligerently. 'And went like that.' He drew back his arm. 'I didn't see it was a chain in his hand; I thought it was a knife. So I shot him. Yah.'

Gradually the others emerged from the ward, and we drifted out into the car park. Dawn was breaking over the city, a fresh orange splash across the pale-pink sky. Cigarettes were lit, and presently everyone remarked what an unusually quiet night it had been. 'I'm sorry,' said Peter, 'you didn't get to see much action.'

Tanya was already up when we arrived home, putting on make-up for an early-morning audition. Her eyes widened when we described what we'd seen.

'Shacks? They live in shacks on the Cape Flats? I thought they lived in flats.'

⋆   ⋆   ⋆

I have no idea how South Africa is going to defeat its gangs and warring vigilantes. The violence that night was so careless and complete, it felt likely to go on for ever, the police resembling less a force of law and order than just another gang of armed men marauding through the drug deals and shootouts, helpless and anarchic. And even when they do manage to catch someone, the courts cannot always be relied upon, for they are buckling under the weight of so much crime.

On our last day, Abdu-Salaam Ebrahim was again due to appear before magistrates. A week earlier, a court in Wynberg had been bombed just as two Pagad members were due to appear, and today we found giant rolls of razor wire blocking each end of the court-house street. Six armoured vans stood parked in front of the court-house steps. Inside, the entrance to Court 17 was guarded by two white plain-clothes policemen – mountainous gorillas cradling automatic rifles. Inside the court room itself were eight more burly plain-clothes officers. They looked like American farm boys, thighs straining under blue denim, hair blonde and skin tanned. Chewing gum, raking the room with their eyes, they lined one wall of the court room. Two dozen coloured officers in uniform stood shoulder to shoulder at the back of the room, fencing in the public gallery; squeezed on to its pews sat grim-faced women – Pagad supporters – scarves on their heads and handbags on their laps. Faces became corrugated with tension as the room grew airless with expectation.

After an age, a magistrate swept on to the raised platform at the front of the court. Everyone rose, and a muffled gasp fizzed through the room as Abdu-Salaam Ebrahim was led into the dock. In a crisp white shirt and heavy beard, he cut a surprisingly mild, rather bookish figure, the Qur'an clasped behind his back in the fingers of his cuffed hands. Silence fell. The judge beckoned Ebrahim's lawyer to approach the bench, and after a brief exchange of whispers announced that the hearing was adjourned. They hadn't been able to find an 'appropriate' magistrate; it would have to reconvene tomorrow. And so the coils of razor wire were rolled away, the battalions dispatched, and the astronomical expense poured away down a drain. And it would all happen again tomorrow, by which time the state might or might not have found the right magistrate. As the court emptied, Paul and I seemed alone in registering surprise.

Outside in the sunshine, we spotted a man leaning under a tree across the street, waving. It was Gansie Uys. We made our way over and were greeted by a gummy beam and an enthusiastic bear-hug.

We asked why he was there. Swigging on a beer, Gansie explained that a friend was due up in court that morning, so he had come to deliver two parcels of drugs to be taken back to prison.

'But how?'

He twinkled and giggled. 'You only need a bit of money. Watch.'

Minutes later, a police van pulled up and armed guards led out a dozen prisoners, shackled together with ankle-chains. As they shuffled up the steps to the court house, Gansie sauntered over and joined the rear. We watched him wink at a guard. As the chain gang filed into the court house, he quite openly slipped two large parcels into the arms of a prisoner.

CHAPTER 17

Mapogo-a-Mathaga

On our final weekend in the country we found ourselves with a pair of Es from Armien and without the energy to take them. Our enthusiasm for Cape Town's clubs hadn't recovered since New Year's Eve; and, while Armien had claimed the pills were 'magnificent', he did talk a lot of rubbish so we were somewhat sceptical. We had heard a good deal about something called Kwaito, however, a South African version of house music being played in Johannesburg. We had heard, too, about a Jo'burg club called Foundation. And we had also heard about a vigilante organisation there, called Mapogo.

Founded in the rural Northern Province, Mapogo-a-Mathaga had grown in three years from an informal outfit into a populist organisation with a membership of some 60,000. According to the leadership, it was now advancing southwards on Johannesburg and Pretoria, its target the urban drug barons and gangs. Like Pagad, Mapogo's mission statement was ruthlessly unequivocal. If the police were neither able nor willing to punish criminals, then Mapogo would do the job instead. Mapogo had recently been in the headlines, after one of its members was arrested for beating a suspected criminal and throwing him into a river infested with crocodiles. A number of other Mapogo members were in prison charged with beating criminals to death, and even the organisation's president, John Magolego, faced a murder charge. A newspaper contact in Johannesburg passed on his telephone number, and I called. It was an awkward conversation. Magolego was guarded, his voice a long-distance treacle of vanity and menace, but eventually he agreed to be interviewed. We were to meet him in a town called Middelburg, fifty miles northeast of Johannesburg, on Saturday.

We flew up early that morning and under a cloudless sky drove out through golden rolling maize fields of farming country. Middelburg is a typical Boer market town of featureless, single-storey buildings, agricultural stores, wide streets and pick-ups driven by large men with bushy moustaches, dressed in khaki shorts and shirts. The women had severe fringes and heavy, lumpen bodies, lost in shapeless smock-dresses. Blacks in tattered jeans gathered purposelessly in the shade outside bottle stores; whites kept moving, their eyes trained straight ahead. We looked for the BMW garage where Magolego had told us to find him, and there was no problem working out who he was when we pulled on to the shiny showroom forecourt. He was surrounded by four black bodyguards, all carrying pistols in holsters.

John Magolego reminded me of Toad of Toad Hall. He was a short, very black, dandy little man with a rounded belly, dressed in a crisp white shirt, with gold cufflinks, tie-pin and watch and shiny slip-on shoes. After formal, slightly jerky handshakes on the forecourt, he led the way with pointy little steps to a steakhouse. The restaurant was designed in the style of a barn, heavy timbered and poorly lit, the walls hung with paintings of wagons and other Boer iconography. Magolego led us to a table at the back, where he ordered for himself and his four bodyguards without consulting them.

His manner with the white teenaged waitress was oddly childlike but abrupt. 'Lady, what is this "prawn cocktail" thing? What is that? We want a nice meal. We would be happy to receive it in a short space of time.' He turned to us. 'Now! Let the interview commence.' Magolego answered every question in a sing-song voice, sometimes chuckling, sometimes stern, but overall the balance tipped towards humour – 'ha-ha-ha!' – which was odd, in view of what he was saying. He was less sinister than he had sounded on the phone, but I think this was because he was trying to be charming.

'We are not an underground movement,' the president began. 'We are trying to solve this country's problems.' Four years ago, he had been a small-businessman in the rural north. Driven to distraction by robberies, and frustrated by the courts' failure to convict criminals, he and a handful of local entrepreneurs banded together to form Mapogo. The strategy was straightforward enough. Every time one became the victim of a crime, he would round up the others by two-way radio and they would track down the culprit. 'In rural areas, we all know who the guilty man is. Information gets around. We all know who the criminals are. When anything happens, we know where to look.'

Having found their man, they would drive him into the veld and beat him with a *sjambok*, a stiff leather whip, until he confessed. Then they would administer his punishment.

'We believe in corporal punishment, and, my dear, we do not spare the rod. Our punishment is always the *sjambok* on the buttocks of the criminal. The criminal must lie on the floor and he must feel the pain.'

What if he says he didn't do it? 'What, he doesn't want to tell the truth?' Magolego looked indignant. 'Then yes, yes! He must get some strokes of the *sjambok* then. It's the key to unlock the door. We must open his door so we can visit his brains and make him tell the truth.' Failing that, the Mapogo members would go and search his house for evidence.

'But surely you don't have search warrants?'

'But who is there that can stop us from searching?' The law, I suggested. Magolego pulled a face of mock incomprehension, chuckled, and shook his head. 'We are going against that particular law, because it protects the criminal. If you haven't stolen anything, then you can say "Come in and look! See, I am innocent!" We don't consider that a criminal has human rights. A person who commits a crime forfeits them. You cannot respect him; he must never be treated as a VIP.'

'What about the right to silence?'

'Ho-ho-ho!' Magolego's eyes streamed with laughter, and he laid down his cutlery to wipe them. 'Oh no, we don't want that, no, no.' Magolego wished to go further than that and abolish defence lawyers altogether.

'Why should I catch the man, and then let somebody help him to escape his punishment?' He found the convention inexplicable. 'These lawyers, they just help to perpetrate crime. Look, if I know you have stolen my car, and I've seen it in your possession, then what the hell do you need a lawyer for? That's my car! And everyone knows it's my car. And I've seen it with you! So the lawyer is just someone who tries to get you off when you are guilty.'

Magolego had become quite worked up. Coughing politely, a body-guard intervened to ask whether we had anything like Mapogo in our country. We cast about for an answer, and came up with the Guardian Angels. There was general incredulity and disgust at the news that the force was unarmed, but Magolego was eager to know more. What he really wanted, he explained, was to bring together all the vigilante groups in the world. 'We can have a summit,' he declared. 'Yes, a summit, like the UN. And also, we must have a national chairman of the world. And I assume they will choose me. Because I am the king of the vigilante groups in South Africa!' He beamed, and proposed a toast to himself.

Magolego expressed bewilderment at the charges of murder and assault facing his members as a result of their activities, but did not deny that some deaths might have occurred. 'Yes, yes,' he puffed impatiently. 'When people are angry, at times they can overdo it, of course. But the *main* aim is not to kill. Why, even a doctor can take a patient to the operating table and try to cure him, and instead the patient dies. But that is OK, because he was *trying* to cure him. There will always be casualties, you see, but we are like the doctor.' He winked, and on cue his entourage laughed, familiar with the analogy. 'Yes, we are only trying to cure the criminal.'

Mapogo had made its president a rich man, for a slice of every membership fee went directly to him. He toured the country, holding meetings modelled upon religious revivalist conventions, urging audiences to open new branches. Run at local level by their members, these had now spread to districts of Johannesburg and Pretoria. His organisation, he puffed with pride, had outgrown rural crime, and was ready to take on the urban drug barons and gangsters. He was hugely impressed with People Against Gangsterism and Drugs, and had been in touch about strategies and partnerships. The urban side of things was where the big money lay. That was where the real criminals could be found – with the drugs.

'You can always find more monkeys where there are more peanuts,' he chuckled, dabbing his mouth with a napkin. 'Am I right?'

The meal was over. Would it be possible to arrange an interview with a member in Johannesburg? He shook his head; that would be too 'sensitive' at this stage. But he would try to find a member in the Northern Province to speak to us, and would get back to us after the weekend. We left him in the steakhouse pondering the possibilities of a global Mapogo via the Internet, and drove to Johannesburg to go clubbing.

The journey into the city was unnerving. The northern suburbs of Houghton and Sandton looked not unlike parts of Surrey's stock-broker belt, their leafy, landscaped avenues lined with heavily fortified houses nestled behind electronic gates and rolls of barbed-wire along garden walls. Further south, though, the stillness gave way to a busier muddle of bumpy streets, and when we pulled on to Rockey Street in Yeoville the pavement was suddenly thick with crowds of young men. Spotting us, they began to holler and wave. For a second I thought they were parking attendants, then realised they were trying to sell drugs. First touting like hookers, peering in through the windscreen, the crowd then sprang in front of the car and pressed their wares up to the window. Our guide book had described Yeoville as racially mixed and lively, but it was printed five years before our visit and things had evidently changed, for the dealers clearly assumed the only reason a white person would be driving down Rockey Street was in order to buy drugs. By the time we reached our guesthouse we were quite badly shaken.

So it was with fairly weary reluctance that we dragged ourselves out for the evening to Foundation. I think we were both secretly relieved to find the club deserted, but we had heard of another club called Enigma in the same district of Rosebank, so forced ourselves back in the car to give it a try. Rosebank is one of the smarter, rather sterile areas to the north of the city centre, and Enigma fitted in there well, for it was like a provincial eighties wine bar, chrome and black, with little round tables topped off by candles. African bar staff in matching floral uniforms narrowly outnumbered their customers, young black men – all eight of them. Hovering at the door, we only decided to stay for just one drink for fear of looking rude.

The DJ, a lanky young African, wasn't playing Kwaito, but an intricately rhythmic strain of garage, with delicate vocals overlaid with disco and latin beats. Between record changes he would leap out on to the tiny dancefloor, bringing the total there to four – but the dancing was fluid, endlessly imaginative and rippled with comedy. The four spooked each other, pulling faces and shimmying together, then spinning on their heels and strutting to the edge of the floor, twirling round to double up in giggles.

There is always something enchanting when a tiny group makes a dancefloor their private playground, and we were charmed – but still shattered. After taking half an E, I hadn't felt a thing. Paul hadn't touched his, and I couldn't even bother to do my other half, so I was on my way to flush them down the toilet when Paul said what the hell, he'd give his a go. With a shrug I handed it over, took my other half and sat down to finish my drink, expecting to be home within the hour.

Half an hour later Paul, me, the DJ, the bar staff, the bouncer and the rest of the club were all piling into cars and tearing off to Foundation. I don't think I'd ever had an E like it, and have no idea how we failed to crash the car, for the roads were a spangle of disco lights and Paul was dancing with both hands and feet as he drove. We burst into the club and found ourselves in the scene we had come to South Africa searching for. Packed solid with smiling, stylish blacks and whites dancing to deep house, Foundation looked like a commercial for the beauty of clubbing.

We danced until we could hardly stand. Late on, one of the men we'd come with tapped Paul on the shoulder and held up our car key; Paul had been so off his head he'd left it in the car door. The man dropped it into his hand with a twirl and a grin – 'Don't worry, you are with nice moral ethnic people now.'

A pink dawn was breaking over the city as we arrived at our guesthouse. Paul got straight on the phone to Armien. 'Mate! Those Es, they're fucking amazing.' And Armien, surprising to the very last, coughed modestly and insisted that they were nothing special.

It was a glorious, bolt-blue Sunday. Johannesburg is always described as a charmless city, and that's about right, but after Cape Town's elegant segregation it looked electrifying. Between the fortified northern white suburbs and the mayhem of Yeoville is a real African city where blacks lead normal urban lives, crisp with confidence, a world away from the cowed parking attendants of Cape Town. The night in Foundation had seemed to cleanse away layers of ugliness we'd seen in South Africa, and when we returned from lunch and found a message waiting from Magolego, I was inclined to ignore it. Part of me wondered how seriously to take what he'd told us. It scarcely felt real any more, just the fantasies of a trumped-up little despot.

We rang the number anyway. A man called Peter Drake answered, and as he talked I grew more and more doubtful, for his voice was gentle, articulate and rather eager. He sounded hopelessly sweet-natured, and quite ill suited to the role of vigilante, but he said that, yes, he was a branch leader of Mapogo. If we liked, we could come and speak to him at his farm, near Tzaneen, four hours' drive north through the veld in the heart of the Northern Province. We agreed to go the following day.

The land north of Johannesburg is featureless at first, one bland mile after another of even maize fields, the sky above stretching to infinity. As we drove, the landscape grew hilly, and we passed African settlements scattered across scrubby red fields – forlorn housing, though less squalid than townships, some of it traditional African mud huts but most of it concrete cubes or tin shacks. Bulky, bearded Boer farmers passed by in pick-up trucks, and African farm workers walked single file along the roadside, shirts off and heads down, in the dry dusty heat. Later, the road began to climb, and as dusk fell the land grew lush, green and cool. At the top of a wooded mountain pass we turned off down a rutted red-earth track thick with sub-tropical vegetation, and at the end lay Peter Drake's farm. When the farmer appeared on his porch, smiling through the gloom of an African dusk, no doubt was left in my mind that there had been a mistake.

Peter Drake was a tall, muscular man in his forties, dressed in regulation khaki shorts and shirt, with generous features, a kindly gaze and a close resemblance to John Malkovich. Shooing away a scramble of dogs on the steps, he took our coats and bags and ushered us inside. It was a traditional South African farmhouse, functional and rough around the edges, its large, spare rooms dominated by solid handmade furniture. Although comfortable, it had been undisturbed by any great attention to ornament. In the kitchen sat the farmer's wife, Karen. She was a slight, demure woman in a modest smock-dress, brown hair cut to the shoulder and unstyled, her face free of make-up. On her feet at once, she began warming a meal for us on the range. In the next room, three pretty daughters lay sprawled on the floor in jeans, watching cricket on the television. Throughout the evening they drifted in and out, lighting up their father's eyes, bringing teenage smiles and updates on the score.

The four of us sat around the kitchen table. Peter Drake was unusually relaxed about being interviewed. He spoke easily, neither guarded nor prone to exaggeration, never giving the impression that he had paused to consider how his words might strike us. They were his unmediated thoughts, offered with absolute faith in our complicity. Not once did his voice betray a hint of anger or violence; there was no hate in his eyes, and his tone was that of a decent, honest man. He was deeply hospitable, called his wife 'my sweetheart', and gave the impression of someone who seldom lost his temper. He appeared quite unhaunted by demons, and spoke with confident grace. I say all of this because it probably won't be apparent from reading what he said.

Had we met him under other circumstances, I expect we would

have thought him a very fine man, but there were times that evening in his kitchen when I thought I must be dreaming. But here is what he told us.

CHAPTER 18

The Nazi Gestapo Guy

'When I heard John Magolego was coming to Tzaneen,' Peter Drake began, 'I thought, This is like Father Christmas coming here.' Peter had seen Mapogo in action on the television, beating a suspected thief until he begged on his knees for forgiveness. 'That made sense to me. I know the black man through and through, I understand him. And I looked at the television, and I thought, That is what the uneducated black man in this country understands.'

Peter ran an old family farm, growing eucalyptus trees and fruit. He employed around sixty men and, like the other white farmers in the valley, had grown tired of them drinking and fighting and stealing. The final straw came when he'd caught one red-handed stealing a few avocados, and the police prosecution failed on a technicality. One thief had even taken to stealing the copper wire from the telephone lines, and still the police did nothing. 'I actually caught the bugger stealing it. Right there, on top of the telegraph pole. I shot him as well.'

'You'd had to lie under the pole all night for weeks,' added Karen indignantly.

'Yah, that's just it.'

So, Drake and the 15 other white farmers rounded up 600 workers and went to hear Magolego speak at a Mapogo meeting in the valley.

'It went down very well with everyone there. Everyone – including the blacks.' Peter told his men afterwards that they must either join Mapogo or leave his farm. They had to pay a 50 rand membership – 'That's important, you see. The average guy gets paid 200 rand a month, so it has to be a decent membership fee. Magolego explained to me, if you make a chap pay for his membership, he will cherish it.' Peter selected eight of his farmworkers, his 'top chaps', to make up his Mapogo committee; and the next time a crime was committed on the farm, they were ready to swing into action. They caught a man snaring a bush pig, held a trial, and sentenced him to twenty-five lashes.

'We call it a *kgoro* – a tribal court case. It would be like a normal court case, only very condensed. The victim puts his case, and then the accused is brought in. If he denies it, we say, OK, tell us who saw you not doing it. It's a fair trial, you see. Eventually the perpetrator admits he did it, usually, and the committee decides how many lashes he should get. For smaller crimes, like stealing a penknife, it might be fifteen to twenty lashes. If he did it twice, though, it could be fifty to a hundred and fifty, and then he's lucky if he's alive. The idea is, if you hammer the smaller crimes, the crimes don't get bigger. It's called zero tolerance. I think it began in New York.'

'It's like beating a dog,' Karen murmured. 'You have to do it quickly, so they learn their lesson.'

'Where does this all take place?' I asked.

'Oh, we drive the criminal out to a forsaken spot. And we always wear balaclavas. That's a must.'

Paul asked if the bush-pig poacher was surprised by what happened to him.

'Oh yes,' said Peter. 'He was very surprised. In fact, he was quite indignant when we gave him his beating. He thought we should give him a chance. But in Mapogo, we say we do give you a chance, because we don't give you as many lashes as you probably deserve.' He paused to sip his coffee, and looked thoughtful.

'It is ruthless, the beating. But that's how these chaps grow up. They understand power and control and respect, you see. You have to understand: the black man, he's brutal. When I see how my committee guys are willing to give a guy a hiding, I see how these black atrocities get committed in Africa. You just wouldn't believe how brutal they are.' Peter's guys are so brutal, in fact, he has to stand over them while they administer the beating he's ordered, to make sure they don't go overboard and kill the man. 'I'm like the Nazi Gestapo guy,' he remarked lightly. 'I monitor the beating.'

The windows of the Drakes' house were heavily barred. On the sideboard in the kitchen lay a rifle, a bulletproof vest, and a two-way radio connecting the household with a chain of other white farms along the valley, so that assistance could be summoned swiftly in an emergency. To demonstrate, Peter broadcast a request for responses, and a crackle of taut, pseudo-military barks came echoing back through the night. Karen smiled tightly as she counted them off on her fingers. The family had rehearsed a drill in the event of the house being attacked, choreographed to cater for every eventuality. They had a special procedure if the intruder tripped the lights, and a concealed hole tunnelled into the ceiling for the children to hide in. They also had five guard dogs, two of them a Rottweiler and Great Dane cross. These wouldn't live more than a few years before their legs dislocated under the unnatural weight of their hulking bodies.

And all this was necessary, Peter was sad to say, because of democracy. The vote had 'undermined the black man's historical blood-lines and traditions,' and produced a Third World government incapable of imposing law and order.

'You can't tell me you can teach an illiterate individual First World principles like democracy. He has to be educated first, and I'd say eighty per cent of our population are illiterate. The system simply doesn't work. If a criminal gets caught by the police, he gets off on a technicality.' Peter looked hurt. 'Even if he goes to jail – well, he has been taken to a life of luxury. OK, there are guards and rules in prison. But he's used to abiding by rules. And while he's inside, what does his wife do? She becomes a harlot. And her daughter. Her son starts breaking into houses, to get money for the family. You see, by removing one criminal from society, you make at least three. In Mapogo, we say no. Give him a hiding instead.

'I don't like our way, but it has to happen – it's a system devised by a black man for the black man, and it works. You know, crime rates have plummeted here since we got into Mapogo. You'd be amazed at how many people wave at me now when I drive down the road. The blacks love what Mapogo does. You see, the blacks are like children – you have to be harsh and hard. And fair, obviously.'

There were risks involved, Peter willingly conceded. Mapogo was an underground organisation, and therefore open to abuse. If Paul was his friend, for example, and someone was bothering Paul, Peter and his guys could take the man out, no problem. But Magolego had a strong commando force for dealing with that sort of thing.

'For example, there's a town north of here. It's right on the way to Rhode–, I mean, Zimbabwe. Some guys started a branch up there, and it came to our attention that the method of investigation was a bit much. If a criminal wouldn't talk, this one guy would defecate on the ground and rub the guy's face in it. Now that's all wrong. We don't want to humiliate the guy.'

'Well,' put in Karen softly, 'not to that extent, anyway.'

'No,' agreed Peter earnestly, 'because what happened then was, the black people there lost respect for Mapogo – and once they've lost respect, they won't tell you anything. So it had to be sorted out.'

And then there was the case of the missing branch-funds. A local Mapogo chairman couldn't explain where the money had gone, so he was hauled up to Mapogo HQ and never seen again. 'So you see,' the farmer smiled, 'even if you are a Mapogo chair, you are not above the law. It might lend itself to abuse, but in the end it's self-regulating.'

Paul asked if a white had ever been beaten by Mapogo. Peter nodded readily.

'You wouldn't believe it, but yes. Not by my guys, luckily, but a group north of here. This guy was buying stolen beer for his stores, and he got the hiding of his life. He's a nervous wreck now. He's the only one, but you see, it can happen. The blacks ask us all the time, "Why don't we see whites getting lynched?" But I explain to them, there's thirty million blacks in this country, and only seven million whites, so it stands to reason, doesn't it? And secondly, the whites have grown up in a more law-abiding way.'

But Peter had a problem. To his distress and disbelief, the police had recently begun to crack down on Mapogo's activities in the region. He told us the story of a friend, Chantelle, the wife of a Mapogo branch-chair in a white town some miles away. A little while ago, the police had accused the branch of beating two men to death, and arrested eight of its black committee members. They impounded Chantelle's computer, and three months later came to arrest her.

'This is where harassment comes into it. They came to arrest her on a Friday, so she wouldn't have seen a magistrate before Monday, at least. As a white woman in jail among blacks, she would definitely have been raped.' But Chantelle had got wind that the police were coming, and had fled to the Drakes' farm to hide. Four months later, though, the police managed to arrest her.

'Luckily, thank God, she's asthmatic, so she conveniently developed an asthma attack and went to hospital instead. Her doctor helped her to stay sick, so she was kept in hospital.' He shook his head sadly. 'You know, this is a woman who owned her own house and ran two businesses. She has three children. Her husband has a job in the mines. That's sick. That's what I call harassment.'

The case against Chantelle now appeared to have been dropped, but it had worried Peter badly and in the past six months he had scaled his activities right down.

'I don't want what happened to Chantelle to happen to me. I've got three lovely daughters. Chantelle says that when this case is finally over it will have cost her 25,000 rand. It's too much money.'

'And for nothing!' added Karen.

Chantelle's eight workers were still in prison awaiting trial for murder. I asked Peter if his committee guys were worried about being arrested.

'Oh no, these guys are used to living in danger. If they die tomorrow, they don't have a problem with that. They don't have any value on life, black guys. They can't, can they, or they wouldn't be able to kill so easily. I mean, Paul, if you or I were going to kill someone, we would just kill him, wouldn't we? These guys, they'd kill his baby too. They've got no feeling.

'But what frightens me is, if my committee guys got arrested all my top management on the farm would be gone.'

Peter paused, for his eldest daughter had padded in to report a fallen wicket. Her father gave her a kiss on the forehead and waited until she had left the room. Dropping his voice very slightly, he leant forward towards us across the table.

'I'm sad to admit it,' he confided, 'but lately I've had to resort to torture. You hold the guy down, put his T-shirt over his face, and pour water over his mouth. The blacks, they can't swim, and they're terrified of it. They sing like a canary. Then, if they go to the police and say Mapogo assaulted me, the police say show us your wounds. And he hasn't got any. I have to do it myself, though, 'cause my guys don't know how to.' He paused again, took a sip of coffee and shook his head.

'I tell you, the thing that shocks me is having to degrade myself to the level where I'm the one who has to actually go out and lynch people. That's the government's job.'

It was nearly midnight when we finished, and the Drakes insisted we must stay. Peter wouldn't hear of a hotel, and Karen was quite insistent. 'You must understand,' she said. 'South Africans are very hospitable people.' She checked herself. 'Well,' she corrected, 'South African farmers are, anyway.'

Karen showed us into a classic farmhouse bedroom, with bare wooden floorboards, an old iron bed, and a chamber pot. After she had said goodnight and closed the door, we sat on the bed and stared at each other in silent disbelief, too scared to whisper a word. Paul put a finger to his lip and shook his head, and we lay awake in the dark, listening to the eerie orchestra of an African night. Every now and then the dogs would go berserk in the yard, and we would sit up rigid, wide-eyed, picturing ourselves trying to persuade an intruder that we were nothing whatsoever to do with this family.

At six the next morning, Karen was frying home-made antelope sausages in the kitchen. Over breakfast Peter offered us his particular take on apartheid and its ruling National Party.

'Decca, I never believed we would have a black government. I know how strong the Nats were – I learnt that years ago. I spent two years in the armed forces under them, and they brainwashed me. I tell you, the way they brainwashed me was phenomenal.' He sounded less angry than impressed. 'I firmly believed I was doing the right thing. I would have died for my country, but I wouldn't do that now, not now that I know what the Nats were up to. I hate the National Party, because they insulted my intelligence.'

This surprised me, but not as much as his explanation for the change of heart.

'Oh, it was the Truth and Reconciliation Commission, of course. When I started hearing the facts about what the government had done to people, I couldn't believe my ears. I'd say that was true of all South Africans. It was just such a shock to hear the truth.'

'I'm sorry, Peter. Do you mean that you feel the truth about apartheid was concealed from people like you?'

'Oh God, yes.' He stopped eating and raised his eyebrows. 'Apartheid was terrible! And the facts were all controlled. But then again,' he reflected, buttering his toast, 'in a sense that wasn't a bad thing. Because with democracy and free speech came the rot. And it's that rot we're having to deal with now.' The only long-term solution, he firmly believed, was education of the masses, but Karen wrinkled up her nose.

'But we are *trying* to educate them, and it just isn't working. I think they are just too far behind,' she sighed.

'Mmm, that's true,' Peter agreed easily. 'The black kids don't want to learn; they just go to school to disrupt class. They are dirty.' He sighed. 'And their upbringing from their parents is very doubtful, I'm afraid. I don't see why my daughters should have to sit next to *kaffirs*.' He laughed. 'You know, my daughters don't like it when I call them *kaffirs*. They say they're people too.' The farmer shook his head, chucklingly indulgent of such cute sentimentality.

The big mistake of the apartheid regime, Peter thought, was to give it a name. He was sure the same thing went on everywhere else in the world, but that foreigners were shrewd enough not to call it apartheid. 'You should be able to open a business, and instead of saying "no blacks", just say "right of admission reserved", and then not have to give a reason. It should be left to the individual.' Paul asked Karen if she'd like to go back to apartheid. She stopped clearing the table, and thought for a moment, one hand cupped around the back of her neck.

'I probably would prefer it,' she decided. 'Yes. It was better.' She paused. 'It did cause a lot of grief for the blacks, I suppose.'

After breakfast, it was arranged that Peter would round up his committee for Paul to photograph. Peter thought the ridge above the farmhouse would make a nice view. We climbed into a 4×4, and in the fresh morning sunlight slowly bumped up a steep track behind the house. Peter steered with one hand, and with the other pointed out of the window at his land. 'And that's another thing,' he complained, halfway up the track. In the land-claims court set up by the new government, a number of blacks had claimed that sections of Peter's farm had been stolen from their ancestors. 'But they don't have any documentation! They just have graves. They point to the land and say their ancestors were buried there.' Karen snorted, but Peter didn't actually dispute what they were claiming; he merely pointed out their lack of white-man's evidence. A technicality defence, you might say.

'And now the new government is trying to put a tax on the exotic trees we grow. They say the trees soak up all the water, so none runs down to the homelands where the blacks live. Can you believe that? We are being taxed on the rain.'

'A tax on the rain!' sang Karen.

We climbed higher still, the track now an overgrown tropical tunnel of tangled vines scraping against the windscreen. Peter brought his workers up here every now and then, and they sang songs. 'The black man loves to sing – it gets his blood up.' Was it hard, Paul asked, to keep up morale?

'Oh,' Peter said mildly, 'only if they are not paid enough. I don't pay my men enough, but they can leave if they want to. And they don't. I won't let the unions on my farm, absolutely not. If I hear a man's in the union, I make sure he gets a visit. I send my committee round and they tell him, "I wouldn't stay on this farm, or you never know when you'll be burnt alive one night." Yah, I'll burn a union man's house down, no problem. I can't have that on my farm.'

At the peak of the ridge, the track opened out into a grassy platform bordered by ferns and clusters of boulders. Far below, the farmhouse was a small red speck. Beyond, the emerald valley stretched out beneath us like a kind of paradise. Paul and I walked to the edge and gazed down in wonder, lost for words at such loveliness, Peter and Karen at our side. Glancing across, I realised they were just as spellbound, drinking in their land with fierce, hungry eyes.

Peter's committee men were already waiting, squatting on boulders dressed up in Mapogo T-shirts and balaclavas, brandishing *sjamboks*, ready for their photo-call. Peter posed first, sitting on a ledge with his rifle on his knee, gazing out over his land. When the committee's turn came, they mocked up one of their number as a criminal and pretended to beat him. They lay him on his back, knees pinning him to the ground, and crowded round, the leather whips raised over their shoulders. Karen and I were sitting out of the way, talking about her children, but when she glanced over and saw this she burst into peals of giggles. 'Oh *look*!' she squealed, pointing and sniggering. Karen was a mother and a ballet teacher, but profoundly childlike. She didn't say a great deal, but her sweet, pretty face turned sour whenever she thought about blacks.

As we bumped back down the track I asked Peter if he ever thought about giving up and leaving.

'Oh, sure,' he shot back. 'If I could sell this property for a decent price, I'd be out of here tomorrow, but I wouldn't get enough money to get into somewhere like Australia or Europe. What you have to do is, you send your child into the country to marry, and then maybe you get in that way. I'm hoping to get my eldest into au pairing in Germany. She's the pretty one, and I'm hoping she'd meet a guy there and marry him. My second one, she's very bright; she could study abroad, then hopefully marry someone there. That's what I'm hoping.' There was a pause.

'I. Don't. Want. To leave this country.' Karen spoke in a low voice, staring down into her lap. 'I will stay and face it.' Peter turned to her and sighed.

'You see, Karen – Karen doesn't read newspapers very often. You don't know what's going on, do you, my sweetheart? Her knowledge is what I tell her. It doesn't really affect her. Until the day she gets attacked.' Karen smoothed her hands down her apron and looked out of the window.

Karen and Peter were relieved to hear that we were flying straight out of Johannesburg. A dreadful place, Karen shuddered. She'd heard it was full of people who took drugs. When we turned the car to leave, Karen and Peter were still plying us with more bags of lychees through the open window – about 700 lashes' worth, I'd say. As we bumped away down the track, they stood on their porch, arm in arm, waving until we were out of sight.

THE PROMISED LAND

CHAPTER 19

Altered States

Sunlight dappled the wooded pass as we wound our way down the valley and with each bend, as the Drakes fell further behind us, we breathed more easily. For the first few miles we were hollowed by shock, but as the land opened up beneath us the mood became first light-headed and then slightly hysterical. 'We're *very* hospitable people,' I shrieked. 'I'm like the Nazi Gestapo guy,' growled Paul. We drove on, past Pietersburg, and Nylstroom, and the road for Johannesburg grew straighter and wider.

It would have been nice if the sensation of having stepped outside our world could have lasted. However dark or surreal it had been inside the farmhouse, there had been comfort in the certainty that these people were absolutely mad, existing far beyond our lives, beyond even our imaginations. As we cut south through golden miles of maize, on our last day in South Africa, the hysteria softly subsided. We fell silent, still thinking of the Drakes, and a profound uneasiness began to settle.

Like many people of our age, Paul and I had belonged to anti-apartheid campaigns. We had sat down in a variety of streets to demand democracy, had come to the country full of slightly self-righteous hope, and been shocked by whites who sneered at the new regime's disgraceful failure to maintain the meticulous crime statistics of the former police state. Couldn't they see what the government was up against? A better question might have been couldn't we. The Drakes' farmhouse and Cape Town's ecstasy didn't exist in separate universes, however much we might wish them to. We had wandered a long way from the hunt for the perfect E, but perhaps not as far as we had thought.

The scale of problems facing the new South Africa is overwhelming – and their connection with the drug trade is substantial. Without drugs, the gangs would be comparatively helpless. Without gangs, Pagad might not exist, and Mapogo members like Peter Drake would be denied their grander *raison d'être*. Without gangs and vigilantes killing people, South Africa would be a different country, and would finally stand a chance of building the democratic dream we'd been grandly boycotting Barclays about for all those years. I was so pleased with myself when I closed my Barclays account, I nearly opened another just so I could withdraw my custom again. I wouldn't have been seen dead buying a Granny Smith's apple. And yet, unaccountably, I had come to South Africa and casually bought a Hard Living gangster's drugs.

Paul's willingness to give my judgement the benefit of the doubt never wavered on our journey. I can't think why, as my status as all-round drugs expert had been exposed as far back as Detroit, but his generosity was limitless. We were halfway back to Johannesburg before he made the obvious remark, and then it was an apology.

'Sorry, Dec, this is probably a stupid question. But could you just run through why it was OK for us to buy Es from Armien?' I don't think it had even occurred to him that I might not have any idea.

Most of the arguments against ecstasy have always struck me as unproblematic. The Leah Betts objection – that it can kill you – is unarguable. But so can all kinds of things, and this is seldom thought to be grounds enough for prohibition. Addictive drugs do present serious problems, but ecstasy is not among them, neither does it inspire antisocial behaviour. People on ecstasy may bore you, but they are unlikely to hit you. For that matter, if anyone on E ever does hit you, you should probably consider yourself lucky – think what they might have done if they hadn't been on one. The philosophical misgivings about ecstasy are more interesting, I think, but these too are inconclusive. Even if happiness through artificial means were shown to be quintessentially harmful, it would be arbitrary to confine this notion to drugs; and having widened the net, I'm not sure where it would end. Only one argument against ecstasy really seems to hold water – the one I had always managed to avoid addressing.

Anyone who takes ecstasy contributes to a violent economy, operated by and for the benefit of criminals. That is the stark reality of the matter, and it is the ethical problem clubbers are least comfortable with. The popular solution is to ignore it. That was certainly my strategy, and it was surprisingly easy to employ. In Manchester we bought our drugs from each other, and seldom came across gangsters, so it was perfectly possible to shut one's mind off from the thought that the pills we purchased from our lovely friends had been whole-saled by some of the nastiest people in the city. Our world comprised of Strangeways and the gay village, situated at an optimum distance from the city's underworld, allowing the gangsters to occupy, if any-thing, a vaguely glamorous space in our imagination. Near enough and bad enough to thrill, they were sufficiently remote – and, ulti-mately, controlled – not to frighten.

London's speed garage club scene could have been more problem-atic. If the aesthetic undertone of Strangeways was camp, in garage clubs it was gangster chic, and there was always a certain amount of ghetto-fabulous bravado. But oddly enough that solved the problem, for since everyone was posing like a gangster, the reality element could also be passed off as an act, a subcultural fashion statement. The fact that most of the ecstasy around came from Holland probably also helped. Sponsoring a cottage industry of Dutch chemists felt less sinister than subsidising South American cartels, and the opportuni-ties for hiding one's head in the sand were endless.

Only now, in South Africa, there was very little sand left. We could hardly pretend we thought Rashid Staggie and Gansie Uys were statesmen of the new democracy. They were monsters. For the life of me I couldn't see how to defend subscribing to the gangster economy, and this threw into sharp relief their question of whether it was accept-able anywhere. What did we think we were doing? It was a long drive back from the Drakes' farm to Johannesburg, and every mile brought us closer to the conclusion that it was probably time to go home.

I would like to imply that this was a crisis of conscience only, but a more accurate account of our situation would be less high-minded. The truth was, we weren't sure we were enjoying ourselves. It had hardly been a lavish ecstasy romp. Paul couldn't decide whether to feel cheated or vindicated, but either way there was no doubt in his mind. Clubbing was not all it had been cracked up to be. I was troubled by how few of the clubs I had warmed to, and had started to suspect that ecstasy, far from being bad for you, is only a problem when it's been too good. Manchester had made me so fussy that I was trailing round the world holding every club responsible for its inexcusable failure to contain the membership of Strangeways.

Nostalgia is inseparable from clubbing, both its magic and its poison. Partly because of the rapid pace of change in club culture's short life, and partly due to the peculiar chemical quality of ecstasy, most clubbers are terribly susceptible to the condition of premature nostalgia. The condition has the pleasant effect of flavouring clubbing with delicious poignancy; on a good E in a good club, you enjoy the double delights of the intoxicating present, and an advance preview of the pleasure of the memory. That is the up-side. The down-side is its tendency to make clubbers old before their time, grumbling like pensioners that nothing is ever as good as it used to be. It is not an attractive attitude, and without a doubt I was guilty of it – not circling the globe anti-clockwise so much as trying to turn back time.

And there was something else. Before setting off, it had crossed my mind that an ecstasy marathon might become somewhat exhausting. In the event, the clubbing itself had taken surprisingly little physical toll, but the process of going at it with a view to writing everything down afterwards had practically destroyed us. It was such an unnatural thing to be doing. Unfortunately this wasn't something I'd picked up from the few travel books I'd read in our haste to leave England. Travel writing had come across as a beguilingly leisurely activity, soaked with dreamy reflection – whereas in our experience, it appeared to be sending us mad.

Actually, mad is not quite the right word. A better description would be a loss of the ability to taste mood; there had been so much strangeness, it was becoming hard to distinguish between bizarre and banal. It is interesting but unnerving when you can no longer assess atmosphere, for there is a real danger of inappropriate behaviour, and I'd begun to worry that we could no longer trust ourselves. Like a person with no sense of taste who bites into an onion, I could see myself absentmindedly breaking into dance at a funeral. So if only for fear of losing our judgement for ever, I thought we ought to head home.

And then we got to Amsterdam, and had to change our minds about everything all over again.

A soft, grey, drizzly dawn swaddled the damp city in darkness. We were shocked by the darkness, physically stunned. Where had all the light gone? It looked like Amsterdam had been swallowed into a nuclear winter, a natural disaster. And everything was so tiny, and so *old*. Dappled grey streets flanking chocolatey canals appeared to be lined by dolls' houses. They were tall, but the charcoal and cream and timber fronts were so narrow it was as though the breath had been squeezed out of them. Some tilted at impossible angles, as if drunk. Dim light glowed through the shuttered windows in the cold morning mist and the sounds of a city awakening were muffled; the clanking of tram bells rang out softly through the fog, and the distant putter of mopeds ruffled across the water. Bicycles swished by, silent, over the cobbles. Even at midday it was still dark, but the mist had lifted to reveal gothic grandeur, the fairytale magnificence of the Royal Palace in Dam Square, and the intricately gilded façade of Centraal Station. And so many people, in such a miniature place! Tall, fair, upright, they filled the streets, weaving between the bicycles and trams and traffic in a complex system of ancient humanity. Even the colours blended into a harmony of taupe and brown and oak – barely colours at all, but an antique sepia photograph.

The first days in Amsterdam had a dreamlike quality. We climbed a creaky flight of tiny steps to an accommodation office, and twenty minutes later were being handed the keys to an elegant apartment on Nieuwezijds Voorburgwal, in the heart of the city. The landlord was a property magnate with the manners of a church minister, courteous and kindly, and quite offended by our suggestion of something as tawdry as a deposit. He would appear each week with freshly starched linen, concerned to hear that we were enjoying ourselves. Paul hurt his back, and within an hour a doctor was at his bedside, attentive, solicitous, anxious to leave us his personal number in case we should need him. He drew diagrams on our maps, pointing out the best Saturday market, and his favourite coffeeshop for apple strudel. I telephoned a club promoter, and she met me in the bar next door to our apartment, a shock of pink hair and platform trainers offering sociological analysis of the city's club scene like a thoughtful professor.

We hired bicycles, heavy iron steeds, and sailed around the city along the canals, past the boutiques and cafes of the Jordaan, through the gracious Vondelpark, among the stark black trees of mid-winter. In the frosty morning we bought cheese and flowers in the farmers' market near the Westerkerk, and in the afternoons drank cocktails in the art-deco chic of the Hotel American. Cycling under the archway beneath the gothic splendour of the mighty Rijksmuseum at dusk one evening, we found an ice rink in the middle of the park. Encircled by a halo of white fairylights, we skated in the crisp night air, strains of opera music drifting over the ice.

All talk of going straight home was forgotten. I could not believe we'd never been to Amsterdam before. It lies just over the water from London, but everyone I knew who visited the city always came back full of nothing but the delirious thrill of *buying hash in a coffeehouse!* God, they went on about it, and this had put me right off, unable to imagine anything worse than a city full of gunslinger spliff-heads. Having arrived, though, it was astonishing that decriminalised cannabis had been what they were all so excited about. Of all Amsterdam's distinctions, it is the least extraordinary.

Almost a million people live in Amsterdam, but it feels more like a village than a city. After growing up in the countryside, I probably have a weakness for urban villages; the attraction of the gay village in Manchester for me was less the gay half of the equation than the village, with its ultimate and eccentric conjunction of characters. Amsterdam is multicultural, certainly, and cosmopolitan, but nothing is ever more than many minutes away. Everything has been built on a human scale – except that the people of Amsterdam seem to be not quite human. It is as if they have extra genes, ones that the rest of us have been denied, for their behaviour confounds every assumption about human nature. They disprove laws of urban living you would have thought were immutable.

One example of this would be their attitude towards people like us. Every Friday, British voices fill the Damrak, the wide avenue leading from Centraal Station into the city. Bearing Nike holdalls and beery grins, the stag groups and sixth-formers and office outings come spilling off the trains, armed for a weekend of riotous misbehaviour. All weekend they fall down drunk, throw up in the gutter, crash about getting lost. They fall off their bicycles, misread traffic signals, ride on the wrong side of the road. They buy drugs from junkies on street corners and have sex with prostitutes. On the ice rink in the park, they are the only ones who must approach the activity in the manner of bumper cars. They are fools.

And the Dutch? They behave as if this is fine. When I collide with another pushchair, having still not learnt to master my bicycle's brakes, the smiling parents wave me on with a chuckle. In vomit-smeared doorways are cheerful notices: 'OK, let's try this in English. Please don't leave rubbish here.' Bar staff greet goggle-eyed teenagers in Stoned Again T-shirts with amicable grins. And we, who scream like banshees if a French schoolboy so much as gets in our way on the Tube, cannot believe our eyes. Why are they behaving like this? They are not like Americans, stuck in a Have a Nice Day mantra, unable to help themselves. They aren't like the Thais in Ko Samui, slavering for the tourist dollar. The explanation appears to be that the Dutch really do not mind.

Tolerant is not enough of a word for what the people in Amsterdam glow with. Tolerance would suggest disengagement, but they are sharp and involved; a grander word is required, less passive, more magnificent, to capture the astounding grace of their make-up. The grace is present in their very movements, for they do not even walk as people do in other cities. In London it is all elbows and pout, but had we walked around like that here we would have looked hilarious. The pace isn't indolent, but there is something profoundly calm in its stride, purposeful rather than pushy. It breaks all the rules. Amsterdam has none of the haughtiness of Paris, the immodesty of London, the salesmanship of New York – but, stranger yet, these people know they are blessed and are not even smug about it. They stroll about like a therapist's model of well adjustment, undamaged by all the usual urban scars of ambition and greed and fear and the drive to *get on* and to *make something of themselves*.

You might have thought that if a city without greed could exist, it would be boring. That's the implication of London's culture, and its strategy for ensuring that its residents do not take up arms against its viciousness. Coming to Amsterdam, we felt like *Daily Mail* journalists who slave for years under an office culture known as 'creative tension' only to move papers and discover that it is possible, after all, to think up headlines without being made to cry. People in Amsterdam would be puzzled by such lies, but, in spite of their innocence, they are also unshockable. To be uncorrupted, yet not the slightest bit naïve, is an extraordinary achievement.

When Charlotte and I used to talk about looking for the perfect E, we agreed that it would be prudent to set off in an anti-clockwise direction. The logic was that were we to start looking in Amsterdam, we would probably find it, and then the rest of the trip might not happen. Most of the world's ecstasy is made in Holland. There are said to be factories in the former Soviet Union now producing pills on a scale to rival the Dutch; but even if this is true, they are not producing ecstasy of anything like comparable quality. Pills do not come with a 'Made in . . .' stamp, so this cannot be easily verified, but received wisdom in club circles is usually reliable, and the opinion is that Amsterdam pills remain the finest in the world.

The city's only world-famous club, the RoXY, had burnt down shortly before our arrival, but every coffeeshop and bar groaned with flyers for other venues, and we carried them home in great, hopeful armfuls, assembling piles on the living-room floor to help draw up a plan of action. We combed the record shops as well, noisy temples of vinyl full of boys in puffa jackets, and in one, we came across a flyer for a club called The Zoo. It is hard to explain exactly how you can judge a club from its flyer, particularly if it's written in a foreign language, but there are general themes. Computerised sci-fi graphics usually mean techno, for example, while ethnic mysticism often translates as trance. The Zoo flyer had neither, and merely indicated that it was an after-hours venue in the red-light district, but there was a knowingness in its simplicity that reminded me of Strangeways.

'S'wicked.' We looked up. A pink-faced, rather chubby young man behind the counter was pointing at the flyer. 'I'm tellin' ya, it's wicked.' Matty, it transpired, was one of the DJs at The Zoo, and something of an evangelist on the subject. He had moved out from Kent the previous summer, and by his own account of the matter was never going to go home. They would have to carry him out of The Zoo in a coffin. When pressed for details on the club's extraordinary charms, though, Matty grew tongue-tied – partly from shyness, I think, and partly from a slight issue with vocabulary. 'It's just . . . it's just wicked.' He studied us for a moment through the only fringe of his brown, pudding-bowl hair. '*You* will *love* it.' He shrugged. 'S'just wicked.'

When Saturday night came, Paul's back hadn't recovered enough for dancing, so we wandered along the canals, among the crowds in Rembrandtplein, lit by more strings of fairylights tangled through the trees. Through the drizzle the neon lights of the bars glowed fuzzy in the damp air, reflected back in the still, brown waters of the canals. In the red-light district, gaggles of men clustered around brothels, gawking at prostitutes in their underwear in windows. Sweet clouds of cannabis smoke filled the air, and dance music spilled out of pub doors, followed by drunken girls, slipping and giggling on the wet cobblestones, holding each other up and shrieking with laughter. The centre of Amsterdam is so tiny that on a Saturday night the scrum should be overbearing, but the watery silence of the canals somehow muffles it, softening the dissonance into something atmospheric, almost picturesque.

When I woke up on Sunday morning the city had turned crisp and frosty and still. Leaving Paul to sleep, I slipped out and criss-crossed the quiet streets, back to the red-light district. On a side street off Oudezijds Voorburgwal, a straggle of drug dealers were still standing, strung out and wild-eyed, muttering 'pure Colombian' (a likely story) to anyone that passed. Slumped against the wall, filthy, in rags, they cut about as desperate a figure as a drug dealer can, and it was a mystery why they weren't simply mugging tourists. It would be easy to pick off the odd lost, drunk clown as he lumbered by. But even the street-corner drug dealers are a law unto their own in Amsterdam, and as I passed they merely smiled and held out small bags of white powder. I shook my head, and they wished me good morning.

The Zoo stood on the far end of Oudezijds Voorburgwal, facing on to the canal. It could easily be mistaken for a lock-up garage, the only indication that it was open a short, bulky bouncer standing outside, stamping his feet in the cold, hands thrust into the pockets of a heavy overcoat. For a moment I wasn't sure that he would let me in, but I offered Matty's name. Grinning, he pushed open the heavy metal door. A wave of moist, smoky heat hit me first, then the thud of a bass line, and when my eyes cleared I found myself standing in what looked an awful lot like Strangeways.

CHAPTER 20

Sunday at The Zoo

Paul was still asleep when I came flying in and landed on the bed, bursting with news.

'You'll *never* guess what.' I jumped up and danced around the room, spilling out the wonders of The Zoo. The people – charming! The music – a joy! The toilets – crammed! He rubbed his eyes and peered over the top of the duvet.

'Have you had drugs?'

'No! I'm *telling* you. The club is *perfect*. It's like Strangeways – it's like Endup in San Francisco, only smaller. And there are drugs galore.' Paul sat up on his elbows.

'So why didn't you buy any?'

'God, I didn't even think to.' I'd been too bowled over to give it a thought. 'But by the look of everyone in there, sweetheart, getting hold of some decent Es is not going to be a problem.'

I could hardly wait for the next weekend, when I could show Paul what I'd found. By Wednesday, though, his back was deteriorating. It was an old problem, and a doctor in Glasgow knew how to put it right. There was nothing for it but for Paul to fly back to Scotland – which meant that he would miss the weekend. We phoned Manchester. The call lasted about thirty seconds, and on Thursday evening at Schiphol airport, minutes after I had waved Paul off, out through arrivals staggered Terry.

'Right!' he declared, lighting a cigarette and ripping off three nicotine patches. 'Let's go and bloody well buy some drugs.'

★   ★   ★

It was quite a weekend. As far as Terry was concerned, there was honour at stake; the fiascos of San Francisco were to be avenged. Smoke literally steaming out of his nostrils, Terry charged. We spent Friday night in the gay bars and clubs along Reguliersdwarsstraat, all day Saturday in recovery, and that evening presented ourselves at a club called Escape. Escape is the city's biggest dance club, a two-tier, velvety palace of neon and glitz. If anywhere in Amsterdam was going to be haughty, it would be here – but although the dancefloors glittered with girls in diamante and boys in Dolce & Gabbana, the spirit of Escape was closer to the free-for-all of an old-fashioned rave. We processed the alcoves and balconies, and soon seemed to have half the club fetching drugs for us, introducing us to a variety of dealers who all looked like film stars and behaved like party hostesses. How could they help? Were we having a nice time? Would we like a drink?

I have no idea how many pills we'd had by the time we stumbled out of Escape and proceeded to The Zoo. The only thought I remember as we clattered through the red-light district was that if Paul didn't come back soon, I would probably be dead. In a better state, I might have had time to worry about whether The Zoo would live up to my billing, but it would not have been necessary, for as we fell into the club a look of sheer delight spread across Terry's face. 'Now *this*, Decca,' he giggled, struggling to get his coat off. 'Is the *very* thing.'

The Zoo consisted of a single, rectangular, low-ceilinged room, with a bar at the near end and the DJ booth at the other. Generous, battered leather sofas were tucked into raised alcoves on either side; a basic lighting rig hung overhead. Helicopter's house classic 'On Ya Way' belted out through speakers, and the club was clouded with a sweaty fog of cannabis smoke, poppers, perfume and dry ice. In the steam, every last inch of space was crowded with dancing – a joyful, reckless abandonment of dancing. There must have been about 200 people, gays, straights, black and white, in kitten heels and army boots, miniskirts and combat trousers. Coats off, we dived in.

The details of that morning in The Zoo are inevitably hazy. I remember people falling asleep on top of each other on sofas, and others swinging from the lighting rig. I spent a long time in the toilets talking rubbish with a drag queen, and Terry got off with a very pretty blonde boy who admitted towards the end of the night that he was actually a soap star. ('Are you famous, then?' demanded Terry. 'Oh,' he blushed. 'Only in Holland, it is nothing.') A redhead in a black cocktail dress had to be carried out, having danced herself into a fever until she couldn't stop whooping and had begun to hyperventilate. Another woman I ended up beside on a sofa had come to The Zoo by herself – a very rare occurrence and the best recommendation that could ever be made of a club.

We bought a bucketload more drugs, from whom I had no idea. At some point in the morning we met The Zoo's owner, a slim, mild-mannered man no older than myself, who talked with self-deprecating passion about the loyalty of the crowd. An artist called Igor in a pinstripe suit explained the meaning of *gezellig* – a subtle but crucial Dutch concept that translates into something like cosiness and is the cultural aspiration of Amsterdam. Matty bumbled by every now and then, beaming and sweating. 'See what I mean? S'wicked, innit?' Come to think of it, Matty's command of English was probably weaker than anyone else's in the club, although by dawn mine must have come a close second. The Dutch are effectively bilingual – but much more remarkable than that is what they actually say.

Nightclub prattle between strangers is fairly inane at the best of times. Usually this is no bad thing; several Es in, the last thing you want is to be cornered into intelligent conversation. What happens is that you bat platitudes back and forth, to the tune of I Like You, and reserve your judgement for body language. How people dance is always their most authentic expression in a club; what comes out of their mouth is just window dressing. That is the usual rule, anyway, but apparently not so in The Zoo.

The Dutch are not confrontational. On the other hand, they have no use for platitude. They are the opposite of Americans, whose social impulse to please is so strong that you can get them to agree with almost anything if you smile hard enough. People in Amsterdam are quite different. Rather than agree with everything you say, as a method of communicating friendliness, they listen closely to it and then tell you what they think. It's the strangest thing, and takes some time to adjust to. I would be blethering away, then be taken by surprise to find the conversation had moved on into something both real and interesting. More bewildering still, it would be quick and humorous. And this with clubbers even more off their head than me.

We tumbled out of The Zoo at lunchtime, into bitter February sunshine. 'Right,' said Terry, giving himself a brisk shake. 'Where to next?' I stared at him in horror – then settled the question by passing out on the cobblestones. Terry carried me home, put me to bed, and headed out for a sauna.

★　　★　　★

Paul returned from Glasgow later that evening, just as Terry was crawling in. Terry had now been in Amsterdam for three days and still hadn't slept; but whereas I couldn't get out of bed without being sick, he was shortly off again for another night of clubbing. He flew home the following morning, looking somewhat green, and that afternoon Charlotte arrived from London. I still couldn't get out of bed, but Paul took Charlotte for supper and filled her in on our journey's progress.

Charlotte's relationship with clubbing is enthusiastic, but has always been more conceptual than actual. Being of an intellectual disposition and a fragile constitution, she has tended to find nightclubs terribly *interesting* rather than enjoyable. Since leaving Manchester with me, she has followed developments in clubbing more as an inquisitive observer than a committed participant. Charlotte is probably more interested in what people are like before they have taken drugs than afterwards, and so was intrigued by our account of Amsterdam's unnatural emotional wellbeing. Over breakfast the following morning, I could see her mentally rolling up her sleeves. 'Well! I think we'd better get to the bottom of *that*.'

Actually there was nothing unnatural about it. Far from hiding secret genes, the Dutch in Amsterdam originate from the same gene pool as Afrikaners in South Africa – which should give genetic determinists something to think about. Perhaps it was because we'd grown so accustomed in South Africa to insoluble mysteries that we had not seen at once why Amsterdam is an enchanted city, and its people so contented. It is the same reason why Cape Town and its people are not, and it is of course politics.

Until the 1960s, Amsterdam was a broadly conservative, traditional trading city. What happened next was something approximating a cultural revolution, in the course of which Amsterdam became known as the 'Magic Centre' of Europe and a magnet for radical ideologues. It began with a group called the Provos, mischievous pranksters whose activities included disrupting the wedding of Princess Beatrice to a German by throwing live chickens at the royal procession and shouting 'My bicycle back!' – a reference to German soldiers stealing bikes in World War Two. In 1970, a similarly spirited group occupied Dam Square and dedicated it to environmentally minded peace-lovers. They were the anti-capitalist eco-warriors of their day – except that they were more conventionally successful, and soon began to win seats on the city council. Public opinion was hardening against the capitalist orthodoxy of putting commuters in high-rise suburbs and building ugly motorways into the city centre. In 1975, a protest over plans to replace a central neighbourhood with executive offices exploded into violence. It proved to be a turning point, and was followed by a prolonged chapter of squatting, rioting and looting, and a reappraisal of political values.

By the 1980s, Amsterdam had arrived at a new consensus. Faith in rampant commercial growth had been replaced by belief in a city run by neighbourhood councils, where people could walk to the shops and cycle to work, and afford to live in a canal-side apartment as opposed to a towerblock. Today, the police ride bicycles, drugs are considered a practical rather than moral matter, same-sex marriages are recognised . . . and so on. Most of it is banal – rent controls and effective public transport – but as an illustration of how politics can make better people, it is nothing less than electrifying.

And problematic.

For me, one of the great attractions of ecstasy in the beginning was that it was unequivocally of our time, belonging only to us. Our generation has had to put up with a great deal from its parents, whose belief in the abiding supremacy of sixties' youth culture is unshakeable and often insufferable. Until dance culture, the sixties had faced little competition – and didn't we know it – but with ecstasy and house and club culture, we truly believed we had a social revolution of our own. We weren't in any doubt. When the first outdoor raves broke out across the country in 1988, it wasn't many minutes before we had christened it the Summer of Love. If in retrospect that seems presumptuous, it was modest in view of what clubbers thought they had on their hands. Nothing was ever going to be the same again. Ecstasy had changed *everything*.

The assumption wasn't as absurd as it sounds. One year earlier, nightlife had looked condemned to a joyless eternity of Malibu and Phil Collins. Nightclubs were gladiatorial – boys beating each other up, girls slagging each other off in the toilets, the two circling each other warily all night until the ten-to-two lunge for a slowie on the dancefloor, with a quickie in the car park afterwards and recriminations for weeks. 'Slag.' *'Wanker.'* And then, just twelve months later, the very same people were conjuring complicit magic out of a warehouse near Rochdale and thinking they could die of happiness. We loved each other! We wanted the whole world to love each other! We thought the whole world really would love each other, just as long as it had a good DJ and some decent pills.

Alas, the prophecy has not gone according to plan. The whole world does now have some excellent DJs, and some splendid pills, but what it has managed to make of them is decidedly patchy. This would be disappointing enough in itself, but even more upsetting to see is the distribution pattern of success and failure. Ecstasy has not been the all-conquering revolution we once thought it would be – for there is no disguising the fact that clubbing has only fulfilled its promise in those cities previously visited by the sixties, and where something of that decade still survives. Our parents can rest easy. Clubs in San Francisco and Amsterdam are better than clubs in Ko Samui or Cape Town or Chicago, but not on account of the quality of ecstasy. The matter was decided before I was born.

If there is any consolation to be taken from the disagreeable evidence of clubbing's limitations, it regards the moral question of ecstasy. Leaving South Africa, we had touched on the same conclusion reached by those parents of my friends who went off the rails on ecstasy at university: Just *stop taking it*. That had looked like the obvious solution to them, and for a brief spell to us too. But it wasn't. Clubs and drugs are not the variables that determine the happiness and health of an individual or city; it is quite the reverse. Likewise, a liberal attitude to drugs is not the reason – whatever dope-smoking sixth-formers may like to think – why Amsterdam is so civilised. It it the other way round. Drugs are logically no more the problem in South Africa than they are the solution in Amsterdam, for in either instance they are only the by-product of something altogether bigger and older. Getting rid of ecstasy wouldn't alter the essential truth of either place.

I have to say that to arrive at such a conclusion was not an unwelcome turn of events. In fact, it suited our personal interests so nicely it was rather suspicious. But it did not apply exclusively to our chosen vice, and the same logic bore out in other examples that we had no interest in letting off the hook. Bar-girls in Ko Samui had upset me profoundly, and prostitution seemed then to be the toxic root of the poison on the island. Yet months later we were breezing round Amsterdam's red-light district without a thought of degradation. For all of Amsterdam's apparent vice and licence, we found ourselves behaving better here than we had anywhere else in the world. We weren't rude, didn't drop litter, didn't shout at taxi drivers. Dignity is so deeply encoded within the city, it cannot help but be transmitted – regardless of whatever else may be going on. This works both ways. People don't behave badly in Ko Samui because of prostitution. The island is degraded because it knows nothing but money.

CHAPTER 21

The Last Dance

In the final week the weather turned bitterly cold. We passed the time huddled in coffeeshops, exploring various plots for a finale. There were some complicated telephone calls to Armien, in an attempt to track down the source of his brilliant Es, but the plan came to nothing. His pills had arrived in Cape Town on a flight from Amsterdam, but he was wary about identifying the supply route, and I think began to panic that we were setting him up. I tried to call an old dealer from Strangeways in Manchester, thinking there would be symmetry in ending the journey with an E from his Amsterdam source, but the number was out of service. Terry and I had bought some magnificent pills the previous weekend, but of course we had taken them all. I was fairly sure that a man in The Zoo had sold us some blinders, even better than Armien's, but couldn't for the life of me remember who.

Paul's temper degenerated throughout the week and not without justification. Having returned from Scotland fully recovered, he heard all about the weekend's high jinx, and now we had only one weekend left and no ecstasy crescendo lined up. The last minutes were ticking away. All the way round the world, time had been slipping away. It haunted us, a ticking clock, for there was only so much time in each place, and never enough, and we always seemed to be leaving just as we had begun to arrive. Ecstasy's greatest wonder is the sense of timelessness it creates, and in the very surge of its rush there is a magical calm as time ceases to exist. Yet, in our search for the perfect E what preoccupied us always was time, and it was running out. After all that we'd gone through, it seemed that our very last night would be no less haphazard than our first. We were back to square one, trailing around after strangers on the off chance that they might be selling decent pills.

It was late on Friday afternoon when I found Ali's telephone number. Paul and Charlotte had gone ice skating in the park, and I was alone in the apartment, making a dispirited start on the packing to go home. I nearly threw the number away, for it was scribbled on a cigarette paper, scrumpled up in a corner of my sock in the laundry basket. The red ink had turned pale pink, and had started to run, but I flattened out the paper on the kitchen table and there it was, the name Ali and a ten-digit mobile-phone number. I could have kissed it.

When a man's voice answered, I introduced myself as someone he had met at The Zoo. Dealers do not always like receiving such calls, understandably, but Ali was grace and charm itself – 'Hello Decca! Of course! It would be no problem to meet for a drink.' He named a cafe, and said he would see me there in half an hour. Scrawling a quick note to Paul and Charlotte, I wrapped myself up, and jumped on a tram.

Night was falling. Through the frosty tram window the city looked like a fairy-tale – fur hats bobbing along the Rokin, the lights of the grand Hotel L'Europe blinking ripples in the canal. At Rembrandt-plein the tram clanked to a halt, opposite the Café de Kroon, glowing like a lantern in the dusk. It was only then that I remembered I had no idea what Ali looked like. One of Amsterdam's famous Grand Cafe's, de Kroon was crowded with Friday-evening drinkers, and through the smoke I scanned the wicker chairs and glass tables, but saw no face I recognised. And then, standing at the top of the stairway, waving, there was Ali.

Ali had one of those lucky faces that tell the truth. His brown eyes twinkled in the candlelight, his coffee-coloured skin shone, and his movements were generous and easy. We bought drinks, found a table, and made small talk. He had just come from work, he explained, teaching sport to underprivileged children from ethnic minorities. Ali himself was originally from Morocco, had come to Holland by way of France, spoke four languages and was training to become a social worker. He looked like a Premiership footballer and spoke like a saint, eloquently outlining the cultural problems facing the children he coached.'It is an anthropological challenge, yes? Is that how you say? Really, they are fucked.'

Fuck, fuck, *fuck*. I excused myself and slipped away to the toilets. What an idiot! How embarrassing. Ali wasn't a drug dealer, he was just somebody we'd met in The Zoo. I'd got the whole thing muddled up, and now here we were having a drink, and he was so sweet, and I was going to have to make up some awful lie to get away, and come to think of it this was going to look pretty funny to Paul. *Damn*. When I returned to our table, Ali was searching in the pockets of his tracksuit.

'Sorry,' he smiled. 'For a moment there I thought I lose them. How many was it you wanted?'

Paul and Charlotte gathered round in the kitchen. Feeling like Jack and the Beanstalk, I opened my hand to show them two large white pills.

'And *these*,' I burst, 'aren't even the best ones!' Holding out my other hand, I showed them two small, pale yellow pills. 'Get this: Ali isn't just a dealer. Him and his friend *make* their own Es. His friend's a chemist or something. The white ones are the Es me and Terry bought last week, and they're unbelievable. But these ones, the yellow ones, they're his *homemade* ones. And he didn't even want any money for them! They're a gift.'

The personally designed E is the stuff of clubbing fantasy. If only such a thing were possible to order, it would be chock-full of nothing but lovely MDMA. We have all dreamt about this E, and bullied our friends with chemistry degrees to try and make one. I knew a few who'd even had a go, but it's harder than you'd think, and the experiments had never to my knowledge been a great success. Raw materials are the principle problem, but the precise chemistry of the process is a delicate matter, and knowing your way around a test tube is no guarantee of success.

Paul examined the round yellow tablets, holding them up to the light. They were faintly powdery. Professional ecstasy factories are fitted with expensive pressing-machines that produce smooth, tight pills, but a DIY operation turns out something dustier, and Ali's pills left tiny traces of yellow on our hands. Paul studied them doubtfully.

'And he *gave* them to you?'

Charlotte, being more familiar with the superstitions of clubbing mythology, was in raptures. 'Dec! They are *it*!'

When ecstasy first appeared in Britain, it was expensive. The standard price was £15 a pill, and it was possible to pay £20 or even £25, but the clubs were so flooded with empathetic generosity that clubbers would buy them for each other, and most dealers were moved to give the occasional one away. These days you are unlucky to pay more than a fiver for a pill, but the decline in quality has meant that strangers seldom give anything away any more. Es may be cheaper, but clubbers have got much meaner. When Charlotte and I began taking ecstasy, a gift from a friendly stranger had a magical quality, to be cherished like a lucky charm, and the superstition surrounding the gift of a pill still survives, even if the practice has not. It is, everybody agrees, always the very best E.

Charlotte has always been at her happiest in a club when she has bought a pill but not actually taken it. Often she will dance all night, then come home to discover her E still in her pocket. Having gazed in awe at Ali's homemade gift, she was satisfied that the hunt was over and the journey complete. Leaving us to the final task of taking them, on Saturday morning she left for the airport. We would see her in London the following night, when we would be home.

We spent the afternoon devising our plan. We would go out early to Escape, and take the white pills at first. At four o'clock, we would come home, collect our bag of records and the yellow pills, and go to The Zoo. We called in on Matty at the record shop to ask if he would mind playing some of our tunes in the club, and although slightly surprised by the request, he agreed that he would. 'No problem. Wicked.' Matty did wonder what we were doing with a load of records, though – as had we, some considerable time ago.

This was the bag of records we had packed painstakingly, with such hope, before setting off on our journey. The idea had been that we would carry them clubbing everywhere, so that when we found the perfect E we would have the perfect tune ready to dance to. Exactly how we would persuade a DJ to play our records when the moment arrived was a problem we had planned to solve once we were under way. In Chicago there had been some giggly discussion of strategy, and we amused ourselves no end picturing various DJ-booth scenarios. But lugging the bag about was a real nuisance, and none of the clubs had looked the least bit likely to share the joke, even if we had found the perfect E. As it was, by then we hadn't found a thing. In San Francisco we decided the records were a stupid idea, and the bag had been abandoned at the bottom of the suitcase ever since. At last, the moment had arrived.

Reaching Escape just before eleven, we were dismayed to find shivery queues tailing all the way across the square and out of sight around the corner. But it was to be one of those magically flawless ecstasy nights: for reasons we will never know, the woman at the door waved us to the front and in. Inside, we were swept up into the club's heat and colour. Ali's Es came on quickly and strong, and soon we were dancing on the stage, scampering along the balconies, declaring everyone we spoke to quite the loveliest clubber we had ever met. '*And this E*,' Paul mouthed as he danced on a podium, '*isn't even the homemade one!*'

At four in the morning we came tumbling out soaked in sweat. The fairylights of Rembrandtplein were glittering in the frost, and suddenly we were freezing cold. As if expecting us, at that second a cab drew up and carried us home. The cold had brought us round with a shock, though, and by the time we had showered and changed the white Es had all but worn off. We lay on the living-room floor, gazing up at the ceiling, and paid garrulous tribute, as only clubbers can, to the multiple beauty of Escape. And to Amsterdam – and our journey, and each other; and, and, and . . . *well*! Wasn't this just the *best* time ever.

I rolled over on to my front. Having spread a magazine on the carpet to catch any crumbs, very gingerly I unwrapped Ali's yellow pills. 'Hold on!' Paul leapt up, and returned from the fridge with a bottle of champagne. Laughing at ourselves, we stood and made a formal toast to the pills. We kissed, added a toast to Charlotte and Terry – and then took them. I checked my watch: a few minutes to five. The Zoo was about to open; it was time to go.

We came up on the Es as we were crossing Dam Square. Still icy and dark, the empty black square was silent as we scurried on, bundled up beside each other for warmth. Icicles glistened on the Royal Palace, and a clock somewhere struck five-fifteen. Paul was first to feel anything. 'God, Dec. Bloody hell.' I turned to look, alarmed, but seconds later understood, and as we crossed the Damrak into the red-light district I felt as if a thunderstorm of MDMA was showering joy through my mind. It was unlike anything I'd ever known. We stared at each other, speechless.

The Zoo was already crowded when we got inside, hot and smoky and frenzied. Near the door I bumped into the owner, then Igor at the bar, the crazy redhead, the drag queen from the toilets, and Terry's soap star. There were kisses and hugs and hellos, a great fountain of delight. Eyes shining wide, Paul gazed at the bacchanal. We surged through the room, turning circles of happiness, and had almost reached the toilets when Paul spotted Matty.

'Oh!' he exclaimed. 'Dec, we forgot the records.'

Being on ecstasy is not like being stoned. You do not find everything equally hilarious, good luck and catastrophe alike. You do, however, find that there are very few things more urgently pressing than dancing. And so when Paul exclaims that we have forgotten the records we have carried all the way round the world, we both laugh at our silliness, and continue to dance. It is hot and steamy and feverish, and presently we are dancing on the bar. But we do wish Matty would play one of our favourite tunes, and in due course Paul wonders why we don't just nip back and get them. I think that this is an excellent idea. We blow Matty a kiss, and skitter out on to the icy cobbles.

It is bitterly cold, but we do not feel it as we skip through the back streets. The lights from the doll's houses along the canals are dancing in the water, glowing in the frost, and it is so pretty that we stop to stand and stare. Nothing has ever looked so beautiful to us, or so perfect. The twisting, narrow streets are empty, and we are so enchanted by the stillness that at first we do not notice we are lost. When we do, we are amused. We hoop over this bridge, then double back over that one. We stop to look up at the stars, and are so happy we forget that we are lost. When we remember, we are puzzled that everywhere now somehow looks the same. We pass a policeman on a bicycle, and ask him the way home, and when he tells us we find we are going in completely the wrong direction.

Dawn is breaking when we arrive home and collect the bag of records. We think it will be easier to find our way back now, but here we are again, lost in the sparkly maze of canals that look exactly like each other. This time there is no policeman on a bicycle, and we criss-cross over the cobbles, and peer across bridges, and the club is nowhere to be found. It is still very pretty, but we are quite cold now, and would like to be back inside the lovely Zoo, hearing our lovely records. After a while Paul says he thinks we are going round in a circle, and when I think about this, I agree that he is probably right. We turn around and try again.

And here it is! Only, we cannot understand why there are all these people outside. There are so many people outside, dozens and dozens, standing in front of The Zoo. There is Igor, putting on his coat, and there is Ali, getting on his bicycle. And now here is Matty. 'Sorry, mate,' Matty says. 'Sound system blew, dinnit? Had to close. Nightmare.' And I say, 'But we have our records. Look!' Paul holds up the bag, and pulls out 'The Promised Land'. And Matty looks down and says, 'Oh mate, sorry about that. Next time, eh?' But we have run out of time.

★   ★   ★

The last E was something clubbers often talked about. When would it be? Would we know it was our last as we took it? Or would it be only when we looked back, remembered, that we would realise. No one could ever decide which would be the less unbearably sad. And so a part of us was always in mourning for the end.